MARTHE ROBIN

Thomas Lafleur CSSp.

Marthe Robin

A Prophetic Vision of the Gospel Message

Bernard Peyrous

With the collaboration of Marie-Thérèse Gille

Translated from French by Kathryn Spink

VERITAS

Published 2010 by
Veritas Publications
7–8 Lower Abbey Street
Dublin 1
Ireland

publications@veritas.ie
www.veritas.ie

ISBN 978-1-84730-237-3

Originally published in French under the title *Vie de Marthe Robin*, by
Éditions de l'Emmanuel/Éditions Foyer de Charité, 2006; © 2006 Éditions
de l'Emmanuel, 20, rue Jean Baptiste Pigalle – 75009 Paris (France);
ISBN 2-915313-63-6.

Copyright © Bernard Peyrous, 2006
This translation © Kathryn Spink, 2010

10 9 8 7 6 5 4 3 2 1

A catalogue record for this book is available from the British Library.

Designed by Lir Mac Cárthaigh
Printed in Ireland by Hudson Killeen Ltd

*Veritas books are printed on paper made from the wood pulp of managed forests.
For every tree felled, at least one tree is planted, thereby renewing natural
resources.*

FOREWORD

Marthe Robin was born in 1902 into a small peasant family in an obscure rural village about eighty miles south of Lyon. Some might call this family dysfunctional. Her father had fits of anger against his young daughter because of her sickness and her brother committed suicide. She herself was sickly as a child. Her illness progressively developed to become chronic with a severe handicap, her legs totally bent under her body.

Yet this quite uneducated and extremely disabled woman became the centre, and I would say the heart, of a vast movement which renewed the hearts and spirits of many people in France and elsewhere during and after the pre-Second Vatican Council days. This movement began with the creation of a small religious school for children in her village, Châteauneuf-de-Galaure, with the help of a priest from Lyon, Père Finet. It developed into a retreat centre, run and animated by a community of lay people consecrated to God, at the head of which was a priest. In 1940 this form of community was totally new in the Catholic Church. The talks given by Père Finet during the retreats provided not just doctrinal formation or pious spirituality, but a theological vision which was deeply living and brought the retreatants to a desire to follow Jesus and lead a life of holiness.

This retreat house in Châteauneuf was and is a 'Home of Love', called in French a 'Foyer de Charité'. This love radiated through the teachings but also through the bonds that united members of the community. Didn't Jesus say, 'They will know you are my disciples by the love you have for one another'? As the community became known, people from all over France and even from other countries came to follow these retreats which gave a vision of hope for the world.

Marthe Robin lived a deeply spiritual life. It became clear to her that she had been chosen by Jesus to be an instrument of his love. Our Lady appeared to her a number of times, revealing to her how much she was loved by God. She grew in this love and became, little by little, identified with Jesus. Jesus did not bring life to this world just by his teaching and his example but also through and in his sufferings on the cross. Through his death he gave life to the world. Marthe had a special love of Mary, the mother of Jesus. Wasn't she the first to believe in him, to trust him and to love him? Didn't she live with him for about thirty years in Nazareth, during which she was led by him into a deep union with the Father? Wasn't she at the cross when other disciples had fled? For Marthe, Mary is the model and mother of all believers. Her unique role in the vision of God is to help people deepen their union with Jesus and become like him.

This identification with Jesus brought Marthe to suffer with him, even to suffer his suffering. Like St Francis of Assisi she carried in her body the marks of his wounds. This special grace is called stigmata. Blood would flow from her head and her body every Friday as she lived the Passion of Christ.

This book, written by Father Peyrous, goes through the life of Marthe step by step, through her physical and spiritual growth and the growth of the initial community and of other communities born from it. Today there are over seventy 'Homes of Love' throughout the world, in about forty countries.

As with other saints and people in the Church, the appearances of Jesus and Our Lady to Marthe bore extraordinary fruit. They were the source, not only of the amazing influence of these 'Homes of Love', but of the deep wisdom of Marthe Robin herself. Many thousands of people over the years came to her for advice; she prayed for them, and she revealed to many the way in which to follow God.

Numerous bishops and theologians as well as medical doctors came to verify and witness to the mystical realities that she lived. All found her humble and wise; all found strength and consolation in contact and in conversation with her. Marthe did not want publicity; journalists or people seeking the extraordinary were kept away. She was a hidden source of love for many in the Church.

Marthe is well known in France and in the French-speaking world but is practically unknown in English-speaking countries. That is why this extremely well documented book by Bernard Peyrous and the excellent translation by Kathryn Spink is not only timely but necessary. This hidden, simple woman has a message from God to give to all people. Like the prophets of Israel and like many saints and holy people of God she helped many to become united with God, to live the message of the Gospels in a new way, and to be transformed by the intense love of God for each and every person.

She died in 1981 but the fruits of her life continue to grow and deepen throughout the world. Her great love and respect for people and for the unique call of Jesus for each person can help bring Christians from different Churches together. Her message grew out of her deep love of Jesus and for the Catholic Church but it is also for all Christians. We are all called to love Jesus, to suffer with him and in him, and to offer our lives to the Father, so that the kingdom of God may come. Marthe Robin can be a beautiful model and source of inspiration for many Christians in the English-speaking world. Like Thérèse of Lisieux, she can help us all to become better disciples and beloved friends of Jesus.

I personally had the joy and privilege of meeting Marthe a number of times. She was so simple and friendly, capable of laughter and fun, yet always pointing towards Jesus. She was not some 'holier-than-thou' mystic, pronouncing great words of holiness. She loved l'Arche and Faith and Light, and all the people with disabilities that live with us; for she herself was so severely disabled. I am grateful to Jesus for having revealed himself to me and to so many others through her. In her union with Jesus she has carried our communities and helped us all to grow in love and wisdom.

JEAN VANIER

Request from Père Bernard Michon
Priest responsible for the Foyers of Charity

If you are in a position to send us an account of any 'graces and favours' obtained through Marthe's intercession, we will forward it, as required, to Mgr Lagleize, our bishop in Valence. Alternatively you may send it to your own bishop who will, if he thinks fit, pass it on to the Congregation for the Causes of Saints.

CONTENTS

INTRODUCTION
'Our Dear Marthe'

There are some people who leave a trail of light behind them. This is unquestionably the case with Marthe Robin. Although she died in 1981 she is still present in the conversations, memories and lives of thousands of people. Some of them knew her personally. Others have heard her talked about so vividly that she still reaches them through what is said. In the course of some fifty years this gravely ill woman received over one-hundred thousand people in her room. With a remark, a question or sometimes simply by listening, she changed many lives. She was without doubt one of the most influential figures in France in the second half of the twentieth century. In an era of crises, doubts and questioning, she was like a manifestation of Divine Providence when no one wanted to hear about it, when Providence as an expression of the presence of God had been dismissed. Better still, she bore witness to the love of God to hearts that were both distant and hungry. To give just one example among many: a young man came to see her and poured out everything he could think of against God: evil, injustice, death etc. ... all the objections to the existence of the God of goodness preached by Christianity. Marthe Robin listened to him in silence, a silence that was perceptibly respectful. When he had finished she said simply, 'And yet …' Her visitor discerned in this very brief response something that was beyond his pain and criticisms. At a single stroke he was acceded to another world; there is a light beyond our darkness. His life was completely changed. He became a friend to Marthe and went on in his own way to help her in her work. 'Our dear Marthe!' A great many people have used this expression because she seemed so close to them. Rarely has anyone called forth so much admiration and affection without seeking to do so and despite the fact that her living conditions seemed to preclude publicity or the opportunity to wield any influence.

It is not surprising then that so much has been written about Marthe since her death. Even while she was alive, people tried to discover things about her that she did not wish made public. Marthe Robin was discretion personified about things in general and even more so about what concerned her. The work she founded, the Foyers of Charity, reflected this same reserve. Some thirty articles did, nonetheless, appear about her, and after her death came an uninterrupted flow: nearly thirty books, some of them translated into many languages, and over a thousand articles. There have also been radio and television programmes about her here and there. Marthe Robin is thus one of the most publicised twentieth century French women. She is known all over the world from Columbia to China. For some she is a saint; for others an enigma. Yet others reserve their judgement. For many hers is a particularly interesting example of human existence. How could a person living as she did, lost in the Drôme countryside, confined to bed and without education, engage the interest of great intellectuals and ordinary people alike, and make herself understood and appreciated by all? What was her secret? What motivated her? Where did the source of her influence lie?

It seemed only natural that a few years after Marthe Robin's death the procedure for her beatification should be begun. The *processus*, to use the accepted term for the preparation of the inquiries to secure beatification, was an opportunity to gather not far off a thousand testimonies, amounting to hundreds and hundreds of pages. Her writings and correspondence were collected up, studied and subjected to various expert appraisals. In all the material put together and transferred to Rome to be used in the cause for beatification came to over seventeen thousand pages. Of course a good part of the information, involving people still living or only recently deceased, remained and will remain private for a long time. But from their statements it has been possible to extract material for a biography of Marthe Robin that is better informed and more complete than previous publications. Hence this current work.

Using what I can pass on from the *processus* documents, I hope that people will understand that I have still maintained some measure of discretion. I have tried, nonetheless, to make Marthe Robin, one of the most astounding spiritual and human examples in contemporary French history, more comprehensible. In conclusion I may perhaps be permitted to say that this biography is a token of my gratitude. I owe much to Marthe Robin. I too am among those who would call her 'our dear Marthe'. No one will be surprised, therefore, that this biography, though based entirely on verified documentation, is also permeated with the affection one may have for someone who is both very close and revered.

BERNARD PEYROUS

— PART ONE —

THE AWAKENING OF A SOUL

CHAPTER I
A Small Village in France
(1902–1917)

People's life stories are often intertwined with that of their place of origin. Marthe Robin is no exception. She was a child of the small French village of Châteauneuf-de-Galaure.

I. Châteauneuf-de-Galaure

Marthe Robin was born in 1902 in Châteauneuf-de-Galaure, in eastern central France, the former province of Dauphiné, in the *département*[1] of Drôme and the diocese of Valence, seventy kilometres south of the city of Lyon and forty-six kilometres north of Valence, which is the *préfecture*[2] and the seat of the bishopric.

Châteauneuf is situated in the valley of the Galaure, a small tributary of the Rhône into which it rushes some twenty kilometres to the west. The district encompasses two sorts of terrain: the valley itself which is fertile and flat, and the hillsides above it. As for the actual village, the old part is situated on the hill slopes. A more recent part has been built alongside a secondary road which runs through the valley. In former times it was dominated by a château which gave it its name: the new castle[3] or manor house, which over the years belonged to the Moirans family and then to the Montchenus. After that it fell into disrepair with only a section of the main building and the stables remaining. Apart from the main agglomeration which had 676 inhabitants at that time, Châteauneuf was made up of two separate ones: Saint-Bonnet-de-Galaure with 539 inhabitants and Treigneux with 137. Saint-Bonnet subsequently became an independent district. At the beginning of the twentieth century the three units, Châteauneuf, Saint-Bonnet and Treigneux, were three separate parishes. Châteauneuf was then a rural district with most of its occupants, apart from a few craftsmen, living off the land. This was right in the depths of pre-First World War France, in a world that was slowly paced and linked to the soil, in which people worked hard for a living and had no State assistance on which to rely. It was a society with well-established reference points; everyone knew who they were and what they had to do. People did not call morality, or the love of work or homeland, into question. Most residents expected to marry locally and carry on the family farm. As we shall see, however, the world had already started to change.

On the hillsides above the valley were several hamlets with a few houses clustered together. In a place called La Plaine (meaning the plateau), one of these hamlets was known as Moïlles. It was made up of three farms: the Achard farm and two others very close together, occupied at that time by cousins: the two Robin families. They shared their agricultural buildings under the same roof. The well was also communal. Moïlles felt quite a long way from the village two kilometres below. The landscape was completely different. It was not at all like being in the valley. From the hillside when the sky was clear the view was vast. To the east you could see the Jura Mountains, the Alps with Mont Blanc, the highest point in Europe (4,807 metres), the mountainous mass of La Chartreuse above Grenoble, Le Royans and Le Vercors. To the west, beyond the Rhône, the mountains of Vivarais with Mount Pilat were visible, and the view to the south stretched as far as Mount Lozère – approximately two hundred kilometres of mountains lay to the east and a little less to the west. Later Marthe Robin was to say: 'From the poplar (about three hundred metres from her farm) you can see a quarter of France.' An obvious exaggeration, but indicative of what the locals said. Sometimes on the hillside the view was limitless and the air invigorating. There was nothing to obstruct the wind from the mountains.

Marthe's father, Joseph Robin, and family owned their farmhouse and thirteen hectares of agricultural land. It was not a large concern and land on the hillside was less fertile than in the valley. The Robins were not rich. Their farm might even be described as modest but they had a home of their own on their own land. They were not part of the agricultural proletariat, nor could they really be described as poor. They had what they needed to live, even if it was at the price of much labour and devoid of luxury. The children went to the primary school which at that time provided an excellent foundation for the rest of life. But it was a not very cultured, perhaps even rough, environment.

As I have said, the world had started to change. The Galaure Valley was affected by the anticlerical struggle that defined a good part of life in the Third Republic. In the nineteenth century the State had not involved itself – or involved itself very little – in education. Consequently districts had often turned to religious who were inexpensive and provided an education acknowledged to be sound and reliable, and that gave the children religious instruction. The Third Republic drove these religious out and replaced them with teachers from training colleges that were, according to the teacher, novelist, playwright and filmmaker, Marcel Pagnol, 'anticlerical seminaries'. At Châteauneuf, after the Brothers and Sisters had left, the lay school became a centre for subjecting children to anti-religious propaganda. An anti-Christian group was formed in the village and brought pressure to bear on the local people. A Masonic lodge even set itself up in Châteauneuf and more or less controlled the elections. On one occasion Marthe Robin was to have her Catechism book torn up in one of the village streets. In 1961 she recounted: 'One day I was on my way to Catechism class. I had a copy under my arm in a brown cover; a gentleman from Châteauneuf asked me, "Where are you going?" I answered him quite proudly, "To Catechism." "And what's that?" He pointed to my Catechism book. "Show it to me." I handed it to him. He took it and tore it in two ... But I was so attached to that book that I kept it after that, torn as it was, as a relic ... I must have been seven or eight years old.' Faith in the Church diminished and religious practice waned. Men went less frequently to Mass and whole families dropped away. In Châteauneuf the number of Easter communicants fell from 105 men and 200 women in 1897 to 37 men, 92 women and 47 children in 1926. The clergy spoke out adamantly against the drive to de-Christianise. True, religious life still went on: all the children were baptised, people married in churches and there were very few civil burials but there was a real crisis in the very heart of the countryside.

II. The advent of a child

In those days women gave birth at home so Marthe Robin was born in her parent's farmhouse at 5 p.m. on Thursday 13 March 1902. She was the last child of her parents, Joseph and Amélie, who had married in 1889. Five children had preceded her: Célina, Marie-Gabrielle, Alice-Victorine, Henri-Joseph and Clémence. Their father had a reputation for being an affable, kind man, very good with his hands but authoritarian, and their mother was a smiling, friendly woman. It would seem, however, that husband and wife went through a difficult patch. Amélie Robin is purported to have had an affair with a farm-hand employed by the Robin cousins. Word went round the family and the locality that Marthe was not her father's legitimate daughter. She herself is thought to have believed it. Although several testimonies seem to imply Marthe's illegitimate conception, however, there is not enough evidence to be completely sure.

Even if the affair did take place it seems certain that the father forgave his wife. He recognised Marthe as his daughter. More than that, there were occasions when he showed special affection for her. Similarly Marthe's mother really loved her daughter and was to prove it. Marthe would speak of her parents as the 'two people I cherish most on this earth'. Child upbringing was very strict then. 'I wasn't a spoilt child,' Marthe was later to say. But if her background was tough, it was not without qualities of the heart. Her parents were generous to passing beggars, especially during the First World War, and they taught their children to be generous too, even encouraging them to give the beggars some of their own food.

Marthe Robin's childhood was that of any little girl living in the country, following the rhythm of the seasons and the work in the fields, close to nature and animals. As soon as children were capable of doing so they used to help with small jobs. As a very young girl, in summer she would take drinks out to the men working the threshing machine. Little by little the children learned to cope in a number of domains and do useful things with modest means. The farm was like a very small family enterprise in which everyone had their role. Grandfather Robin lived on the farm, as was usual at the time, and helped out where he could (his wife Thérèse had died in 1888). In November 1903, however, the household was disrupted by typhoid fever, brought on by polluted well water. Four people were affected. The grandfather died of it. The two frailest children – Clémence, who was five, and Marthe, who was one – were taken seriously ill. Clémence died on 12 November 1903 and Marthe was believed to be lost. After two months of illness, she started to recover but was to remain frail throughout her childhood.

Fragile as she was, Marthe still had to go to school. Her sisters had gone to a Catholic girls' school but it had been closed by the anticlerical government in 1905, so she was obliged to attend the State school in the lower end of the village in the valley, near the station. From the age of five she used to walk the two kilometres in the morning and afternoon. On the way back there was a very steep slope to climb. At midday she would eat the snack she had brought with her at one of her friends' houses. She stayed on at school until she was thirteen which was not compulsory at the time and took her beyond primary education. The fact that her schooling was slightly extended suggests that her parents considered she had the ability to study. She was frequently ill, however, and could not pass her school certificate, an exam to which great importance was attached at the time.

We know virtually nothing about Marthe's experience of school. She does not seem to have been unhappy there, much less traumatised by it. In those days a close eye was kept on children and any aggression between them was curbed by strict supervision. Boys and girls were segregated. Marthe seems to have been a rather happy, even somewhat mischievous, pupil. She was always to have a sense of humour. Some effects of the instruction she received would no doubt remain with her and form foundations on which she could build: a sharpened sense of historical chronology and geography, the love of appropriate and precise words, a supple, simple and direct use of the French language. By the time she left school, her intellectual world was limited, but it was still much better organised and effective than that of most contemporary children of the same age.

Marthe had good relationships with her family. Henri Robin, her brother, was described as 'timid', which could imply many things, including limited intelligence and difficulty in relation-ships. Perhaps he was also a little crushed by his father's personality. He would never really be able to work out where he belonged and problems arose as a result. Marthe was later to say: 'I loved my brother very much because he was timid and his timidity made him awkward. I always defended him.' With her sisters Marthe had excellent relations. In 1908 the eldest, Célina, married Claudius Serve and went to live in Saint-Sorlin. Marthe felt her elder sister was being taken away from her and reacted badly to the marriage. She was very upset. It was only from seeing Célina happy with her husband that she derived some consolation. She stayed in their home on several occasions. The second daughter, Gabrielle, loved a young man and wanted to marry him but fell pregnant by him. His parents opposed their marriage. She gave birth to Gabriel-Raymond in 1914. The father acknowledged the child as his but died in the war in 1916. Marthe remained close to her sister and nephew. Alice, the sister closest to her in age, was in the same class at school. She married in 1924.

III. The discovery of a relationship with God

In the meantime something different, something that transcended all this was beginning to happen to Marthe. Even as a child she had known about prayer: 'I always loved God very much indeed as a little girl … All my life I have always prayed a great deal, in my bed and everywhere.'[4] But she was coming to know God more closely. Initially there did not seem anything exceptional about her compared with friends born at the same time. Her parents were believers but not practicing. Her father did, however, receive Holy Communion at Easter, which allows us to suppose that her mother did too. Although baptised, her brother Henri did not go to Catechism classes. Marthe suffered greatly over this spiritual deficiency, and in 1930 was to say of her family: 'What I ask above all else is that my good parents return to the faith and to religious practice.' Cousin Ferdinand Robin in the house next door was indifferent to religion. The neighbouring Achards had no faith. By contrast her sisters Alice and Gabrielle went regularly to Mass on Sundays and Marthe definitely accompanied them.

At first Marthe went to Catechism classes in Saint-Bonnet because the Moïlles hamlet was part of that parish, but it was much further away than Châteauneuf and in the end the priest,

Abbé Hippolyte Caillet, agreed to Marthe's going to Châteauneuf where Abbé Cluze was the parish priest. Abbé Cluze taught Catechism with the help of his housekeeper. Marthe was somewhat put out when she had to recite her lessons by heart, as was usual at that time. She was always to show signs of an exceptional memory. But she did not much like the highly moralising and guilt-provoking way the Catholic faith was presented. 'There is no love in this Catechism,' she was later to say, which was exactly right. The Catechism did have the advantage of being very precise and quite complete, but it was not infused with any perceptible feeling of spiritual inspiration and the religious faith it presented was restricted in form. What Marthe was seeking was an experience of God. It was not long in coming.

Marthe made her First Holy Communion with a friend on 15 August 1912. She did so late because she had the measles on the day originally set for the ceremony. This was her first contact with God: 'I think Our Lord took possession of me at my First Holy Communion. I believe he already took me to himself at that moment. My First Holy Communion was something very sweet.' At that time children were given a Rosary. Marthe had certainly not been given one previously by her family. She made a habit of reciting it: 'When I was little and used to go on errands to the village I would always have my Rosary in my pocket and used to say it as I walked along.' Her Solemn Communion took place on 21 May 1914. It seems that Marthe had a real desire for Holy Communion then, and that on Sundays when she was looking after the livestock she would still sometimes arrange things so that she could go and receive the Eucharist. She was already experiencing intimacy with God and was able to identify his hand at work in her environment: 'The desire to pray I sometimes had was definitely something that he himself was bringing about in me. As soon as there was less sensitivity on my part, he would call me back to him through this desire, and it was like intimacy with God. I think I felt God; it was more than prayer. What's more I found him everywhere in nature, which helped me greatly to see him beyond it, even as a little girl. I found him in my neighbour and especially in priests. His[5] person would call me to prayer without anything being said to me: the sight of a priest always moved me. Why? It was not for me to understand. What did I know more than others? I loved sick people very much and I would have crossed hills and vales if I had been allowed to, to go and see someone who was ill, not to nurse them but to love them.'

When she left school in 1915, Marthe helped on the family farm. She learned the thousand jobs that countrywomen do, looking after the livestock for example. She was charged with tending and milking the goats, and would always retain her love of animals. She also learned to cook. She learned to embroider. Pretty embroidery work of the kind done in the countryside was a way of earning money and of passing the time when rural labour died in winter. It was also a way of expressing herself, of doing something beautiful. Marthe became very adept at a craft which exercised the fingers in a particularly precise way. She and her thimble were not to be separated.

Mutual support was strong in the country. Marthe used to go down to the village to do the shopping. Her sister Gabrielle was a seamstress. Marthe would deliver the dresses she made to the clients. The husband of her sister Célina, who had become Mme Serve, went off to war. His wife, who had two small children, one of them a baby, had to work in the fields. Marthe spent six months with her during the winter of 1915–1916 when the second child was born. She was to go back there in the following year. She looked after the house. 'I often did the cooking with Robert in my arms,' she was later to say.

She then went through a relative cooling-off period: 'I was lukewarm for a while around the age of fourteen but it didn't last.' She swiftly returned to the faith of her childhood. So at the time when her personality was being formed, Marthe appears to have been an intelligent, happy girl, open to the future, helpful, ready to tease in a way which suggested a sense of humour and a pleasant way with people. She had a temper. When she was younger it was not unknown for her to stamp her feet in anger. She was fearful by nature and did not like making the long trip alone to Saint-Bonnet to fetch string for the tobacco crop, but she went nonetheless. She learned to overcome her feelings and obey. She was a wholesome, devout little farm girl no doubt like many others in the France of that time.

NOTES

1. Administrative division.
2. Location of the main administrative office for the *département*.
3. *Châteauneuf* in French.
4. Here and on numerous subsequent occasions, Marthe, like Père Finet, refers to 'Le Bon Dieu', which literally means 'the Good God'. In French, however, 'Le Bon Dieu' is much more commonplace than 'the Good God' in English. The translator has therefore opted to refer simply to 'God'.
5. The priest's person.

CHAPTER 2
The Sudden Onset of Illness and God's Preparations (1918–1928)

Many people's lives are disrupted at some point by serious illness. There is life prior to it and life after it. It becomes necessary to adapt physically, psychologically and socially to a different way of being. Many are unable to do so or only manage it partially. Or maybe they are unable to integrate a particular dimension, such as the spiritual. In any event, becoming ill implies going through advancements and setbacks, revolt and acceptance. Illness is a whole world in itself. This was the world that the adolescent Marthe Robin entered in 1918.

I. Manifestations of illness

During the summer of 1918 Marthe Robin did not feel well. She suffered from headaches, fever, ocular pain and vomiting. In a big city she would have received treatment. In an isolated country hamlet people grinned and bore it, and hoped that it would pass. On 1 December 1918, however, came the first major episode in her illness: 'Before mid-day I collapsed on the floor and was very ill, crying out for a doctor.' This happened in the farmhouse kitchen.

It seemed serious and the family did its duty. Marthe was examined by Dr Pangon and Dr Allemand from Saint-Vallier, a

village about fifteen kilometres away. They thought it might be a
brain tumour. The situation worsened rapidly. Marthe fell into a
coma which lasted four days. They thought they had lost her and
she received the last rites. She emerged, however, from this acute
period and recovered a little for a few weeks. But again the illness
advanced, so much so that for twenty-seven months she was in a
state of lethargy. In the family, for want of a better explanation,
they referred to it as 'sleeping sickness'. Marthe was confined to
bed and could not bear light so the room was plunged into
darkness. She even wore a blindfold. Paralysed on one side, she
was in great pain day and night. Her niece Marcelle wrote:
'Marthe was in her room in the dark, on the kitchen side. She
used to cry out. I could hear her crying out all the time, she was
in so much pain, the poor thing. We didn't dare go near her bed
she was yelling so much, the poor girl. She suffered day and
night.' She herself said: 'If you were to plunge me into your
boiling laundry, I couldn't be in any more pain.' At that time
there was not much to relieve pain and no Social Security. How
was the family supposed to pay for protracted treatment or
hospitalisation? They were very worried. Henri was in the army at
that time. Between 15 May 1918 and 2 June 1919 he wrote some
fifty postcards to his family. In them were twenty-nine references
to Marthe's health.

In July 1919 the illness became even worse with muscular
contractions, sleep problems, digestive difficulties, and problems
with her sight to the point where she could not see at all for some
months. People tried to help her as best they could. She was
given injections and a little chocolate (considered a medicine in
those days) to suck on because, although she was able to absorb
fluids, they had great difficulty in getting food into her. She was
not completely unconscious. One day when her sister Alice was
close to her, Marthe told her softly, 'I sense when it is you'. She
would go through intervals when she was able to speak a little
better.

April–May 1921 saw a period of remission. Marthe began to walk again. Her vision was restored, leaving her just short-sighted. As soon as she had recovered the use of her legs she went to several places of pilgrimage. During the summer of 1921 she visited Notre-Dame de Chatenay near Lens-Lestang and Notre-Dame de Bonnecombe near Hauterives. She might have been taken for cured but then, in November 1921, the illness took hold again. Once more her legs became paralysed and linked with this she had pain in the back. Then, as before, she was able to walk, although her legs were swollen and painful.

The following year was more peaceful and Marthe resumed work at the farm. 'Marthe used to embroider to make money for medicines to give herself some relief,' said one of her friends. 'Mlle Caillet used to give her embroidery to do. Marthe Robin's work was much better than anyone else's.' When the work was delicate, customers would say, 'Give it to your little invalid'. 'I saw Marthe on her feet, looking after her cows not very far from her house … She was dressed soberly in black.' Another friend, Madame Bonnet said: 'She was very good with her hands and worked well. She didn't want to be dependent on her parents.' Every Thursday she used to go for her injections in Saint-Vallier, which was not unproblematic because she had to go by train and she had difficulty in walking to the station. So whenever he could, her father would take her down by cart.

In October 1923 she went for resin bath treatment in Saint-Péray in Ardèche. She gave her niece a humorous account of the way she was made to sweat: 'We are popped into a nice cool oven … and we have to stay there dutifully for half an hour, while we turn into fountains. You see, sweetheart, it's no picnic, but you're there to be cured and the disease is very much worse.' A little while later she wrote to her: 'I can tell you that today I was baked for the eighth time. I think I'll soon be done to a turn.' She was close to her family and in anticipation of her sister Alice's wedding, she wrote to her uncle: 'On that day we shall dance, uncle. I shall hold you to it, so don't you forget. Keep it well in mind.' So she was hoping to get better in the future, even in the near future.

Unfortunately her hopes were not to be fulfilled. Gisèle Boutteville, who first met her in 1924, said in 1926: 'What a change there was in her! She had been very ill, even partially paralysed, I believe, and there she was in her armchair behind the kitchen window with the shutters already half closed, afraid of the light.' Her nephew, Raymond Gaillard for his part described how: 'Her father, M. Robin, used to carry her over to sit there [in the armchair]. Marthe would read, sew and embroider. She had to be helped to stand up and walk over in extraordinary pain and sit in front of the clock to have her meals at the table.' Raymond Gaillard 'lost his appetite' at the sight of her. In June 1926 she wrote: 'I am more and more out of sorts.' Still she kept up her embroidery. In September that year she said: 'The more needlework I can do, the better it will be for me and mine, and also for my morale because I often run out of courage … I have worked and still work a little despite the fact that my hands often want to shake.' In March 1927 she said: 'My health is always precarious and the constant pain in my head bothers me a lot.' In July 1927, writing to the pharmacist in Saint-Vallier, she described her condition more precisely: 'Sir, in your last letter you asked how my health was. I have to say it is still the same. I get up (or more accurately someone gets me up) every day around ten or eleven o'clock when I am put in my armchair, and I don't budge from it until it is time for me to go to bed, which I do, not without tears, despite all my assiduous taking of tablets and pills. My nights are generally bad. The warmer it is, the more I think I suffer, although this winter was tough for me because I had a very long and painful bout of rheumatism all over my body, which kept me in my bed for a long time, unable to move.'

In October 1927 a fresh crisis occurred characterised by very sharp pains in the stomach and digestive bleeding. The doctor diagnosed a likely tumour. Very soon it seemed that nothing more could be done. For the second time Marthe was given the last rites. She was at death's door and remained in a form of coma for three weeks without being able to absorb anything. Yet once again she emerged from the attack.

She had nevertheless been greatly affected by it and did not really recover. After May 1928 she would never again be able to stand. The paralysis of her lower limbs would not go away. Her legs progressively folded under her and she was in constant pain. She was given what tranquillisers were available, prescribed morphine and belladonna suppositories, and offered chloroformed water to take. 'All that did reduce the pain but it was still terrible,' she wrote. 'I am still suffering almost constantly and only feel alright with the help of sedatives, by getting through bottles [of aspirin].' She was so ravaged by rheumatism and stomach problems that she sometimes cried out with the pain. She would force herself to eat a little despite frequent bouts of vomiting. Her head ached even in the semi-darkness of the room.

A medical interpretation

It is always difficult to reach a diagnosis without actually examining the patient. Taken as a whole, however, the various testimonies relating to Marthe's illness are noticeably consistent and cover a lengthy period of time. In 1942 Marthe was also examined by two doctors from Lyon using the most reliable methods known at the time, and they provide useful information for comparison with other sources.

Marthe Robin's illness should not be attributed to mystical phenomena. To do so would serve to confuse and make its pattern incomprehensible. The mystical phenomena, as will be seen later, occurred in a sick person and did not 'replace' the illness. Marthe Robin did not, for example, experience a state of ecstasy for twenty-seven months as has sometimes been suggested. She was well and truly ill during that period, with phases of lethargy. It is essential to establish and separate the different planes from the outset.

Without resorting too much to medical terminology and specialist discussion, it would appear that what Marthe Robin had was encephalitis, probably in the form of von Economo's disease, an inflammatory infection of the nerve centres. This went on developing throughout her life with phases of remission. The effects were extremely incapacitating and painful. As far as the pain was concerned a doctor specialising in palliative care estimated that she went to the very limits of human endurance. The fact that the illness had alternating phases of advancement and abatement so that there were times when it was possible to believe things were improving and there were indications of partial recovery, added to her anguish. Anyone with any idea how a seriously ill person clutches at hopeful signs, may well imagine that Marthe vested a great deal in any apparently positive developments. These signs would come to nothing, however, and the illness would start up again until fresh indications of recovery appeared. Encephalitis does not take its toll on the body alone. It affects the whole being and especially the personality. Sufferers do not just feel ill in part of their body. Rather their whole being seems to be giving way. They lose their bearings and in the end may self-destruct before the violence of the onslaught. Life loses its meaning. They may then sink into madness or succumb to death. Marthe must, as we shall see, have done the opposite and opted for life.

For the time being, however, she had become an invalid and left the world of normality behind her. She got by as best she could with problems assailing her from all sides.

II. The reactions of her family and those around her

At a time when there was no Social Security the Robin family could not send Marthe to hospital. Prior to 1901 it might perhaps have been possible to find a convent-run clinic or nursing home to take Marthe free of charge, but the expulsion of religious communities in that year as part of the struggle against the Church had weakened the French medical network. There was no alternative but for Marthe to stay at home with her family. She could no longer look after herself so her mother was obliged to give precious time to her that she would otherwise have spent working in the house. Marthe cost money. Marriage was no longer possible. Nor would she be able to go on earning a living doing embroidery. The door to the religious life was closed to her for health reasons but also because of the expulsion of the congregations. To pursue a vocation she would have had to leave France. So the family found itself at an impasse.

At the time this was not unusual. Most disabled people were kept at home but this could sometimes be demanding. With the best will in the world people were required to adapt. Illness did not disrupt the life of the patient alone but that of those around her too. Real problems resulted. Her father and mother had already had their difficulties: the tiff that had gone on between them for a while, the death of Marthe's grandfather and of little Clémence, the war to which Henri had been called up for several years and the illegitimate conception of Gabrielle's son. This was the last straw. 'What have I done [to God] to have such a daughter?' asked her father. Emotionally, doubtless out of self-preservation, Marthe's father and brother distanced themselves from her. 'How hard it is for me to deal with people who are indifferent and sometimes hurtful,' Marthe admitted, referring to her relatives. Her mother, however, looked after her daughter. When she talked about her she called her 'my little one', a term of affection, an affection she was always to show her.

The strongest reaction was her father's. Unable to take anymore, in 1927 Marthe confided her hurt to her friend, Mme Delatour in connection with an attack of toothache which had been going on for a week. 'I had to say all kinds of things[1] to my father and shame him into going and getting me some help – it must be easy to have a heart so hard that nothing moves it, not even his own flesh and blood when he sees it lying on the cross … I pity my poor, unfortunate father with all my heart for really being so hard. It's true that in the five years since I've been ill he has troubled himself no more over me than over his dog, but perhaps you think and perhaps you'll say that it is not nice of me to talk like this. It is really despite myself that I do so and only to you as a much-loved sister and without any rancour. Only it does have a bearing on my heart because ultimately there is a limit to everything and my poor little life has seen some very hard things … I wish him only happiness and tenderness, I who find loving so sweet, but I can no longer show him love: it is beyond my capabilities but because I am a Christian I feel simply indifference.'

There are witnesses to confirm what Marthe said. Gisèle Boutteville who went to visit her was to recall: 'Marthe's father talked about his other children but not about Marthe. I asked him for news of his family. First he answered me in patois. Then he talked about Mme Brosse. About Marthe he said nothing. "And Marthe?" I said to him – "Oh Marthe …" I can't say they were very appealing … Her mother was pleased I'd come but M. Robin, the father couldn't care a jot and the brother even less.'

If the family did not help Marthe very much, at least not on an emotional and psychological level, others around her were no more supportive. In the surrounding countryside people did not know what to make of this seemingly strange illness and were harshly judgemental. This was the point at which 'hysteria' as classified by Charcot and the Salpêtrière School of Psychiatry was making its mark on a half educated public. It proved a very useful way of explaining away any phenomena that were difficult to understand and people were quick to apply it to Marthe. Marguerite Lautru, who had come to Châteauneuf as a midwife at the request of a doctor in Hauterives, remembered that 'she had no or virtually no visitors. Not even M. le Curé to whom I had often spoken about Marthe. He used to encourage me to visit her (he only came to see her in the last months before I left), but some of the local practicing Christians criticised me because they did not think she was of any interest ... Sometimes their judgement was even more disparaging. People said she was hysterical and added that this was Dr Modrin from Hauterives' diagnosis.'

The result was that Marthe Robin received no visitors. Her classmates, possibly afraid of contagion, did not come to see her. And so she was completely isolated for days on end, alone with her suffering and her boredom. A few words from her describe those long periods of solitude:

During the week I work away quietly but I have relapsed into the sad solitude of other years, with no one to pass away the hours with a good chat. (1927)

As for me, I think this Sunday will be just like all the others and I also think I shall not see a living soul apart from those who live in the house. (1928)

No more visits, not one. You'd think everyone had passed the word around to leave me to my embroidery and my thoughts ... (1928)

My days go by with uniform monotony and all the same, with three quarters of my time spent by myself, because my mother doesn't just work in my room. (1928)

As for me, tomorrow will be like every other day, grey and uniform; and my day will be spent in my mother's company, which will hardly change us. (1928)

Marthe was sharing her mother's room but experienced such pain during the night that she admitted: 'At night I suffer, I suffer so much that I bite on my sheets to avoid waking her.'

It was the local priest's role to visit the sick in his parish. This was something of which the formation of priests was very mindful and many devoted much of their time to it. Until 1923 the parish priest was Abbé Payre who did go up to see Marthe, but he was succeeded by Abbé Faure who was to be the priest at Châteauneuf until 1955. He was an energetic man who set about renewing his parish and counteracting its de-Christianisation. He created a Catholic Union for men which at once acquired fifteen members, and a Sunday school with ten children. He gathered around him people of good will, long crushed by anti-religious propaganda. He was a strong personality, a little gruff, whom people were quick to liken at times to the Curé d'Ars. He was probably the sort of man needed in this strained context to stand up and make his mark, but he was wary of mystics. As a seminarian he had asked God for the grace not to have to be confessor to any. With hindsight this probably meant that he put his trust primarily in the ascetic life and personal effort as a way to God. You had to get a grip on yourself and carry on regardless of the price. This was the approach advocated by Catechism in the diocese.

His relationship with Marthe was difficult at first. He did not understand her. 'M. le Curé's heart of gold is hidden behind an oak exterior and I'm afraid he doesn't always understand me,' Marthe wrote. 'Sometimes he makes me repeat what I've said. I think he is scolding me with his somewhat harsh voice and my heart swells and it's impossible for me to answer him. M. le Curé thinks I'm sulking and we part without understanding each other.' To her friend, Jeanne Bonneton, who spoke of his kindness, Marthe responded: 'Well, when he comes to my house, he leaves his kindness at the door.'

In the barely religious setting already described, moreover, Marthe's family did not take kindly to the priest's visits. They were probably afraid people would say they had become 'calotins', meaning pious or close to the Church. 'If M. le Curé comes again

I'll fire a shot at him,' Henri is purported to have announced. So Marthe told him not to come anymore. He was hurt. He did not understand. Only in 1927 did relations begin to improve when Marthe was apparently dying and he gave her the last rites. In such circumstances a visit from a priest was admissible to the family. What happened between Marthe and her visitor on that occasion? We do not know but some connection was established and Marthe modified her view of him: 'I know M. le Curé is a holy priest, entirely devoted to his duty, rally round him, he deserves it … Don't you think M. le Curé has changed? Well, he'll change even more. He will become patient. Don't be afraid of him. Open yourselves to him when you have problems. He will understand you. He will always give you good advice,' she said then. In Abbé Faure she had at last found true spiritual support.

First friendships

Marthe had a good and sensitive heart. She was focused outwards and interested in others, craving affection from and communication with them. During her course of treatment at Saint-Péray she made two friends. The first was Mme du Bay, a baroness from Alboussière in Ardèche, who was a woman of faith with a fine religious library. Mme du Bay was certainly touched by this very sick girl who was at a loss and unable to 'integrate' her illness into her spiritual life. She spoke to her about the Passion of Jesus. This gave Marthe a key to understanding and undoubtedly had an impact on her. The second friend was Mme Delatour from Saint-Claude in the Jura, with whom she would have a very intimate correspondence between 1923 and 1928. This correspondence was a source both of relief and of encouragement for Marthe. Mme Delatour was like a sister to her, in whom she could confide everything. She also helped her by finding her needlework to do.

There was also a girl from Lyon, Gisèle Boutteville, who spent part of the summer in Châteauneuf with friends, who came to see

Marthe and became a great friend of hers. This relationship was to last until Marthe's death.[2] We have Gisèle's account of their first meeting in 1924 when Gisèle was seventeen: 'She seemed extremely happy to see visitors and I can't express how I felt when my friends introduced me to her by name, telling her that I came from Lyon, but I was also and above all profoundly struck by her gaze which saw right into my very depths. She didn't stop thanking me for coming and I was even a little embarrassed because the joy, as I told her, was all mine … We chatted like that at length, all together, in complete simplicity and without her talking about herself at all. She would have liked us to stay longer because, she told us, she saw very few people and her life was very lonely.'

In 1927 Francine Bonnet, a dressmaker and wife of the village joiner, met her. The couple were friends with the local priest and were faithful Châteauneuf parishioners. 'I gave her small jobs to do for me personally. She was very grateful and thanked me so tenderly that I grew fonder of her and soon took her for my best friend,' she wrote.

Shortly before Marguerite Lautru left Châteauneuf she went up to see Marthe.[3] This time it was Marthe herself who described their meeting to Mme Delatour: 'On Monday, a first visit from someone whose acquaintance I had made: I was all alone in the house at the time so we introduced ourselves to one another very properly. I had given up expecting her. She had been due to come for a year. She's the Châteauneuf midwife, a young woman of twenty-four. She left me with a very warm memory of her visit. She's very well brought up and speaks admirably well.'

These friendships were extremely precious to Marthe. They opened her up to life, preventing her from closing in on herself and sinking into her suffering and problems. They fed her curiosity, for Marthe took an interest in what was going on in Lyon. Above all, they helped Marthe to feel that she at last mattered to some people. She was recognised for what she was, and not just as 'the millstone' or the 'odd one'. She could talk and partially confide. As we have seen, Gisèle Boutteville, young as she was, was struck by the penetration of Marthe's gaze. This was because important things were beginning to happen within her in her relationship with God. Heaven was beginning gradually to unveil itself.

III. Embarking on the interior life

When she recovered from the first phase of her illness, Marthe Robin went, as mentioned, to several places of pilgrimage. It is not unusual in popular spirituality for people to turn to Mary when circumstances become more difficult. But Marthe had already heard the call to give herself completely to God. Around 1921–1922 she considered becoming a Carmelite. She even mentioned it to her parents but her father's reaction was negative in the extreme and from then on he gave up all vestiges of Christian practice.

Marian graces between 1921 and 1922

Her parents' attitude could, as quite often happens, have disrupted her spiritual progress, but this was not the case. Instead Marthe's inner life was to take on a more accentuated Marian direction.

Marthe had always loved and prayed to the Virgin Mary. What happened now, however, was completely different. Little by little Mary was to manifest herself to her. The Virgin's first appearance to Marthe may have occurred on 20 May 1921. Marthe's mother and her sister Alice noticed something, following which Marthe's health improved noticeably. We do not have much information about this first 'contact' but it is by no means inconceivable. We do, however, know about another that followed quite soon afterwards.

Marthe actually received a great and direct Marian grace. At the time she was sleeping in the same room as her sister Alice, who witnessed it. During the night of 25 March 1922 Alice was woken by a loud noise, and saw a great and very beautiful white light but said nothing to her sister Marthe. Marthe said to Alice one day: 'Yes, [the] light [was] beautiful but I also saw the Blessed Virgin.'

We do not know in what form Marthe 'saw' the Virgin Mary. There are several types of 'visions'. What is important is that these phenomena are not neutral. They bring about a profound change in the soul of the person experiencing them, especially a familiarity with Heaven. That person begins to know the 'other world'. It is equally significant here that contact with this 'other world', which effects entry into the beginnings of the mystical life, occurred through the ministry of Mary. From then on the Virgin Mary was to be Marthe's guide and comforter. Little by little she was to introduce her to her vocation and provide her with the means to fulfil it. God's power was slowly to be made manifest in Marthe's weakness and lead her along a path on which, humanly speaking, no-one can embark alone. The fact that Alice was present, even if she saw only part of what happened, is valuable in helping to confirm the authenticity of the phenomenon.

Marthe Robin's relationship with God was so strong that she wanted to give herself to him completely. Given that poor health meant that the religious vocation she had envisaged was absolutely out of the question, how was she to proceed? While she was staying with her sister, Gabrielle, mother of Raymond Gaillard, she ventured into her attic, where she found a religious book and chanced upon a passage that leapt off the page at her: 'Why seek happiness when you are made for suffering?' Abbé Faure was later to write in his notebook: 'It was there that God was waiting to show her her vocation. Touched by grace from on high, she understood immediately that God did not want to make her a nun but a victim for the conversion of sinners.' That grace was completed with Marthe's receipt of a 'wound of love', an ecstatic pain, in November 1922 in front of the altar of the Blessed Virgin in the church at Châteauneuf.

Marthe Robin was beginning the mystical life, that is to say a life of relationship with God which is not the result of human effort but of God's direct intervention, a life in which one is no longer governed by moral law but by that of love, in which also one emerges from darkness into new light, progresses from distance to proximity, from absence to presence, from the unknown to discovery. Little by little one comes to know who God is. This does not happen all at once. Even if there are apparitions or visions it takes a long time for God to take over a person's interior world. It is a process which involves the laying of foundations which will subsequently make it possible to get through more arid periods. In this contact with God, love is so powerfully revealed that an individual may feel capable of doing great and even slightly crazy things. This is what Jesus Christ himself did when he gave up his life for humankind, so one may well think oneself able and feel called to do the same.

The beginnings of light on her vocation

This was how Marthe interpreted her mystical contacts of 1922. The revelation of the love and proximity of God enabled her to come up with an answer to the major question of what she should do with her life, given the state she was in: she would give her life as Christ had done, and in doing so she would participate in the salvation of humanity held captive by sin. Conversations she had with Mme du Bay in Saint-Péray pointed her in the same direction. Mme du Bay was able to introduce her to the 'victim spirituality' very much in vogue in the Church at that time. Part of humanity was rejecting God. Others must therefore give their lives and make the ultimate sacrifice with Christ to compensate for this lack of love. Marthe had to do something with her suffering. This was how she began to find meaning in it. An emotional encounter with a priest, a hospital chaplain in Angers, who, like her, was undergoing treatment at Saint-Péray in October 1923, provides evidence. He was obviously physically very ill. They had some very deep conversations about Marthe's vocation, and then: 'On the evening he was leaving he came to say goodbye. He opened wide his arms and I rushed into them. "Ah," he said, "I shall die at peace and happy because I have held in my arms someone crucified like my Jesus."'

That sentence is extremely significant. Light had been shed on Marthe's life. She had needed to talk to a priest about it. She had confided her inner evolution to him and he in some sense validated it, recognising it as authentic and encouraging it. Hence his paternal gesture as he was leaving and the attitude of total trust on the part of the young girl. Oscillating between phases of illness and hope, she was nonetheless prepared to embark on the path Providence was suggesting to her by way of her health. She was in no doubt then that God was going to ask much of her and that real heroism would be required of her.

Something she did in August 1925 shows just how courageous she was. Abbé Faure had arranged for her to have a place on a Lourdes pilgrimage organised by the diocese. Lourdes' reputation implied that going on such a journey meant the chance of a miraculous cure. Even more profoundly, it meant visiting a place that had been blessed by the Virgin Mary's presence. For a soul devoted to Mary it was a joyous prospect. Yet Marthe gave up her place for Marie-Louise Costet from the neighbouring village of Saint-Martin-d'Août. The priest did not understand and took it very badly. Another suggestion that she travel to Lourdes made on 24 September 1928 by Jean Signé, Gisèle Boutteville's fiancé, was not taken up. Marthe wanted to remain at her post, in the farmhouse.

Marthe Robin's struggles and the act of abandonment of 1925
The conflict was not over yet, however. One part of Marthe acquiesced but another rebelled. For one thing the illness

progressed. Her whole body reacted with anguish and fatigue, which could not fail to have an impact at the spiritual level. There are indications of this in her letters of 1926 and 1927 to Mme Delatour: 'Life is just one black nightmare for a person in pain.' 'What can I tell you about me? My life is always the same, grey and monotonous, bringing far more sadness than joy; but I don't think anything can get to me anymore. I can see clearly that I am destined to drink from every bitter chalice and in long draughts.' 'Oh my dear friend, what a horrible existence we all have, thanks to the terrible disease that rheumatism is: but let us take courage, we can hope to go straight to Heaven, having done our purgatory on earth.' This was more the language of extremely painful resignation than deliberate offering.

On 15 October 1925 Marthe read on a holy picture a prayer of abandonment by Père de Bouchaud. It was the year Thérèse of the Child Jesus[4] was proclaimed a saint and the feast day of Saint Teresa of Avila. She chose this time to write her own act of abandonment to the love and will of God. For seven years her illness had been getting steadily worse. For seven years Marthe had been confronted with suffering that affected her body and soul. On this way of suffering Mary was a maternal companion to her, granting her signs of her presence and tender concern: 'No appeal to Mary is made in vain. I am firmly confident that she will answer my prayers because I believe the only hope left to us is to turn to Divine Providence which never abandons anyone.' When the act of abandonment came into her hands and Marthe read it, she found there the desire inscribed within her: the will to abandon her life to the one she loved and who loved her. Marthe wrote it out again, making some personal additions which already reflected the experience of a soul abandoning itself like a child to the Lord's will of love: 'I must become another him, another Jesus. So: abandonment, abandonment to love, abandonment full of love, wholly to Jesus.' She was to renew this act of abandonment daily. A few years later she would be able to say to her parish priest: 'Be pleased, Father, I have abandoned myself fully into the hands of God.'

She loved the Eucharist more and more: 'I took Communion very fervently not long ago. I was very content and emerged from it more courageous and more valiant; I can assure you that I was really content. How sweet the kiss of Jesus was to my heart and you can imagine how I took advantage of his presence to ask from the depth of my being and with so much love, for the graces I desire for those I love.'

Contact with Saint Thérèse of the Child Jesus
A flare-up of her illness in October 1927, during which she was once more thought to be lost, was the occasion for a further step. Her condition was extreme. Convinced she could not go on, she prepared to die – happily so, because it meant the end of her terrible struggle and her suffering. Then, as can happen with the apparently dying, she came back to life. When she emerged from her coma she confided to her family that Saint Thérèse of the Child Jesus had visited her several times and talked to her about her vocation. She had told her that she would not die yet but would live and carry on the saint's mission throughout the world. Later she was to add with a laugh, 'Oh the rascal, she left it all to me'. In 1931 she was to say: 'I often talk about her. She is such a "big sister" to me, so close, whose doctrine entirely based on love was so beneficial to my soul during the time of great darkness and no less great solitude, in which I found myself. Her autobiography *The Story of a Soul*, which I would sometimes chance to open, gave me solutions full of light and relevance.' Again she was to say: 'I have to say that I love her so much and yet it is she who closed the gates of Heaven to me. I was happy ... ready to go.'

When people return from the gates of death, they are often more disposed than previously to do what is essential. Life is simplified. It becomes clear what things are fundamental. They know too that the time now granted is a gift from God to them, and to others. They want to make the maximum use of it in the furtherance of their mission. Marthe emerged from her coma more determined and with a clear indication from Thérèse of the Child Jesus what her mission was to be. We have to remember that Saint Thérèse, who suffered greatly with her tuberculosis and was made a Doctor of the Church, was above all a doctor of love. In her, suffering was transcended by the experience of God's love and faith in the heavenly Father. Thanks to her Marthe would not merely offer up her suffering but would aim, in all simplicity, to transform it into love.

The attempt to understand her experience of God

What was Marthe to make of these phenomena? She talked about some of them to her family but they were quite incapable of understanding. In fact, what she told them must have made them even more uncomfortable about her illness. They must have thought her somewhat unhinged. She definitely spoke to Abbé Faure about her experiences too, which may well have been at the root of their initial lack of understanding. He was probably disconcerted and attributed her experiences to non-supernatural causes. Not until 1927 did Marthe receive any help from him. She had had no religious education. She had to put her experiences in context, read material that might enlighten and help her. Books were brought up for her from the parish library: 'I read some good works,' she said. The experiences of others were helpful to her. We have seen that she copied out and changed Père de Bouchaud's act of abandonment. We have also seen how in one of her letters she used the vocabulary of Thérèse of the Child Jesus, referring to 'the kiss of Jesus'. She immersed herself in *The Story of a Soul* and some of its expressions would later find their way into her writing. How could they not? She was serving an apprenticeship in a world she did not know, a vast and complex world in which she had everything to learn. She did so without facile curiosity, without seeking the extraordinary, only in order to meet her life's needs. Her intention is well summed up in something she wrote in her Journal at that time: 'I want to lead many, many souls to Jesus only by my love and by the total offering of my life as a sick person, not having any other will save that of my God, or rather by uniting my own will totally to that of my God.'

Thus God intervened more and more in Marthe's life with precise moments of mystical union. The period of great conflict was not yet over, however. It was leading up to a gift but, despite her good intentions, all was not yet completely accomplished. God had not yet conquered her completely. How moreover was it to be possible? God was asking her to agree not to get better, to accept the suffering inherent in her illness, to unite it all to the suffering of Christ and offer it up for the salvation of the world. How was she to take a step so contrary to all natural human tendencies? It was not enough to want it. A force from on high must take hold of her and give her the necessary strength. Her anguish was not over. When, much later, she described this period, Marthe was to say of it: 'Everyone can and should fulfil their vocation, but not me … I grappled with God … I would not wish any of you to struggle against God.' Yet in the midst of this decisive combat, Marthe Robin still advanced. She did not lose her faith or her love, or even hope. A foundation of peace was probably laid in her. A spiritual and human base was created, upon which God would be able swiftly to work.

NOTES

1. Probably harsh words.
2. Gisèle Boutteville, who became Mme Signé, died in 1989.
3. Marguerite Lautru (1903–2001) was to enter the congregation of nursing Sisters in Lyon of which she became Superior General. She remained close to Marthe.
4. Canonised on 17 May 1925.

CHAPTER 3
The Crucial Choice (1928–1930)

On 22 January 1930 Marthe Robin wrote in her journal: 'After years of anguish and sin, after many a physical, spiritual and psychological trial, I have dared to do it, I have chosen Christ Jesus.' At a given moment a decisive shift occurred. We know the date and the circumstances: it happened on Monday, 3 December 1928.

I. The 1928 mission

Marthe's choice arose out of a parish event organised by Abbé Faure: the 1928 mission. There is a tradition in pastoral ministry of missions being a decisive factor in the conversion or re-conversion of parishes. At intervals local priests brought in religious or diocesan priests with a reputation for being 'extraordinary' preachers for a period of a few weeks. Specialising in this kind of ministry, they were usually powerful speakers, who went straight to the essentials, rousing people, confronting them with their responsibilities and steering them towards a choice, a conversion. For many who heard them the mission would end with confession and continue with lifelong commitment. In the field of diocesan missions, the Capuchins were renowned for the strength of their convictions. They had their sights particularly set on a section of the working class that only inner authority and energy would enable them to reach.

At the request of Abbé Faure who wanted to shake up his parish and reverse its religious decline, a mission was preached at Châteauneuf by Capuchins from Lyon. It went on throughout the month of November and finished on 2 December. According to the Abbé it was not a success: 'A few rare returns, but without perseverance for the most part.'[1] It was very unusual for a mission to be so complete a failure. It implied the village was not free and the presence of a Masonic lodge may well have had a bearing.

One of the Capuchins was a Père Marie-Bernard from Marseille (Bernard Spagnol, 1883–1943). He was a deeply committed man who at the time religious were banned in France had been a missionary in Syria. Prior to 1914 he had read *The Story of a Soul* and been transformed by it. He himself had written a book about Saint Thérèse of the Child Jesus.[2] He was also known for his devotion to the Sacred Hearts of Jesus and Mary. All in all, he was a man of ardent faith who had thrown himself into evangelising. He himself admitted that he was not always blessed with great discernment, being more inclined to force than finesse, but in 1928 he was the right man for the job. Having failed with the parish of Châteauneuf, he was to be a channel of grace for Marthe Robin.

The meeting on 3 December 1928
In the course of these missions, the religious would systematically visit all the families. They paid particular attention to the sick, especially the seriously ill. On Monday, 3 December, the day after the sessions officially concluded, Père Marie-Bernard and his colleague, Père Jean, went to visit Marthe Robin. Mme du Bay knew Père Marie-Bernard and it may have been she who mentioned Marthe to him. By then, at the suggestion of her friend Marguerite Lautru who had been a nun for some months, Marthe had been keeping a diary for a while. A few days after the priests' visit Mme Bonnet went up to La Plaine and Marthe talked about their visit: '"Sister Lautru," she said, "told me to keep a diary so I have, but this week I left one page completely blank so

no one will know what happened to me." "Oh, why not write up those pages?" I asked. "Which day did you skip?" – "On Monday (the day on which Père Jean and Père Marie-Bernard had come to see her) I made my confession to Père Marie-Bernard and the page between my confession and my Holy Communion will remain blank. Only in Heaven will anyone know what happened." A few days later I asked whether her page was still blank, whether her humility was still making her hide what had happened. "M. le Curé knows", she told me.'

The Capuchins went back down, much edified by their time at her house. 'You have a great saint up there,' they told the parish priest but he reacted negatively, saying, 'I don't know who you're talking about'. The Capuchins defended Marthe and it would not be long before the parish priest at last changed his mind.

Something had happened to Marthe in the course of that visit, as a result of which she would never be the same again. It occurred in conversation with Père Marie-Bernard. Indeed, a short while afterwards Marthe advised her friend Gisèle Boutteville to go and see Père Marie-Bernard in Lyon: 'He will understand you ... you see, I have another direction in life.' By implication this direction had come from Père Marie-Bernard who had apparently been able to understand her too.

No doubt things had been very straightforward. In the first place Père Marie-Bernard had probably recognised and validated the mystical graces about which Marthe had been unable to speak to anyone since her treatment at Saint-Péray. But where were they leading? Victim spirituality was one thing but it had to be taken further. Saint Thérèse of the Child Jesus had already introduced Marthe to the way of love. But where did that love stop? Where was it going? Capuchin spirituality was based on the experience of Saint Francis of Assisi who had been as it were 'identified' with Christ. '*Franciscus alter Christus*' people used to say in the Middle Ages, 'Francis, other Christ'. In other words what Christ lived, Francis was called to relive, albeit in his own way. Saint Paul said:

'It is no longer I, but Christ living in me.'[3] Francis of Assisi was, like Saint Paul, 'taken over' by Christ, so configured with Jesus that he even received in his body the stigmata of his Passion. Francis' suffering, which was acute during his lifetime, was transformed, transfigured into love. Père Marie-Bernard probably told Marthe that her vocation was to be like Saint Francis of Assisi, so united to Jesus that he wanted to live in her. This was her crucial choice.

Enlightened from on high, Marthe Robin realised that this was her true calling. Everything fell into place. It was as if she had received an outpouring of the Spirit. The Holy Spirit took charge of her and gave her her mission and, at the same time, the strength to respond to it. She took the plunge, and could then rightly say in her journal:

> The more my life is submitted to God and conforms with that of the Redeemer, the more I shall participate in the accomplishment of his Work. Thus by uniting my obscure work, my poor little actions, my prayers unknown to men, all my sacrifices, all my suffering and immolation, and even the apparent sterility of my life, with the oblation of the infinite victim, I am sure of working not only towards my own sanctification but of giving God an immense crown of those chosen by Jesus.

To help her Père Marie-Bernard made a few suggestions. First he asked her not to read any more profane writings and not even religious writings that were not directly related to the spiritual life. He had also undertaken to promote greater trust between Marthe and Abbé Faure so he vouched for her with the priest. Finally he asked Marthe to become a spiritual sister to the Capuchins by entering the third order of Saint Francis. Marthe could not see clearly how that would help her and hesitated but, at Père Marie-Bernard's insistence, in the end she agreed. Without any doubt, in his mind it was a case of providing Marthe with spiritual support, a framework to which she could attach her spiritual life.[4] It was then that something else happened to confirm her completely in the 'plunge' she had just taken. It also provided her with a way of proceeding without submitting herself unequivocally to the spirituality of the Capuchins.

The night of 4 December 1928 and its consequences

Abbé Faure has left us an account of what happened to confirm the occurrence of 3 December. 'She was afraid she had taken too great a risk,' he wrote, 'when on the night of (Tuesday) 4 a.m. to 5 a.m. Our Lord appeared to her and after reassuring her three times, asked her if she would agree to suffer for the conversion of sinners in general and of Châteauneuf in particular, and at the same time he told her that he wanted me to be her spiritual father and there to be a very special union between us. With every affirmative response she felt and experienced a sword being plunged deep into her heart. From that day on she was thus entirely dedicated to God and resolved to accept all trials for the sake of poor sinners, and Our Lord alone knows what she has endured since.'

After that Marthe Robin did not delay. She asked Abbé Faure to be her spiritual father and, extraordinarily, he agreed. It is not easy to be the spiritual director of a mystic. It takes exceptional humility and abilities. Reassured by the Capuchins, however, Abbé Faure did eventually consent despite his fear of mystics. On 16 December she wrote him a letter. Abbé Faure was to attach so much importance to it that he kept it in his breviary for the rest of his life, and it was found there after his death: 'M. le Curé and dear spiritual Father. I am a profligate, as you can tell from the fact that I am calling you "Father!" without your permission and without having asked you whether you are willing. If it is not your wish I am ready to bow to the sentence of your refusal and keep my pain well hidden. But that is not how it is, is it M. le Curé and dear Father? You are willing for me to be in some small way your child.'

Abbé Faure was a good man. He committed himself whole-heartedly to this new ministry. His relations with Marthe soon became open and natural. She had no reservations about confiding in him. In the same letter she added this little note which already suggests intimacy: 'If it is possible for you to come to La Plaine before Christmas I will require a good long time of you. Don't bring your watch. It would be better ... '

Thus Marthe Robin began a radically different life. She was to write about it shortly afterwards, drawing a conclusion from this moment of transformation and at the same time establishing a programme for her future life:

> My whole life has just undergone a happy transformation. And my soul, which yesterday was still shrouded in the most awful darkness, is opening up to new horizons. I also feel completely renewed for the struggle and the suffering.
>
> At one point I was afraid that I would no longer have the strength or will for anything. What a source of anguish! But Jesus has remade me in him and uniquely for him alone. It is like a new life ... I am eager. I am really hungry and thirsty to work for the love and glory of God ...
>
> I am resolved always to live united with God and to make this union daily more intimate and close so that it may become more fruitful.

II. The principal elements of a spiritual life are put in place

Marthe Robin quickly committed all her energy to the new life opening up before her. On 28 February 1930 she was to write in her journal: 'Having made a vow of abandonment to love, let there be no further delay in the perfect accomplishment of this divine ideal.' God was now guiding her directly. This was the foundation period. The crucial choice was confirmed by other successive choices. 'On the eve of Ascension 1929,' her friend Jeanne Bonneton stated, 'the Lord had made Marthe choose between going straight to Heaven or remaining on the earth for a long time and saving many souls.' Heaven was Marthe's ideal: to see God immediately would guarantee her happiness. Remaining on this earth meant accepting to go on suffering, exposing herself to the storms of life, taking a risk. But it would also be the fulfilment of her mission. Once again Marthe accepted that mission.

Union with the crucified Jesus

Marthe's life on this earth was only of interest and even exciting for her because of the highest experience a human being can have: that of already entering into the depths of God. As we have seen, the way God had chosen for her was that of union with Jesus. Whilst remaining herself, more than that, becoming more herself, from then on Marthe Robin would be in constant 'contact' with Christ. Throughout the period in question this 'contact' was sensible to her soul. In the light of their own experiences the Fathers of the Church, the first Christian writers, established a doctrine of the 'spiritual senses'. They explained that the soul has 'senses' just as the body does but that these senses are atrophied by sin. One day God can activate them. Thenceforth, through grace, one is capable of 'sensing God', of 'touching' him, of 'tasting' him etc. This is all the more powerfully so because the 'spiritual senses' are incomparably superior in strength to the corporal ones. This was what Marthe was now experiencing.

Union with Christ may take different forms according to the difference in souls and God's design for them. Jesus Christ is God. He is infinite. No one can therefore know all of his being. He presents only one particular facet to any one person. Another holy person will thus have a completely different contact and way of identifying with Christ. It was union with Christ on the cross that had been assigned to Marthe, a way to which many holy persons have committed themselves but there are still many nuances and variations to it.

For her it was not just a case of union in suffering: it was above all unity at the deepest level of being. Often this relationship of intimacy uses the vocabulary of the heart. People speak, for example, of entering into the mystery of the Heart of Jesus. The symbol of the Heart of Jesus is used by the Church to signify the intimate part of Christ, the greatest depths, that which is most hidden and most precious of what is lived out within him. Being in 'contact' with the Heart of Christ, Marthe was thus initiated into his secrets, she knew his most intimate feelings, the roots of his love. She understood and tested for herself the reason he gave his life for humanity, a giving made manifest in his death, death on a cross. She summed up everything she was going through admirably in a single sentence:

> The Sacred Heart of Jesus on the cross is the inviolable dwelling place that I have chosen on this earth.

These words are like a motto, encapsulating as they do the essentials of her spirituality and her vision of the life that was from then on to be hers. Marthe could accept the surrender of herself to God as, to use the expression of the day, a 'victim of love'. She did not just wish to counterbalance God's justice by suffering and offering it up. Above all, she wanted to go to the farthest extremities of love and discover in herself and receive from God all the love of which she was capable. And she accepted that the way lay through the cross, even if in the eyes of humanity this seemed absurd. Thus she was able to write:

> Oh cross! Cross of my Saviour, cross that I love and bless, my soul's sweet treasure, it is by you that I wish to live and die, for in you and you alone is my way, my hope and my joy for the duration of my sad pilgrimage ... Oh my sweet Jesus! There I unite my pain with yours, my anguish with yours; it is there that I await the last flash of fire which will deliver my soul from its earthly prison and unite me for ever with the one my heart desires.

These words differ from those of the preceding period in that a certain hope runs through them. They are still devoid of illusion. Life in this world will remain painful, full of suffering and anguish. From now on, however, the pain can be accepted:

> Let me, oh adored Master, die entirely to the world and to myself. I accept with love and with ever greater joy the afflictions, hardships, consolations, suffering, dryness, abandonment, betrayal and disdain ... I love them because they come to me from you, because they unite me with you and make me a little like you, oh my divine Redeemer.

This acceptance was possible because it would bear fruit, not human but spiritual:

> What will come of my small wretchedness, of my trials borne with Christ-likeness and love? Surely they may result in exceptional graces of virtue and holiness for me and in the dazzling graces of conversion for those dear to me, and possibly in the marvellous graces of salvation for many, many other souls.
>
> Perhaps it will be through those trials that seem to annihilate me most, to reduce me to incapacity, that the fulfilment of my most ardent desires, my most fervent prayers, my most suppliant requests will come about.

Marthe also felt able now to say that she was happy and did not refrain from doing so. The love in her had become stronger than the suffering and it spread throughout her being: 'Oh Jesus, Jesus, I love you! In all my suffering I am happy.'

The importance of the Eucharist

Where can people be sure of encountering Christ? In the Eucharist. Jesus, really present, takes possession of the hearts of those who love and receive him in Holy Communion. From then on receiving the host in Holy Communion brought to her by Père Faure each week was to be an intense experience for Marthe:

> I am well aware of all that Jesus is giving me when he gives himself to me. I am deeply moved and overcome with respect and love, wondering what I can bring and give, poor little wretch that I am, to this God who fills me with graces, goodness and mercy, to this God full of love who by giving [himself] to me, places in my heart the seal of the elect.

Thereafter, mystical phenomena were to occur quite frequently at the moment of Holy Communion: 'Holy Communion days are days of unspeakable joy, dazzling lights, rapture, union of the soul soaring heavenwards. Oh! How beautiful it is!' she confided to Père Faure. The most significant expression here is the word 'union'. On another occasion, on 9 June 1930, she wrote: 'As soon as the real presence of Jesus-the-Host was in my heart, my soul was overwhelmed by an excess of happiness and joy. The fusion of my soul in God was so complete, so ineffable, that I was immediately absorbed into an ocean of delight and so entered a very heightened state of pleasure and rapture.' Elsewhere she went on to write: 'The divine master takes over everything and absorbs everything. There is nothing left that does not belong to him alone. Only the all-powerful One can give my soul this happiness, only he can contemplate it fully.'

In the course of these 'encounters' God gradually touched every aspect of Marthe's being: her body, her sensibility, her intelligence, her deepest 'I'. Gradually the 'geography' of grace was put in place. Like many saints in the history of the Church, she experienced the Three Divine Persons as united and yet distinct from one another:

> This God of love deigned to reveal the mystery of the Trinity to me and each of the Three Divine Persons spoke to my soul

separately. The First Person said to me: 'You are my blessed child.' The Second Person who is my beloved Saviour said: 'You are mine for time and for eternity.' The Third said: 'I am the Love that burns you and makes you overabundant in the midst of your trials.'

Thus the Eucharist was not a 'place' of union alone but also of instruction. Marthe began to find her way round in this spiritual world of God and identify the different phenomena that could occur there. She took good care not to confuse them. Marthe drew a clear distinction between God's taking over her soul which could be like a state of ecstasy, an emergence from oneself, and a vision which was a phenomenon of a completely different order: 'In this communion I think the division[5] was very intense but short: my soul was suddenly carried away by a love which belonged only to God and which can only be understood in him ... but I did not have a vision.'

The presence of God as Father
The 'meeting' with God begins ordinarily with contact with Christ. Sooner or later, however, there is usually a 'meeting' with the Father also. We have seen that the three Persons of the Trinity had begun to manifest themselves to Marthe. So it was that after the Son, the Father was little by little to give himself to her. He was to do so through her relationship with her spiritual father who was to unveil to her something of the goodness of God the Father.

The relationship between Marthe and Père Faure swiftly became one not just of trust but also of affection. She found in him a 'support', a 'source of consolation', a 'friend' and a 'guide'. Marthe, who had a loving and tender heart but who had difficulty in giving it expression, saw the dimensions of that heart expand greatly. But all this was constantly referred to God. On 21 April 1930 she wrote:

I begged with ardent love for the conversion of my parish, asking again for holiness for my dear spiritual father, entreating him to make him a model priest and a saint ... The divine king of my soul told me he had given him a great demonstration of his love by giving me to him, making me his child for eternity ... 'Continue the mission with him. I leave you to him; my heart rejoices every time he is near you. As your union grows so your two souls will understand each other. As I am One with my Father, I want your two hearts and your two souls to be linked and merge in me alone.'

Their spiritual friendship did not develop without difficulties. Sometimes the spiritual state of the woman he was directing was beyond Père Faure. To his credit, as we shall see, he sought help. But Marthe sensed his lack of understanding and suffered as a result. She was in fact utterly in need of support. Most of the time the mystical graces were not enough in themselves. They had to be identified, approved, and even purified by someone competent. Purely mystical graces are in fact rare. In the case of Marthe Robin, as with other mystics, they passed through a filter of sensibility, culture, vocabulary and desires. These factors have to be taken into consideration. One can otherwise find oneself so devoid of reference points that one is lost and anguished. This is what actually happened at times in Marthe's relationship with Père Faure. In March 1930 she wrote:

No one who has not been through it can understand the anguish of a heart that finds itself plunged into darkness and spiritual doubt without being able to extricate itself or, if it can, is not understood by its spiritual director, be it because he lacks experience, be it because God does not grant him the necessary light to recognise the sad state of that soul, or be it too because he wants to leave it completely abandoned.

Even in the midst of these trials, however, even when the relationship between Père Faure and Marthe was in some ways at a low ebb, it was full of lessons for her. For the first time she was experiencing what spiritual paternity was: a reflection of the paternity of God. Spiritual paternity only exists as a manifestation of the goodness of the Father, his patience, and his trust. It is totally geared to life. A spiritual father encourages the sources of life to flow, and helps to remove obstacles. His sights are set on the future. For this reason he helps the person he is accompanying to become increasingly free. In this way he says something about God the Father. It is important to note this because Marthe Robin had begun to experience with Père Faure a state with which she would subsequently be imbued. Marthe Robin, as we shall show later, was to become one of the great initiators of the 'return to the Father' which was to have a considerable impact on certain aspects of French Catholicism at the end of the twentieth century.[6]

The presence of the Virgin Mary

The Virgin Mary also played an essential role in Marthe's life. Little by little Marthe's mission was becoming clearer. Progressively her 'special mission' as she called it, her 'beautiful mission of love', included a Marian dimension. She wanted to work particularly 'for the divine sovereignty of the Eucharistic Heart of Jesus and of Immaculate Mary'. In other words it was a question of making Jesus better known in who he is and the love he shows especially in the Eucharist, and the role of the Virgin Mary.

Why did she wish to make the Virgin Mary known? Because Marthe Robin knew her herself. She had met her. Indeed, Marthe had begun a life of very close, intense and affectionate relations with Mary who frequently manifested herself to her. This was how Père Faure described one such manifestation: 'On 15 August (1929) at about 5 p.m. the Blessed Virgin appeared to Marthe Robin. She was white, but an incomparable white, in a white robe flanked with a white shawl over her shoulders which hung straight down and came together with two fleurs-de-lis at waist height and two ribbons with golden fringing on the end.'

Marthe also confided in Madame Bonnet about an appearance of the Virgin, describing it to her with the vocabulary and all the precision of a seamstress. In particular she told her about the 'hands which caressed me so much'. 'Did she speak to you?' I asked. 'Oh yes,' she told me, 'then she took the hand I could not move and helped me make the sign of the cross.'

The role of the Virgin Mary is that of a mother who looks after her child's needs, shows her love and comforts her. She also has an educational and formational role. Marthe had everything to learn, not least the attitudes of mind and heart indispensable for her mission. Her only solution was to look to Mary for guidance. She discovered that the simplest way was complete and integral surrender into the hands of Mary. Provided she left everything to her, there would be nothing to fear in life:

> So I am placing myself in Jesus' care, completely under the Blessed Virgin's schooling, to penetrate further and understand better those great mysteries of faith, hope and charity.
>
> Oh my very good, very gentle Mother! ... Take my will, I give it to you, unite it with yours which is also that of Jesus, so that like you, I may lend myself with all my soul to every one of God's designs.

Through this relationship Marthe Robin experienced great happiness and joy. So abundant was the love of the Virgin Mary for her that she received maternal caresses. The Blessed Virgin's goodness was to enable her to persevere with her mission even in the midst of all her health problems.

The spiritual struggle

At the heart of this evolution there emerged a spiritual battle which was to continue throughout Marthe's life. Anyone familiar with the history of spirituality will know that it was inevitable. Often it takes the form of a direct struggle with the devil. Saint Teresa of Avila, the Curé d'Ars and Saint John Bosco are just some famous examples who did not escape the experience.

Some of the devil's attacks took the form of suggestion combined with ordinary human imagination. Thus on 27 February 1930 she wrote: 'The devil sniggers lugubriously into my ears, repeating foul words without interruption or rest: he tells me I should not believe there is a place for me in Paradise. He also tells me that I should not imagine that God loves me. He attacks me too by way of thirst, making me cruelly and excessively thirsty, which is a very painful battle for me.' In such instances it might ultimately be said that Marthe was crediting the devil with things that were only human. But he also manifested himself physically. Thus Père Faure wrote: 'The devil, after reproaching her in the usual way, slapped her face, even breaking two of her teeth, and cursed her.'

People may wonder at phenomena of this kind and attribute them to autosuggestion. Unfortunately not all can be dismissed in this way. There are numerous examples in the Gospels. We may also ask ourselves why God allows them to happen. The lives of mystics involve sharing in the frontline conflict with the Evil One. They are capable of doing more to counteract him than other Christians and part of their vocation is to destroy the rule of evil. Such a calling may be more or less apparent in their lives. In Marthe's case it seems clear.

III. The development of Marthe's illness
It is evident that Marthe Robin had changed the axis of her life completely. From 1928 onwards the new reasons for living that had become apparent to her were so powerful that they enabled her to go on for another fifty-three years and accomplish something great, which was all the more meritorious for the fact that her illness continued to develop in a way that was ever more onerous.

On 2 February 1929 tetraplegia suddenly set in with contractions and muscular spasms. The pain was very acute. Her legs retracted progressively under her. Her hands were affected. In June 1929 she recovered partially for a while and some movement of the phalanxes became possible. From 1930 on she could no longer absorb anything. When people tried to make her drink, she said, 'I feel such a violent pain that it makes me cry out despite myself'. She suffered constantly. On 5 December 1930 she wrote: 'I am having very violent pain all over, principally in my head, stomach and back. Without Jesus it would be unbearable ... With him I say: "*Fiat* and thank you" ... So to me everything is sweet and good.'

Marthe's increasing disability obliged her gradually to give up the sewing and embroidery that were her only means of earning a little money, helping her family and also maintaining some measure of dignity. She did not resign herself easily to total dependence: 'Must I then give up my dear needlework for ever? I did so love it. It preserved a small illusion of activity. It was another reason to live; and it was needlework that taught me the totally divine art of contemplation ... and the no less divine art of being ever joyful. My poor little nature, which has always remained so active and so courageous in affliction, hardly dares to face the prospect of an irrevocable inability to work.'

These thoughts are manifestly very human, in the positive sense. Marthe Robin was not a glorious body. She did not live like the angels. She needed a minimum amount of activity and occupation and her dignity was important to her. It was extremely hard for her to be regarded as a complete cripple. This was a healthy reaction. For this reason and also because of her spiritual mission, she refused to give in and fought her illness with all her remaining strength. 'Two years ago,' she said on 28 March 1930, 'I desperately wanted to die in order to see God, because I had a firm hope of a blessed eternity. Now that I feel I have a mission to fulfil, I am fighting illness every inch of the way, offering up in advance the suffering that my energy and resignation are prolonging.'

※

On the human level, which for Marthe meant that of illness, the years 1929 and 1930 were thus a tragic time for her. She was all too well aware of it. 'Two years of total incapacity are just up. What a cruel experience of renunciation it has been,' she was to say on 2 February 1931. She did not escape into the spiritual at all. She did not create a parallel universe. Thanks to God's palpable intervention, however, they were also years of a great turning point in her life. Now, it should be emphasised, her spiritual life would no longer develop alongside her illness but actually within it. It was from her illness that she was to draw the meaning of her life. She had turned a dreadful situation right round and given it value. From then on she would be able not just to survive but actually to advance with all her energy. In her journal she wrote: 'The physical and psychological suffering works, I believe, very effectively and very favourably on my spiritual activity and, since this new transformation, I think more about souls and unite myself better to them in God, praying more than I did before for all of them but especially for sacerdotal souls, for priests, missionaries, religious, my special vocation, my beautiful mission of love.'

NOTES

1. Returns to religious practice.
2. Entitled *Message nouveau* (A New Message).
3. Galatians 2:20.
4. She was received on 24 or 25 February 1930.
5. Between the soul's senses and those of the body.
6. The rediscovery of God's role as that of a father full of goodness and mercy rather than a distant God of judgement.

CHAPTER 4
The Spiritual Life of Marthe Robin
(1930–1936)

After her 'conversion' Marthe Robin resolved to live. She had received her mission and wanted to pursue it, but did not yet know what dimensions it would assume or what concrete form it would take. She must therefore prepare herself. She had very few resources at her disposal so in the years 1930 to 1936 she put all her energy into her formation and acquiring deeper knowledge.

I. The framework within which Marthe lived

We should note before all else that Marthe Robin was no longer able to avail herself of something that can be a major source of support to Christians: attendance at Mass. It was impossible to transport her. At that time only Camillian priests were allowed to say Mass in a sick person's room and there were none in the locality. Yet Marthe talked about Mass as if she actually attended. Since 1926 it had been broadcast over the radio and she may have followed it by this means. She was, however, brought Holy Communion every week. Thus her religious life went on within the narrow confines of her room.

Given that she was probably destined to remain in the same place (after all, where else could she go?) Marthe first had to sort out the framework within which she lived. She did not resign herself to being totally dependent. Like many serious invalids she drew on what reserves of energy she had to arrange her familiar universe so that it was as functional as possible. This applied to every aspect of life to which she could attain.

Marthe Robin's physical horizons were restricted to her room. She knew it inside out and was familiar with where things were, right down to what was where on her cupboard shelves. She used the senses she still had – hearing and smell – to the full and through them gleaned as much information as possible. She had a very highly developed feel for the human voice. She could no longer move, or hardly, and so cultivated a way of communicating without gestures. She spoke an extremely precise form of French with an intonation and pitch that were remarkably clear and adapted to the individual with whom she was conversing. For as long as she was able to read with the help of a device set up next to her, she read. She knew she was likely to lose her sight so studied the available spiritual books very carefully and, with the help of an exceptional memory greatly enhanced by necessity, she made the elements she found most interesting her own, to the point of learning them completely off by heart. Similarly she wrote for as long as she was able to, fighting paralysis every inch of the way. She even learned to write holding a pencil in her mouth.

By asking Marthe to read only strictly spiritual works, Père Marie-Bernard had risked limiting her outlook considerably, not only from a human point of view but also from a religious one. Marthe Robin followed his directive for we do not know quite how long. It was not, however, to have negative consequences. Her ability to read was restricted and it was precisely in the spiritual domain that she needed to develop herself, so that was what she concentrated on. But Marthe also swiftly began to receive a wide variety of visitors. If only in order to understand the people with whom she was dealing, she was required to take in a wide range of information, which sometimes bore only a distant relationship to mysticism. This was to help her considerably. In fact, thanks to these conversations coupled with exchanges of letters, Marthe was to expand the space in her room. Later she would readily take an unlimited interest in a thousand things and sometimes surprised her interlocutors with her curiosity about subjects far removed from anything they expected of her. In this respect too, Marthe Robin remained very human, and nothing could be further from the truth than to confine her to the image of a mystic out of touch with life.

Marthe's illness developed but it was also subject to involutions and periods of recuperation. Though her legs were paralysed, it is certain that Marthe tried to move about whenever her arms would respond. She did absolutely everything she possibly could to preserve some semblance of normality. Supporting herself on her elbows, she would force her body to twist along the ground. Sometimes she would drag herself across the floorboards of her room to attend to her private needs. She was not in a supportive familial environment so that was what she would do at night whenever she was able. In this way, even if her ability to get about was very limited, she kept a modicum of freedom. It is likely that she recovered this ability, at least for intervals, up to the very end of her life. Thus she did everything she could to preserve a measure of privacy. People were amazed at this but their astonishment is unwarranted. It shows that Marthe Robin was not a glorious body. She was a human being with legitimate needs who fought to meet them. These were things about which she was very modest and did not speak.

When it came to doing anything more, however, Marthe Robin had to rely on others. Given that she had no income and was totally supported, how was she to come up with the resources she needed at least to give to charity, to help the prisoners or missionaries in whom she was very soon to take an interest? For some years she conducted a small trade in devotional items which brought in a meagre income, although there is nothing to suggest that she profited from it herself in any way. She also received donations from benefactors like Mme du Bay. By this means she was able to start some aid and support work which kept her very busy and brought her into contact with a great many people in need.

For everything else, for daily living as well as the work she wanted to do for the Church, Marthe Robin was obliged to go through the people available. Her mother looked after her everyday needs. Marthe also formed friendships that were to become precious to her.

II. Marthe's spiritual accompaniment

These friendships included those with several priests. Fortunately Père Faure was not possessive and did not hesitate to appeal to more competent colleagues when his spiritual daughter surpassed him. First among them was Abbé Perrier, parish priest for the neighbouring village of Saint-Uze from 1913 to 1938. On a postcard addressed to Marthe on the occasion of her birthday, he called her 'my very dear child'. This meant that Marthe did not regard Père Faure's paternal role in relation to her as exclusive. Marthe submitted the first version of the act of abandonment to Abbé Perrier which suggests a real spiritual intimacy between them.

Very different was Abbé Betton,[1] then philosophy professor at the Saint-Paul-Trois-Châteaux seminary. He was an intellectual, well-versed in mystical theology. He was also a spiritual soul with 'antennae' in that domain. He was taken to Marthe by Abbé Perrier. Having gone as an expert resolved to uncover a possible hoax, he would later describe his first meeting with Marthe: 'I arrived in the room and at once sensed such a presence of the Father, the Son and the Holy Spirit that I felt very small, very small.' In his first conversation with Marthe he pointed out a theological impropriety on her part and she submitted to his judgement with humility and straightforwardness. Because of this humility Abbé Betton judged Marthe to be an authentic mystic.

Abbé Betton had an important role to play because it was he who enlightened Marthe about the nature of the phenomena she was experiencing. He explained the existence of different types of visions: intellectual, imaginative and corporeal. Marthe Robin needed to put her experiences into words and, for want of the appropriate vocabulary, could get it wrong. Had she taken a wrong turning in her descriptions of her inner life, the consequences could have been grave. Thanks to Abbé Betton, Marthe very quickly saw the relative value and respective roles of the various phenomena, as is shown by something she wrote in 1930 comparing intellectual and imaginative visions.

During this period Marthe Robin was visited by an illustrious Jesuit, Père Albert Valensin, one of the leading thinkers in the Company in France. In 1936 he was to say of her to Abbé Finet, the priest who, as of that year was to become Marthe's spiritual director: 'Oh, Marthe Robin, I know her. I was taken to see her by Mgr Pic not very long ago. I spent three hours with her.' He likened her to Saint Catherine of Sienna.

Yet relations with Père Marie-Bernard did not continue beyond 1930. A time came when the priest took fright, something not unusual for people associated with mystics. As a consequence he turned for advice to an expert in spiritual problems, Mgr Saudreau, chaplain to the Sisters of the Good Shepherd in Angers and author of remarkable works on the subject. Mgr Saudreau, who was not given much information by Père Marie-Bernard, suggested a sort of test which Père Marie-Bernard conducted with what might be considered a certain naivety: he asked Marthe to have herself photographed and give him a photo. Because Marthe gave him the one he considered least ugly, he thought she was consumed with pride! He believed the test to be conclusive and pronounced a judgement on Marthe as categorically negative as it had been positive a short while previously.[2] This also brought about a severing of connections with the very generous Mme du Bay who knew the Capuchin and followed him. Fortunately neither Père

Faure nor Abbés Perrier and Betton were put off. Nevertheless Marthe suffered enormously as a result, especially in October and November 1930: 'My soul is plunged into bitterness', 'My soul is completely flooded with pain.' The rupture had been accompanied by accusatory meetings and correspondence.

Yet Marthe Robin was in all the more need of support because she had now entered a new phase in her mystical life: like a number of other holy people in the history of the Church, every Friday she relived the Passion of Christ.

III. Mystical phenomena

The stigmata
At the beginning of the month of October 1930, according to the testimony of Père de Mallmann, Marthe received the stigmata. She asked that they should not be apparent. At first therefore her stigmatisation was interior. Only later did the phenomenon become visible.

During the 1930s Marthe's friend, Gisèle Signé, visited her at La Plaine: 'One day, after parting from Marthe and saying goodbye, I left. I was in the courtyard. Mme Robin called out to me, "Little one" and I turned round. "I'd like to tell you something. I'm very worried about my little one. She's bleeding." She indicated the heart, the face (forehead and eyes). I immediately thought, "Those are the stigmata." – "But what are the stigmata?" She thought it was an illness. "Look at this linen," she said to me. It was all blood-stained. "I've washed this laundry," Marthe's mother said. "I've boiled it, I've bleached it but it won't come out. What is it?" – "Mother Robin you should not keep this to yourself. Marthe should talk to M. le Curé about it." She replied: "Marthe doesn't want me to tell him, don't say anything about it to him."'

There is no doubt that this statement is the earliest evidence of Marthe's visible stigmatisation. The most precise description of

the phenomenon comes from Marthe herself. During the medical
examination she underwent in 1942 she was induced to explain
the unusual wounds the doctors found. This is their report of
what Marthe told them:

> In 1931, at the end of October, beginning of November, Mlle
> Robin began to suffer the Passion on Friday and the
> phenomenon has recurred every week since then.[3] At the same
> time the stigmata appeared on the backs of her hands and feet.
> They presented initially as painful reddish blue contusions
> (bruises) and persisted in that form for two years. Then on her
> hands, feet and left side, right next to the medial line, they
> were replaced by painful wounds which remained open
> without bleeding or forming a scab. These wounds would
> bleed on Fridays, and only Fridays, and they disappeared after
> six months. Then the stigmata assumed another character.
> Blood would appear only on Fridays but there were no wounds
> and above all no permanent stigmata. In 1934, 1935 and 1936
> on several occasions the Passion did not involve bleeding: in
> 1936 notably the stigmata did not appear for two months.

We probably have a description of what was happening from
Marthe herself in a text dated 14 November 1931:[4] 'At once I saw
my bed turn into a large thorny cross, a transformation which had
already occurred many times and which became ever more
agonising with ever more love … "That is where I want you
now," an inner voice immediately said. The change came about
suddenly. The intensity of the suffering was such that it caused me
to tremble dreadfully, all my limbs shook and I felt as if my heart
were burning.' Later the philosopher and academician, Jean
Guitton was to question her: '"But," I said to her, "they say that
the stigmata are simultaneously very joyful and very painful." –
"Yes, simultaneously. But you mustn't think of a human or
sensory joy. It is a deep and 'divine' joy, a joy that is entirely

internal. Similarly the suffering is extreme, primarily interior. If God did not support you, you would die." – "But have you seen a lance, a fire?" – "Yes, a burning, interior (but sometimes external) fire. A fire that emanated from Jesus. And I saw it as a dark red light, a light that burned."'

Thus every Friday until the end of her life, Marthe relived or rather shared in the Passion. The duration of the phenomenon was to alter with time and become longer. Marthe remained extremely discreet but as time went on her spiritual father allowed certain persons to be present during her Passion. At the end of 1933, beginning of 1934 for example, there was Mgr Soulas, the vicar general of the diocese, and Abbé Auric. Père Faure or, as of 1936, Père Finet would take notes. Some of those present were to leave sometimes quite detailed testimonies. Over fifty people questioned at the cause for beatification had seen blood flowing from Marthe's wounds. Mlle Faure, for example, a teacher at a private school in Saint-Uze said: 'I saw blood flowing from her eyes.' Canon Bérardier stated: 'We saw her sweating blood from her forehead and tears of blood flowing sometimes thickly, leaving heavy traces across her cheeks, and sometimes mixed with ordinary tears.' Abbé Auric wrote: 'I personally witnessed her face all bloodstained: blood running from the stigmata of the crown of thorns, blood being wept from her eyes onto her cheeks.' During the medical examination in 1942 the doctors also noted the presence of stigmata on her head, face and hands, and a large bloodstain on her chest.

At times, as once on the feast of the Most Precious Blood, there was so much blood that it took several cloths to staunch it. Alice Brosse and Madeleine Cheval sometimes helped Marthe's mother to wash these cloths.

The phenomenon was witnessed by so many that it seems absolutely beyond dispute. In many stigmatics the stigmata disappear and they did not go on throughout Marthe's life, except for those on her forehead which were still visible when she died.

The meaning of the stigmata and the Passion

The death of Jesus on the cross was, according to Christ himself, the greatest act of love he could offer mankind: 'No one can have greater love than to lay down his life for his friends.'[5] In the course of the history of the Church a significant number of people have been led to unite themselves with Christ to the point of sharing in his Passion. We know of several hundred, most famous among them Saint Francis of Assisi and Saint Catherine of Siena. Sometimes this Passion was completely internal. Sometimes it was accompanied by various external manifestations, even to the point of the body of the person receiving Christ's own wounds; over two hundred people have been stigmatised in this way. The stigmata appear in different forms. Sometimes they are actual holes into which a finger could almost be introduced, sometimes they are smaller slits, and sometimes they are simply painful spots. In the lives of the holy people concerned the stigmata themselves may evolve. Often out of humility those who receive them ask that they cease to be visible.

During the Passion, Jesus' various states are relived; his dereliction in Gethsemane, the scourging, the way of the cross, the nailing down, the agony on the cross, the feeling of abandonment by the Father, the surrender into his hands when 'All is accomplished'. The external world no longer exists. For most of the time the person concerned is no longer in the presence of the people around him or her, but in the Jerusalem of two thousand years ago. When the person speaks, it is possible to follow the various stages leading up to a death which seems real. Quite detailed accounts may be written down on the basis of what is said. There is a whole literature based on it. Then, with varying degrees of rapidity the stigmatic comes back to life. Sometimes he or she is able immediately to resume normal activity, although this was not of course the case with Marthe.

Persons reliving the Passion do not in any way lose their personality. Even while unconscious they remain very much themselves. The realities of the Passion are thus sometimes expressed through a specific culture and particular preoccupations. Absolute scientific value should not therefore be attributed to them. There is still a measure of subjectivity about the way in which things are experienced. Thus during the Second World War the preoccupations of Marthe and those around her are apparent during the Passion, at least in the prayers addressed to Christ and the Virgin Mary.

Marthe herself gave an interpretation of her Passion in a conversation with Père Livragne, an Oratorian Father and a great preacher of retreats: 'All Christians are called upon to participate in the Passion, to complete in their body that which is missing in the Passion of the whole Christ.[6] I am just a sign, a reminder to Christians.'

For an example of the way in which the experience was perceived by a witness we can do no better than to cite a highly regarded priest from Lyon, Canon Bérardier, director of charitable works for the diocese and then priest in charge of the parish of Saint-Louis in the city of Saint-Etienne. In 1942 he wrote:

Friday at 4.15 p.m. official time i.e. 2.15 p.m. by the sun. We joined M. Finet who had been with Marthe for over two hours … A continuous moan was coming from Marthe's lips; a lament that could be perfectly noted in a musical score, with crescendos and diminuendos.

This repeated sound quickly seized hold of and haunted the heart. Doctor Ricard told us that this kind of moaning is an indication of pain exacerbated in the extreme. This is how a person moans when he can no longer cry out, an expression of suffering beyond relief.

At the same time Marthe's head moved slowly and regularly from right to left on her pillow, and at times her body would jerk in all directions.

Then we heard Marthe say very distinctly: 'Oh! Go away! Be quiet!' She was addressing the devil and her castigations were not unfounded because a few moments later, the previous painful lament gave way to a sort of raucous, almost savage cry which lasted several seconds. The lament was resumed, interrupted again by a 'Be quiet' uttered in the same threatening tone. Sometimes Marthe would add: 'Oh you! Will you keep quiet! You won't get anywhere!' No doubt at that point Satan was suggesting the temptation of despair to her and trying to persuade her that her suffering was in vain.

Then the moaning gradually subsided. At about 5 p.m.[7] we clearly heard Marthe say: 'Father, why have you forsaken me?' Her head was still moving backwards and forwards. Instead of the tragic lament we had been hearing for an hour there were sharp, broken, quite rapid 'Ah! Ahs!'... Then clearly though softly articulated: 'My God, into your hands I commend my spirit.'

One minute later Marthe uttered a great cry, a strange cry that lasted three or four seconds and with a sudden movement her head fell back onto her left side forming a marked right angle with her body. We were totally convinced that she had just died. Her face was pale, tears and blood had coursed across her cheeks onto the towel round her neck.

Other phenomena

The reliving of Christ's Passion never occurs in isolation. Mystics go through an entire itinerary. Marthe was introduced into a new and extremely rich universe. This universe even became central for her and it was from it that she took her bearings. She had knowledge of God's spiritual world and it was that world that she wanted to make known on earth.

This world manifested itself to her in several other ways. She had 'visions', which is to say that figures from Heaven appeared to her; either they were corporeal visions or they appeared in her imagination in which case they are referred to as imaginative visions; or they related to her intelligence, in which case they are referred to as intellectual visions. These things should not be regarded as being produced by the person concerned. A non-believer could not of course interpret them in any other way, but a believer, especially one with some spiritual experience, knows that these manifestations have a power, precision and higher degree of reality than anything arising from ordinary human experience. Such visions permeate the individual to a depth that is difficult to describe.

Marthe Robin was clearly granted visions in different forms. On several occasions she had intellectual 'contact' with the Trinity. That does not mean that she saw God face to face as in a beatific vision, but she was nevertheless taken into the depths of God. Thus she wrote on 23 May 1932 that after Holy Communion she found herself transported 'to the summits of the divine life, face to face with the truth, in which (she saw) in the depths of eternal love (as far as is possible in this world), God's Being in all majesty, the source of all Life, God in his divine essence.' 'I do not understand,' she added, 'how this could have happened but I am sure of the truth of the miracle.'

She also 'saw' Jesus in visual and intellectual form. On 4 April 1932 she wrote: 'I am sure of the human presence of Jesus at my side … Since my last great vow of abandonment to love, Jesus has never appeared to me exteriorly. I should say that I have had very few corporeal visions. The divine apparitions almost always manifest themselves to my soul.' That is to say that they were intellectual visions.

She had one actual physical contact with the Virgin Mary who looked after her like a mother caring for her child. She felt her touch and saw what she was doing. This is extremely important. Marthe was suffering dreadfully. She needed to be loved and consoled, and to feel it. She could only give what love she received. No doubt the Virgin Mary took care of Marthe more than we can imagine, as a mother looks after her sick child with constant tenderness and attention. Visitors were struck by the way in which Marthe talked about the Blessed Virgin: 'It was as if she knew her very well.'

Marthe also had 'visions' of the angels, of Saint John and Saint Francis of Assisi in ways unknown to us. These two saints are particularly associated with the Passion of Jesus. They were given by God to Marthe as friends to develop, console and help her to bear the suffering of the Passion.

Yet Marthe was well aware that there was a risk of becoming attached to these visions and did not ask for them. What interested her was love and because in her case love was linked to the cross, that was all she wanted. Thus she wrote: 'It is not visions that I want but the suffering of my Jesus, the bare cross.' She wanted these phenomena to be kept secret. 'But what would people think if I were suddenly transported in ecstasy,' she wrote on 16 January 1932, 'when what I want so much is for the great secret of my life to remain unknown to anyone?'

But in order to show people around Marthe the reality of what she was experiencing, God sometimes went a little further, and some people did catch a glimpse of certain spiritual phenomena. One day M. and Mme Signé were in conversation with Marthe when she unexpectedly stopped talking and appeared to them 'illuminated'. The stigmata on her forehead and bloodstains on her gown could then be seen very clearly. After a few moments Marthe resumed the conversation as if nothing had happened. After they had left her M. and Mme Signé talked to each other about their visit and found that they had both witnessed the same thing, although nothing had been said while they were in the room.

Marthe's innermost reactions

How did Marthe Robin react deep within herself to this flood of divine favours accompanied by so much suffering? She was full of gratitude to God for granting her the grace of being so close to him as to share in his Passion. On Wednesday 9 January 1935, she wrote:

Each day I embrace with renewed gratitude and renewed joy the immense task entrusted to me by the Redeemer and thank him for having so prodigiously given me of his chalice, his crown, his nails and his holy cross, for having granted that I might experience and continue his long and painful agony and all his Passion, for having in short so prodigiously and profoundly imprinted in me his suffering and Eucharistic life.

The Lord had indeed become extraordinarily close to her. She was having the greatest possible experience any human being can have: that of feeling God living within her. On 26 January 1932 she wrote:

Never before have I been in a state of such complete transformation into the adorable suffering and loving humanity of Jesus. Of Jesus, assimilating, absorbing, exhausting, melting my whole being in him ... New life in a surfeit of self-abandonment and love! More than ever given up to the transforming action of the Holy Spirit ... To Jesus, to Christ – the Host, in order to conform to his image and be in his likeness.

She was not going through this for her own sake. There are references in her writings to those she loves and to causes dear to her, especially the holiness of priests: 'Ah!' she said, 'I would so like to show everyone the Christ full of love and mercy, in order to draw them to God.' Marthe was becoming more and more conscious of her intercessory role. She held in her prayers the souls she knew but in this respect too she was expanding her horizons. People entrusted their intentions to her, and she took an interest of her own accord in causes outside her immediate environment, beginning with her parish and the holiness of priests. Her room started to become the centre of a prayer network that was to go on growing until her death. Marthe's interior life was not just concerned with her. Her identification with Christ was the implementation of the first commandment: to love God. But she yearned with all her might to put the second into practice: to love her neighbour to the point of laying down her life for others, as Christ had done before her. She did it through the daily offering of her life of suffering. Within her she carried something of the future of the Church and humanity, just as we all do, albeit often without realising it. In Marthe's case the undertaking was conscious and integrated. She entered into a combat that was to affect her greatly, gradually consume her, a combat to which she would give her all to the very end.

IV. Marthe Robin's reading and writing

Anyone attempting to analyse Marthe Robin's activities during the period we are looking at, will be struck by the amount of time she must have spent reading and writing. She must have immersed herself in it for hours on end with remarkable constancy and great energy. Reading and writing did not come easily to her. She had to find the necessary concentration. Not only did she write with a pencil in her mouth but there were probably times when she turned the pages of a book with a knitting needle or something similar held in the same way. Any readers or secretaries to whom she had recourse, had to make themselves repeatedly available for long periods of time. That presupposed much good will on their part and the recognition that what they were doing was important. All in all it took great effort by Marthe and by several other people. The manner in which she accomplished her work was remarkable in itself, quite irrespective of the contents.

Reading

Marthe Robin read or had read to her, a number of books from the parish library. She would like to have gone more deeply into the speculative knowledge of faith. 'What is truer … more magnificently beautiful than dogma? How I would like to study and penetrate the depths of the mysteries! Sometimes I envy those who have the good fortune to do theology,' she said on 22 January 1930, but immediately added: 'But doesn't prayer, divine contemplation, far surpass even the most rigorous studies in knowledge, love and power?' So Marthe threw herself into what she had: books on spirituality, which were in any case better suited to her than theological works and fundamentally more in line with what she was seeking.

The parish library bought up all the latest publications and was well stocked with spiritual books. One of Marthe's friends, Mlle Blanck, who was very interested in mystics, also kept her supplied with books and pamphlets on the spirituality of the Sacred Heart and introduced her to the saintly Italian Sister, Bénigne Consolata of Como. Thus we know of some twenty books at least that Marthe went through. Sometimes they were the work of fashionable authors of the day such as the Jesuit Père Plus, Abbé Klein, Père Désiré des Planches and the Dominican Père Bernadot. They dealt with essential elements of the interior life, with the Eucharist and faith, but they were mostly concerned with different people's lives, their notes and correspondence. Some were very well-known: Saint Mechtilde von Hackeborn, Saint Teresa of Avila, Saint John of the Cross, Saint Marguerite-Marie, Catherine Emmerich, Saint Veronica Giuliani and Saint Louis-Marie Grignion de Montfort. Others were only just making their appearance in the field of spirituality at that time: Madeleine Semer, Marie-Antoinette de Geuser, Gemma Galgani, Consummata, Adèle Garnier, Thérèse Durnerin, Lucie-Christine, Dina Belanger, Theresa Higginson, Elisabeth of the Trinity, and Thérèse of the Child Jesus, 'her big sister' whom Marthe took great delight in reading. But she also had a deep grasp of the contents of the other works made available to her.

Why did Marthe read these authors? She could only have done so with the agreement of Père Faure and more generally of the other priests dealing with her. It was vital for her. Firstly, because

Marthe was experiencing mystical states which were totally out of the ordinary and for which nothing had prepared her. It was important that she found out for herself that others had gone through the same things. In this way she was not abnormal. She belonged to a line of servants of God who were no doubt special but had nonetheless been very much alive and aware of what was going on in the world. Thus her vocation was not 'a case'. Ancient and recent Church history helped to give meaning to the amazing venture in which she found herself engaged.

Secondly Marthe needed something with which to draw comparisons. The mystical life is not a matter of study and theory but of experience. People may hold forth endlessly about spiritual states but unless they have experienced them themselves, at least partially, all talk is empty. They are speaking of a universe that they have not explored. The priests surrounding Marthe were men of God but they were not enough for her. She had to find fellow souls who could tell her what had happened to them and where they had stood in relation to it. She would otherwise have felt lost.

There is a third, even deeper reason, for her reading of these books. Because Marthe was suffering terribly from an illness that was extremely destabilising, at times her personality was in a state of great tension. It is likely that at such times she felt lost and interiorly ravaged. She could have succumbed to madness or death. She had to fight in order not to go under, to maintain her identity and even reconstruct herself. What kept her going was her mystical life. She needed therefore to give expression to that life, to articulate it herself, but she had neither the words nor the knowledge to do so. In that world she was lost. So she had to find the vocabulary somewhere else to express the inexpressible within her. She needed to find formulae, descriptions, studies that would say something about her, and she could not invent them herself. It is understandable that writing was as vital to her as it was for Marcel Proust and other gravely ill people in the history of spirituality and literature.

Writings

Marthe Robin's writings fall into several different kinds. From 1929 to 1932 she kept a personal journal. She dictated texts – prayers, meditations and poems to Père Faure and other writers. One particularly important text is an account of the Passion which because of its length and the care it required, occupies a place apart in her 'works'.

What are these writings about? They are an expression of Marthe's life. In them she gave voice to what she was experiencing, her feelings, desires and love for God. They were not speculative. She had no desire to write books for subsequent use by the Church: 'I am only relating these things for my spiritual father and I know that he will know how to keep my precious and great secret. To write for him, to write out of obedience, is also to pray' (16 February 1932). Sometimes this work took its toll on her because she found it hard to apply herself to it: 'I am finding writing more and more repugnant. Revealing heavenly favours, making known the ever more numerous graces bestowed on me by our great God of love is my most painful trial. Yet I must make everything known to the father of my soul' (23 February 1932).

Père Faure was one of Marthe's secretaries. 'I have never written so much in my life before,' he was to say. Jeanne Bonneton was another. She wrote on small torn off sheets of paper which she would then take down to the parish priest. This explains on the one hand, the existence of isolated sheets and on the other, the presence of the same texts in several places. The first draft was copied out again. And not just copied but sometimes reworked as Marthe Robin tried to find exactly the right expression. The act of abandonment, for example, was to be reconsidered and enriched in this way.

Marthe was enormously reliant on what she had read. She knew some texts off by heart and included passages from them in her own writings. This is a well-established method of composition: the Magnificat and the Benedictus were woven out of quotations from the Old Testament that sprang spontaneously to the minds of Mary and Zachariah. Saint Bernard constantly quotes from the Holy Scriptures which often form the framework for his sermons. The Curé d'Ars put whole sections by authors whose thinking he had totally assimilated, into his. This does not detract from the originality of his thinking. So with Marthe we find several kinds of writings: some are exclusively by her. Others are compositions made up of her own texts mixed with some that she has borrowed. This is the case with the Passion, for example, which draws much of its inspiration from Catherine Emmerich. Simone Ladret has stated that in 1941 Marthe dictated 'Preparation for Easter' to her. Marthe had no books in view. What she dictated came from her and what she borrowed she knew by heart. If we look closely at these intermingled texts we will find that the parts personally composed by Marthe are often still important. They are, if you like, the creative work of several people but Marthe remains the orchestral leader. For instance, she borrows a narrative thread from Catherine Emmerich, completes it, corrects it, inverts certain elements, assumes a certain distance from the archaeology so important to her predecessor, and abandons the framework of Jewish liturgical style to present the same action in the framework of Christian liturgy. Marthe does something a little similar to the Old Testament prophets who used earlier writings, respecting them scrupulously right down to the appropriation of their vision. She had a 'memorial' method of composition, characteristic of the compilation of the Bible.

A thornier question is that of the passages, in letters and notebooks for instance, which Marthe borrows from other authors, attributing to herself the states they describe. Is she lying or falsifying? A lie must first of all be intentional. To whom could Marthe be lying? Her writings were meant only for Père Faure. He could check the quotations Marthe used in books that came from his own presbytery. Indeed, those books are still in the Foyer to this day. There was no intent to deny her sources. Marthe wanted to keep what she was going through secret and was put out when anyone suspected anything of her inner state. This was her reaction all through her life. She was no author seeking acclaim: quite the opposite. She was, however, a woman desperately needing to express herself. Indeed, as has already been established, at times an element of identification was indispensable to Marthe. She was experiencing things which, as someone who had had no education and was conscious of the fact, she did not know how to articulate. Thus on 10 February 1930 she wrote in her notebook: 'How am I supposed to write them down, how am I to know how to articulate all these things that are so far beyond a human being? Nothing comes to mind to convey the slightest intimation of what is going on within me.' Others had found the words. They had said things better than she could so she resorted to those words.

Remuneration for writing is not at issue here: this was a consideration entirely alien to Marthe. Her sincerity is not in question. 'The very numerous samples of her writing we have examined,' a graphologist wrote about her, 'bespeak her slow and steady progression, and the anguish she felt. She is completely frank. Nothing is fabricated to deceive but everything is interiorised apart from the ongoing chant which speaks over and over again of the experience of the Passion and the intensity of her attachment to this mystery. Clear and limpid, the writing is a reflection of her soul.' For his part, Doctor Cuvelier, a neuropsychiatrist and specialist in mystical literature, wrote: 'Marthe Robin moves from memorisation to "memoration", which is to say that through her illness, she incorporates into her personality memories accepted as current reality. Such a process should culminate in mental confusion but here the "me" emerges reinforced. This is where, in our opinion, the intervention of grace is manifest.'

Writing made it possible for Marthe Robin to live. For the long period during which she was trying to find herself, when the mystical life was going on in the midst of her illness, and her very being was under threat, writing was a lifeline for her.

A doctrine according to Marthe?
Marthe Robin had no aspiration to create a work of doctrine. She does, however show real originality on one essential point: the Virgin Mary. Because she is talking about someone she knows, she goes further and is more specific than most authors. This was why she was able to discuss her with great theologians and suggest ways in which they might develop their learned works. She was also able to avoid some of the pitfalls besetting Marian theology at that time. There again, however, it was not a case of doctrine constituted as such. What she had to say about the Virgin Mary was simply drawn from her life with her.

V. Marthe Robin's relationships
Marthe also 'expressed herself' through her connections and friendships. From 1928 onwards she was liberated both interiorly and exteriorly. The ostracism imposed upon her had been lifted. When the parish priest changed his opinion of her, attitudes in Catholic circles also evolved. Père Faure and Abbé Perrier began to talk about her. Père Faure brought the children from the youth club up to see her: 'Marthe tried to encourage us to love Jesus, (to have us) offer up small sacrifices in the way that Saint Thérèse did.' Abbé Perrier brought the children from the choir to her. It is clear that Père Faure now wanted Marthe to have company so he asked people to go and see her. Friendships were formed. This was the case with her neighbour, Jeanne Bonneton, who had seen no more of Marthe while she was ill between 1921 and 1928. Simone Ladret, who worked in the factory at Saint-Uze, was taken to Marthe's house by Père Faure in 1933. She was twenty-two at the time. Marthe told her to come back and Simone was 'very touched and very happy'. Marthe asked her to give the girls in the valley harmonium lessons. After the lessons, 'I used to rush

up to La Plaine ... I would stay for a good while and we would talk and pray.' Simone became one of Marthe's secretaries and was subsequently to join the Foyer of Charity. We know the names of several people from Saint-Uze, Châteauneuf, Anneyron and other local places who now came to see Marthe. Some, such as Mme Besson and Paulette Plantevin, used to come during the holidays. A well-to-do lady from Lyon, the wife of an industrialist, Mme Gorse, brought by Mme Besson, came to Châteauneuf in 1933. She then introduced Mlle Blanck to Marthe in 1935.

It is clear from their testimonies that Marthe loved her friends very much. Paulette Plantevin, who was born in 1907, used to come for extended stays with her aunt, who helped Père Faure and so lived at the presbytery. Père Faure asked her to go and see Marthe to give her secretarial help. 'She immediately became attached to me ... I used to go up nearly every day,' she said. 'We would talk a bit about anything and everything, about what was going on, just like two friends.' Paulette Plantevin used to answer letters at Marthe's dictation and take parcels to the post office. She would help Marthe's mother to 'change the position of the pillow because her head and spinal column had to be supported'. Paulette Plantevin reacted to what she wrote: 'Once I was very upset by what she had me write about the devil and about what had happened during the night. I remember saying to Marthe: "You frighten me". And she laughed. We would often laugh as friends do.'

Marthe remained very reticent to talk about herself in conversation. When people enquired after her health she would say that she had slept badly and that she was suffering a lot but was never more specific. She said nothing about her spiritual phenomena. Even close friends like Marguerite Lautru did not suspect that she had a mystical life. Marthe came across as a humble, tender friend who was fond of people, cheerful and even full of laughter.

She was already starting to have people confide in her, and to give advice and pray for intentions entrusted to her. Her gift for counselling was becoming known. It was to develop considerably in the following years and she was herself convinced that she had a mission to help the souls who came to see her.

According to Paulette Plantevin, 'she loved her family very much.' She was particularly attached to her sister Alice who did not marry until she was thirty and remained with her for a long time. 'They understood each other very well, loved each other very much and my mother never criticised her,' stated her daughter, Marthe Brosse. If her relations did not come and see her for a while, she would worry.

The relative abundance of strangers in a small farmhouse ill-equipped to receive them posed problems for the family. Her taciturn and introverted brother, Henri, had difficulty in coping with the visitors. The imposition of some degree of order on all this began to become necessary.

⁂

By 1936 Marthe Robin had taken the major turn of her life. But where was it leading? She was living in an unknown village in an isolated place. True she had a circle of connections but it was not yet very far-ranging. Things could have remained as they were. Many Catholic mystics have lived lives hidden from the eyes of the world. In Marthe's case, however, despite continued discretion, events were gradually to extend her influence to the farthest reaches of the world.

NOTES

1. Not to be confused with Père Beton, founder of the Foyer of Charity in La Léchère, who is mentioned later.
2. The photographs were taken on 11 August 1930 by the photographer Max Taly of Romans. The photo with the veil does not show Marthe on the day of her consecration to the Order of Virgins, despite what has been written here and there. It is a myth: at that time it was forbidden to make persons living in the world consecrated Virgins (a practice confirmed by a decree of the Congregation for Religious on 25 March 1927). The veil actually represented Marthe as a Capuchin

tertiary. Marthe thought at that time that she was likely to die quite soon. She had had her funeral robe made and intended giving this picture to her friends. This is what Père Marie-Bernard wrote about the photos: 'To expose any vanity, I advised her to have herself photographed: two photographs were taken by the priest (sic), one in which she looked dreadful, and another in which with Valencian lace on her forehead she looked more like Sarah Bernhardt than the poor little peasant girl that she was. Carried away by the temptation to vanity and coquetry she presented me with Sarah Bernhardt and forgot to give me her true portrait.' Père Marie-Bernard's opinion as to the 'dreadfulness' of the photo of Marthe Robin au naturel must be left to him.

3. According to Père Faure the visible stigmatisation occurred in October 1932.

4. It is difficult to specify the precise date on which the stigmata appeared externally after her inner experience of them. In Père Faure's notebook, however, October 1932 appears as the possible date of the exterior appearance of the stigmata: 'No trace of sweating blood for the first time since 1932 (October, I think).'

5. John 15:13.

6. Colossians 1:24.

7. Which corresponds to 3 p.m. by the sun, the hour at which, according to the Gospels, Jesus died.

PART TWO

The Founding of the Foyers of Charity

CHAPTER 5
The Origins of a Great Work

It might have been thought that Marthe Robin's mystical life was a matter for her alone, or again that the grace she received was simply that of welcoming, advising and consoling the people who sought her out, as she was already starting to do. Marthe's charism was not, however, to stop there. People began to see something different emerging in her, something profound, drawn from the very depths of her soul. Gradually the necessary elements for the founding of something new were put in place.

I. Marthe Robin's evolution

'May God make me a true *foyer*[1] of light and love, a word to convey his joy,' wrote Marthe in one of her notebooks on 22 January 1930. On 2 February she wrote something very similar: 'May God make me a foyer to purify the world and set souls ablaze.' Later, on 14 May 1934, she noted that God had told her: 'I have chosen you to rekindle the love that is dying out in the world, to serve as my helper and reveal my Work. I shall make you a flame of the fire that I wish to light on the earth.' On 22 January 1936 there is another quite similar passage written by her: 'It seems to be my mission to spread the reign of truth and love over the earth. I believe I have said it many times but I can't help saying it again: all I want to leave behind as a trace of my passing here below is an immense light of truth and a great fire of divine love. I would like people to love one another as I love them. I would like there to be nothing left in the world but an immense foyer of charity subject to the rule of God and his love.'

In Marthe's texts just quoted the word 'foyer' appears linked with the words 'charity', 'light', 'love', 'joy', 'word', and with the concepts of fire and the reign of God. Was Marthe not being chosen to rekindle this fire, one that must first burn in her own heart, given that she was called to be a 'foyer'? Her love for humanity was such that like Saint Paul she wanted it to give life to others. This was something very powerful. It is as if Marthe was emerging from herself and realising that she was called to a much wider mission of evangelisation.

The great revelation of 1933

These texts come before and after, and in a way form the back-cloth to a revelation from God to Marthe Robin in 1933. It was preceded by spiritual preparation and followed by a whole process of gradual integration. The core of what is known as the 'founding text' containing what the Foyers of Charity recognise as their origin follows in full:

> It was then that he (Jesus) spoke to me about the splendid Work that he wanted carried out here for the glory of the Father, that his reign might be extended throughout the Church and that the whole world might be regenerated through the religious teaching that was to be provided there, the supernatural and divine effects of which would spread to the whole universe ...
>
> At that moment I realised something that I had never previously dared to, or rather that I had hitherto refused to believe, namely that it was in the parish itself that this work that the Lord was calling for, was to be accomplished: his Great Work of Love, about which he had talked to me so often

and on which he was now insisting so much, even asking that the first foundation be effected without delay with the creation of a school for children and young girls, which he promised, together with the very Blessed Virgin to fill to overflowing with his love and their divine protection, saying that one day the school would be one of the branches of the Work which would have an effective radiance.

I was stupefied! ... I hardly dared believe the Lord's divine words, I was so afraid that I was mistaken, realising all the gravity and the incredible consequences of such a communication. And what I could not understand at all was the direct involvement that was being called for by me in all this. But it was not for me to question God's orders. All I could do was bow and obey because I was to announce what had been said to me at once. What agony and torment I was being put through! ... I was choked with anxiety at the mere thought of what I had to say, I was so dreading speaking. But the Lord had insisted with such authority this time that I could wait no longer.

At that moment Jesus opened out his arms in a glorious gesture of benediction and love, looking down at the earth which he was covering majestically with his shadow and surveying it with ineffable tenderness and kindness. After a moment in this attitude, he indicated to me the precise place where he wanted his Work, a place that had to be acquired.

It is clear then that Jesus had been preparing Marthe for a great Work, which she still apparently faced with some bewilderment. This Work was to begin with a school in Châteauneuf itself but would not be confined to that. It was to be started at once.

II. A first fulfilment of God's revelation: the girls' school in Châteauneuf

From the very outset Marthe had given her life and offered her suffering for the spiritual renewal of her home village of

Châteauneuf-de-Galaure, and as soon as Père Faure arrived he too had committed himself to this process of evangelisation. When, in 1928, he had realised who Marthe Robin really was, she had offered her suffering and prayed for him, that he might become a holy priest. With hindsight there is a resonance with the village of Ars, which was spiritually renewed through the charism of the saintly curé, Jean-Marie Vianney, and which is not very far from Châteauneuf.

At that time schools played a major role in pastoral work. People had great respect for teaching and for teachers. What they said was regarded as the foundations for the rest of life. That is why the Third Republic had done everything it could to destroy the influence of the Church in education. It is also the reason why Catholics had sacrificed much in order to maintain a large network of schools. In Châteauneuf there was no Church school any more. Marthe wanted to start one for little girls.

Given the delicate situation in the village, failure could have grave consequences and there was no guarantee of success. In the first place the context was not good. In the 1930s there was a perceptible radicalisation of political positions. In Drôme, between 1932 and 1936, the Communist vote rose from 5 per cent to 19 per cent. There was a fear that confrontation would ensue. A minimum number of children would need to enrol before the school could start. Well-trained schoolmistresses would also be required. Realising she must not be put off by these obstacles, Marthe tried to convince Père Faure of the rightness of such a Work. He spoke to his colleagues who thought the idea a breach of good sense. Then, however, Abbé Marius Perrier declared: 'If Marthe is asking for this, you should do it.' He was alone in his opinion but his moral authority was such that he carried it, and the project was launched.

The only possible location was the old château that dominated the village. For a while it had been used as a dance hall but that had failed, and the building was not in good condition. Fourteen thousand francs had to be raised. Parishioners volunteered to help sort the place out.

It is important to appreciate that Marthe had no intention initially of founding a community arising out of the school. She wanted to appeal to an already existing congregation. At the end of 1933 or the beginning of 1934 she asked for details of a local congregation of nuns. The information she gleaned was positive but then shortly afterwards, following further enquiries, she announced that she had been misled: 'There are a lot of elderly Sisters in this congregation and the young ones are not always well-formed. We shall form the members of the Work ourselves.'

So the school opened in October 1934 with just seven children, one of whom was Marthe's niece. It was barely enough. 'Look with love upon our new school,' Marthe prayed for the foundation. 'Bless the mistresses, inspire them, fill their children with your love … Bless the children at the school and those who are yet to come … Shower the mistresses with your greatest favours.'

It is worth noting that Marthe continued to have difficulty in seeing herself as a foundress. It had taken her some time to commit herself completely to the project. God had shown it to her long before, in 1933, she finally realised that it was to take place in Châteauneuf. Then she had never thought that the school would be run by people she knew. She had gradually evolved and finally accepted the idea of training those involved in the Work. But she did not feel herself capable of setting in motion something that was to have a wide ranging impact, and she still did not seem to see precisely what form it might take. 'I am still very moved,' she was later to say, 'when I think that the Foyer started with the girls' school.'

III. The development of Marthe's thinking between 1933 and 1936

The encounter with Mlle Blanck

Often in life, projects mature through confrontation with other people's ideas. God is at work in a conversation and what he wants becomes more and more clearly apparent through the exchange. It would seem this was what happened in Marthe Robin's case. Meeting a new friend was to make her move forward.

The friend in question was Emilie Blanck. She was born in 1875 and so was sixty years old with a whole religious history behind her by the time she met Marthe in 1935. She was a resident at the Convent of the Visitation, Monté du Télégraphe in Lyon. She belonged to a group interested in mysticism in a city where the spiritual life had always been important. She had been a helper to Mlle Gauthier, had a strong devotion to the Sacred Heart and ran the Sacred Heart Promotional Work, an organisation which published spiritual pamphlets and the life-stories of privileged souls. The Visitation is the female religious order associated with the Sacred Heart apparitions to Saint Marguerite Marie Alacoque in Paray-le-Monial, a small town in Burgundy, in the seventeenth century. By living in a convent of the Visitation and involving themselves in the work of the Heart of Jesus, Mlle Blanck and Mlle Gauthier sought to make Christ's love for the world known and to make the kingship of the Heart of Jesus over people and nations recognised. They were in touch with such places of devotion as the Visitation of Como, Italy where Consolata Ferrero (1885–1916) had lived. The clergy in Lyon mistrusted their taste for the extraordinary. When Mlle Gauthier died in 1929, Mlle Blanck had taken over the running of the work.

Mlle Blanck heard about Marthe Robin through a mutual friend and wanted to meet her. When, in 1935, she came to the region on pilgrimage to La Louvesc, she spent several days in

Châteauneuf and immediately struck up a friendship with
Marthe. From a spiritual point of view Mlle Blanck was able to
expand Marthe's horizons and understand much of what she was
experiencing. There followed a correspondence of trust. Marthe
was delighted: 'I don't know how to tell you what a heavenly
impression the few days we spent together have left upon me.' She
told Mlle Blanck about her interior life and the correspondence
between the two women suggests great reciprocal affection.

Their interaction did not stop there. Mlle Blanck wanted to
found something and told Marthe so. Because Marthe did not see
herself as a foundress she entered into her friend's plans and
volunteered to help her. Marthe used the vocabulary that was
already her own, particularly when it came to the name 'Foyer of
Charity'. Thus she wrote: 'I appreciate that you are still, more
than ever, thinking of "Foyers of Charity."' 'I am still thinking
about the "Foyer."' She acknowledged that the idea had come
from Mlle Blanck. 'I realise more and more that the idea was born
with you, that it (the "Foyer") must come into being.' She
advised her not to begin alone, to form at least one person and
she thought that she could find her some co-workers. She
encouraged her in times of discouragement. She pressed her to
start in Châteauneuf: 'I have spoken to the parish priest about the
Foyer of Charity and I believe he would be happy for it to start in
his parish one day.'

What is striking about this correspondence is primarily the way
in which Marthe remains in the background. How otherwise was
a crippled little peasant girl going to found anything? There could
be no doubt that a cultivated, prominent lady of Lyon had a
much better chance of success. Then there was the fact that Père
Faure was clearly not totally 'in tune' with Marthe. They did not
embark upon the project together. Their affection was real but he
was not made of the right stuff to be a founder. A third factor was
Marthe's insight and expertise when it came to people. She saw
each individual's capabilities and had a great sense of what was

possible. She may not have felt like a foundress but she was already showing she had the abilities to be one.

The project takes more specific form

By the time, a while later, on 19 February 1936, Marthe Robin met Abbé Georges Finet, her thinking would have moved on considerably. She had detached herself from Mlle Blanck and accepted at last that she must enter completely into God's designs for her and for Châteauneuf. We do not know quite how this came about. The Foyers' founding text was in fact reworked by Marthe and Père Finet to take on its final form in 1941–2. This last version specified the role of the priest who was to help Marthe and the form the Work was to take: it was to be a place of instruction in which a community would live together with the preacher, who was to be Marthe's spiritual director. The prayer and offering of all those concerned would be like the Work's 'invisible engine':

> Work to which I was to devote myself specially and give myself in accordance with his commandment and his divine counsel under the direction of the priest whom out of all time he had chosen and selected in his Heart for his edification and to whom he would one day give faithful and dedicated co-workers to help him absolve, instruct and nourish souls and lead them to his love. Co-workers whom his priest would have to choose himself in the light of and by the inspiration of the Holy Spirit, which he would lavish upon him in abundance if he was obedient to his orders, and with whom he would live in the most fraternal and perfect harmony. He told me that the priest he was talking about was the one who would be charged with steering and guiding me, according to his eternal designs in me: adding that he would introduce him to me in his own good time, to let him know his sovereign will for the Work and the immensity of his loving designs for him and for me ...

⁂

By the beginning of 1936 Marthe Robin had finally received God's plan and had accepted the role she was to play in it. Knowing that this plan could only be carried out with the help of a priest who would be sent to her by God, she waited. The waiting would not be for long.

NOTE
1. Meaning 'hearth' or 'home' or in certain subsequent contexts 'spiritual centre'.

CHAPTER 6
A Decisive Meeting (1936)

The founding of the Foyers of Charity was the work of both Marthe Robin and Abbé Finet. Although everything happened at Marthe's initiative, it could not have done so without Georges Finet's unfailing commitment. The meeting of these two personalities in 1936 was therefore decisive. How then did it come about?

I. The circumstances of Marthe's meeting with Abbé Finet

Marthe Robin wanted to place the school at Châteauneuf under the patronage of the Virgin Mary and to have a picture hung there to convey this idea. She wanted not just any picture of the Blessed Virgin but one of her as Mediatrix of all Graces. A Catholic is not required to believe that Mary is the Mediatrix of all Graces. It is not dogma. But Marthe had a special familiarity with Mary and knew the extent of her mission among humankind. She was sure that this mission was universal and that Mary was working with Christ for the salvation of humanity: does a mother not take care of her child's every need? By asking for a picture of this kind Marthe was affirming her personal position in relation to Marian devotion. Such a picture had still to be found, however. And it was not easy. It was the autumn of 1935.

Since 1933 Marthe had been a friend of Mme Gorse through whom she had come to know Mlle Blanck. Mme Gorse suggested that her sister-in-law Mme Relave paint the picture. Once painted, it had to be transported to Châteauneuf, and something of a minor undercover operation was possibly then mounted. It would appear that Père Faure confided to Mlle Blanck that Marthe was overreaching him and that he could not keep up with her spiritually. Mlle Blanck may have mentioned this to M. Roudil, a Catholic printer in Lyon and a friend of Abbé Finet who used to lunch with him every week. So it came about that it was suggested that Abbé Finet transport the picture to Châteauneuf. It would seem that he knew he was going to meet a mystic but not much more. 'I'm leaving tomorrow to see a stigmatic a hundred kilometres away,' he confided to Mother Scat, a nun of Notre-Dame du Cénacle in Fourvière, Lyon, the night before. He set off in his own car probably with Mlle Blanck and possibly M. Roudil. Abbé Finet had lunch at the presbytery with Père Faure. The two men knew each other because Père Faure had previously been to Lyon to ask the deputy head of the private school there for teachers for the school he intended opening. Then they went up to La Plaine.

II. Georges Finet

By the time Abbé Georges Finet entered Marthe's house he already had a very rich past, a past which warrants mention here because he was never to deny it but rather integrated it into the new life he was about to begin. More than that, his past was to determine some of the distinctive characteristics of what he thought and did for the remainder of his life.

Abbé Finet's family background

Socially Abbé Finet belonged to Lyon's Catholic upper-middle class. Lyon was a distinctive town with a very particular mentality. Proud of themselves and their age-old traditions (Christianity in Gaul began in Lyon), the people of Lyon were generally diligent workers, conscientious and thrifty (except on the occasion of impulses of great generosity). Simultaneously mystical and realistic, they cultivated the austere appearance of a serious bourgeoisie (except when they allowed themselves to succumb to jocularity). The Catholics amongst them were manifestly devout and faithful to the Church. The town, dominated by the Fourvière basilica, was a centre of piety and industry. The city's festival, when everything was lit up, was 8 December, the day of the Immaculate Conception of the Virgin Mary. Its geographical and even greater psychological distance from Paris, a city regarded as frivolous and invasive, gave Lyon an independence of spirit conducive to many initiatives. Lyon had also been one of the centres for social, not to say socialist and even extremist, thinking in the nineteenth century. The most diverse trends coexisted there not without the occasional clash. It was a reserved city but one that was rich and powerful in every way.

Georges Finet's paternal grandparents were people profoundly rooted in God. His grandfather, Pierre Finet (1836–1930) was a man of the Holy Family who had inscribed in his diary the prayer to Saint Joseph which Père Finet was to pass on, in slightly adapted form, to the Foyers. He was above all a man of the Rosary, the Rosary as an act of family devotion to which Père Finet would constantly refer, and the Rosary also recited silently alone, a form of unceasing prayer that he passed on to his children and grandchildren: 'Whenever grandfather was alone, he would instinctively slip a hand into his pocket and pull out his beads. How many Rosaries would he say in a day? I have often thought that his grandchildren's many vocations to the priesthood and the religious life must be attributable to those Rosaries.' The Finets had a wholesale grocery and hardware business in the Terreaux district.

Georges Finet's maternal grandparents exerted a different kind of influence. The Beaumont family was wealthier but simpler in style. They lived in Cusset, a suburb of Lyon that was starting to become industrialised, and had a veritable apostolate in the area, supporting and evangelising the workers and encouraging involvement in the parish. This involvement used to culminate in the procession of Corpus Christi, the great feast day of the year, which the Beaumont family was responsible for organising.

Père Finet's family circle was sound to the core. Life was stable and people could count on one another. They could face the future with serenity and determination, and were not afraid of commitment. Of the Finet grandparents' thirteen grandchildren, half gave themselves in the service of the Church. One was killed in 1915 during the Great War. Two became priests: Georges and his elder brother Pierre, a Jesuit. Four became nuns, among them Marie-Thérèse, Georges' sister who became a Little Sister of the Assumption. Like the Beaumonts, the Finet family had a special bond with this congregation dedicated to serving the poorest of the poor. In the course of three generations the two families provided it with five vocations, among them Père Finet's aunt and godmother, Marthe, who died a saintly death at the age of thirty-one. Père Finet's godfather, Joseph, his father's younger brother, had died heroically in 1916 in the attack on the Vaux fort. He had turned down leave in order not to abandon his men at so decisive a juncture, despite the fact that he was married and had children.

Georges Finet's parents, Ludovic and Marie-Antoinette, were united by a deep faith. Temperamentally they were very different and also came from rather different backgrounds, but this did not prevent them from complementing one another and living in harmony.

'A businessman with his feet firmly on the ground,' it was written of Ludovic Finet (1864–1951), Georges' father, 'Ludovic is an upright, just, precise and level-headed man. Reserved on first meeting, like any other good citizen of Lyon, he is also affable, even warm on occasion, and always profoundly kind and attentive to others. He has a very active and helpful temperament.'

Of his mother, Marie-Antoinette (1871–1949) it was said: 'Everything about his mother Marie-Antoinette suggested the milieu from which she stemmed: severe in appearance, always elegantly turned out with a collarette and hat which added to her natural air of distinction. Yet beneath the exterior of an intimidating grand lady she was sociable, full of sensitivity and very generous. "She was goodness itself," the priest would say. She had numerous commitments, both social and in the parish, particularly to the Little Sisters' [of the Assumption] sale.[1] She was also a very welcoming and refined mistress of her household, who opened the family table up to one and all, particularly to family in the widest sense but also to members of the clergy …'

Ludovic and Marie-Antoinette Finet had six children: Pierre, the Jesuit; Marie-Thérèse (Ninette), the Little Sister of the Assumption; Georges; Geneviève who married the surgeon André Ricard and had eight children; Robert, married to Marguerite Birot with nine children; and Simone, married to Marcel Levrat with four children. This list in itself is an indication of the fertile human and Christian background from which Georges Finet issued.

The history of a vocation to the priesthood

At that time women would often give birth in their mother's houses and Georges Finet was born in his maternal grandparents' property in Cusset on 6 September 1898. He was a cheerful, mischievous, bouncing child. He got on very well with his brothers and sisters and was later to speak of all that he had learned about the female world in innocence from his sisters. He was devout and a good pupil. Life at home was happy and punctuated by meals at which people knew how to behave (in true French tradition there was a whole table liturgy) and by family prayer. When he was ready for secondary education his parents elected to have him board at the prestigious Chartreux School in Lyon, near their house. Boarding was considered then to be particularly good training for a man. Georges adapted to it even if he found spending just twenty-four hours a week with his

family very little. His schoolmasters thought highly of the child
and he worked well. He made friends, among them Alfred Ancel,
a remarkably intelligent boy from a good middle-class family, who
picked up all the top marks. Georges made his First Holy
Communion at the age of eleven having undergone excellent
preparation.

Education at the Chartreux School concluded with a retreat to
prepare for entry into adult life. Like many other Christian boys
Georges considered the priesthood but wanted a family and knew
that his father was counting on him to help him in the Beaumont
business. What was more, he already had one brother who was a
Jesuit and in England at that time, and a sister who was to become
a nun. Yet another vocation would be asking a great deal of his
parents. The retreat was held in Ars and was preached by Mgr
Saint-Clair, considered a specialist in retreats for young men. He
placed great emphasis on that purity of heart which creates trust
and abandonment into the hands of God. Georges Finet was to
emerge from this retreat having heard a call to the priesthood and
responded to it for life. In his own words:

> It was between 4 p.m and 5 p.m. [of Saturday 29 May, 1915]
> that we paid a visit to the Blessed Sacrament which has oriented
> all my decisions in life. And it was in the little chapel of
> Providence that the Blessed Sacrament was exposed ... And to
> make even surer that we were fully in Jesus' sight, Mgr Saint-
> Clair had told us: 'Kneel on the actual altar steps, right next to
> the monstrance, near to Jesus'. And that was what we did: I can
> still see the place where I knelt; near the turn of the first step,
> with to my left one of my friends [Alfred Ancel] who had always
> told us he was getting ready to take over from his father as the
> head of large dye and silk factories. And I was also praying.
>
> And it was after this profound half-hour meeting with our
> Lord, as they left the Chapel of Providence that the two young
> men, much to their surprise, confided to one another that they

had experienced a call from God in the depth of their hearts, a call to the priesthood, and that this time they had said yes and it was definitive.[2] All the same they both wanted to be sure that, in their emotion, they had not been mistaken and it was at 6 p.m. that evening, 6.30 p.m. to be precise, that they went in search of the good preacher who had been directing all their exercises. And I noted down his answer to me: 'Yes, be a good priest.' And he added something that was to shape the resolution I made at that school-leaving retreat. That resolution might seem a little strange and yet anyone who had heard his talks would understand what it meant: 'Be a priest with a lot of ambition!' And that is what was to determine my life from then on: being a priest with a lot of ambition who allowed himself to be traversed throughout his priesthood by God's own ambition. That is to say the ambition which relates to God's grand design, God's plan for the whole world, the salvation of souls and the call to all souls.

Georges Finet was overjoyed. 'Oh! My children,' he was to say, 'When you have said "Yes" to God there is such joy in your heart. And in my retreat notes I can sense my heart and soul swelling with intense joy. And I think I can say that that joy has been with me all through my life.'

Back at home in the Quai de la Pêcherie, on the Sunday evening, Georges was met by his elder sister, Marie-Thérèse, the one who was to become a religious. She had been praying for her younger brother's vocation. Just by looking at his face she realised at once what had happened 'and after we had exchanged a few words, I left him alone with father and mother, with no doubt in my mind that he had something private to tell them. I was not wrong. A few moments later Georges called me and I found father and mother sobbing but proud of their son.' 'I knew it,' his mother responded to what Georges had told her. Not for one moment did she and her husband hesitate. They embraced their son tenderly and said: 'You are the third one of our children that God has asked of us. May his holy will be done and adored.' The rest of the family were more surprised. Georges was looked upon as someone who enjoyed the good life and people could not imagine him anywhere else but in the world.

On the advice of Mgr Saint-Clair, Georges Finet was sent to the French pontifical seminary in Rome, which together with the Saint-Sulpice seminary in Issy-les-Moulineaux, was considered France's best training college for the priesthood. Naturally the spirit was very faithful to Rome. Teaching was done at the Gregorian University. It was while he was at the seminary that Georges Finet came across Louis-Marie Grignion de Montfort's *Traité de la Vraie Dévotion à la Sainte Vierge*.[3] This was to prove a decisive step in his life. He decided to submit to Mary the conduct of his inner life and outer actions, and was never to deviate from this commitment. In 1917 he was called up and left for the front as an artillery officer. His captain saw him as a man 'with guts'. The army showed that he had courage and taught him self-control. He also learned to command by winning the affection of men very different from himself in education and convictions. Then, in 1919, he returned to the French Seminary. Fitting back into a strictly disciplined environment that ran like clockwork was difficult. Georges Finet passed his degree in philosophy and theology, however, whilst taking advantage of being in Rome and participating in major events in the life of the Church, notably the canonisation of Joan of Arc and the beatification of Thérèse of Lisieux.

His priestly ministry

On 8 July 1923 Georges Finet was ordained in Lyon. Together with his friend Alfred Ancel, who had been his co-disciple in Rome, he made his ordination retreat at the Trappist monastery in Dombes. He found it greatly moving but after his ordination another emotional experience he was never to forget awaited him:

I will tell you what was in store for the young priest. When suddenly he entered the intimacy of the confessional and heard ... a voice, a voice addressing him. What a feeling it was to hear oneself appealed to: 'Bless me, Father', to hear that word Father for the first time in one's life and to think that from then on we would bear that name because through our priesthood we became fathers, profoundly fathers ... And so that young man who had left everything behind, that young man who had renounced fatherhood, the young man who had renounced having a family was now a father, he had become profoundly a father, he had become a father in an extremely profound way in the very intimacy of his heart, in the deepest fibres of his being ... and little by little he saw all the joys of the world, all the pain of the world entering into his priesthood and calling him: 'Father, Father ...' So at that moment the young man felt an immense song of gratitude in his heart because, having renounced human fatherhood, he knew that in his priesthood he would discover divine fatherhood. As you can imagine, I was overwhelmed.

Even if this is more of a synthetic insight into Père Finet's priestly ministry than a description of exactly what he felt when he heard his first confession, it is nevertheless revealing. Something relating to fatherhood happened to him that day which was subsequently to be greatly developed.

After a journey to the Holy Land, Abbé Georges Finet was admitted to the diocese of Lyon. The post-war years were marked by a desire to rebuild after the sorry pre-war years of anticlericalism. The Church of France could be proud of itself. Many priests and religious had given their lives on the battlefields. It could speak out and show itself in the light of day. Apostolic initiatives were growing in number. In 1924 Abbé Finet was appointed to the working class parish of Oullins, where there was a good priest in charge and an excellent team of assistant priests.

He was full of apostolic ambitions. He got together some twenty boys and prepared them, probably in a somewhat scholarly fashion, to evangelise. He versed them particularly well in the proofs of the existence of God and made ready to dispatch them into the town's cafés. He had drawn up his battle plan, dividing Oullins into sections with a café in the middle of each, and was about to launch his offensive when he was suddenly transferred to the cathedral and a completely different post. Why this appointment when he was so full of zeal? Did the Archbishop take fright at too aggressive a campaign of evangelisation? Whatever the reason, he obeyed and in 1925 found himself at the primatial church of Saint John where he was to remain until 1934.

During that time Abbé Finet began to make an important spiritual choice. He had a real desire for holiness and wanted to lead a radical life. Should he then remain in the secular clergy? Why not enter the Prado to which his friend Ancel had applied? But in the summer of 1925 his spiritual director, Père Albert Valensin, a prominent Jesuit, invited him to a retreat for priests preached by a real Curé d'Ars, Abbé Babolat, who suggested he try for the Society of the Heart of Jesus, an institute for the perfection of priests. Its Ignatian inspired rule was very appealing. Its hallmark was devotion to the Sacred Heart. There were a whole series of stages concluding with a commitment that was possibly even more demanding than religious vows. For some twenty years this way of life helped Abbé Finet and gave him structure. It was as part of this engagement that in 1929, at Notre-Dame d'Ay in Ardèche, he did the spiritual exercises of St Ignatius. This retreat, to which he would often refer, was later to help him develop the retreats on the fundamentals of faith for the Foyers of Charity. He was to remain in the Society of Priests of the Sacred Heart until 1949.

The appointment to Saint John's was no exile; quite the reverse. The primatial church was an extremely dynamic centre of evangelism. Located in a neighbourhood of small traders where everyone knew everybody else, the parish was run by an excellent priest, Abbé J. Gailland, whose parishioners loved him. He led a team of three or four assistant priests who were very close to their parishioners. There was plenty of activity and no lack of good works. Abbé Finet was made very welcome. He was a great success with the female gender but also knew how to protect himself and keep his distance when necessary. He looked very young but the war had given him experience, and people soon realised it. He showed himself to be capable of learning. Required to preach on one important occasion, he chose as his subject the proofs of the existence of God, a subject on which he had done a lot of work in Oullins. A remark from a vicar general on the way out from the ceremony showed him he had missed the mark: 'And in the end I realised that no one had understood any of it … So much so that I recognised something: that I was wrong. I was not a priest in order to prove the existence of God but in order to speak about the Father, the Son and the Holy Spirit, to transmit the message of Jesus. So I changed my approach completely. From then on I would preach about the Father, the Son and the Holy Spirit, and God's family on earth, the Church.' Now he would speak from the heart.

Abbé Finet's ministry bore fruit. He was responsible notably for a group of young men with whom he went deeply into *True Devotion to Mary*. Several vocations resulted, among them that of Père Caffarel.[4] Père Finet had lively and enjoyable ways of helping young people discover a living God. He was to leave a life-long impression on some of them. He visited the elderly and the sick, and spent considerable time in the confessional: 'I would hear confessions for four hours a day, two hours in the morning and two in the evening. On Christmas Eve I could be hearing confessions for sixteen hours.' There he would demonstrate the 'ardent love of souls', which according to Marthe Robin was his most distinctive characteristic.

Marthe Robin, of whose existence he was completely ignorant, was already praying for the man who was to be her future spiritual father. On two specific occasions she was called upon by God to help him. The first was when he was giving Holy Communion to little Lapicorey, a small boy who was dying, and the second was to save him, during a landslide on the Fourvière hillside during the night of 13 November 1930. The first rock fall had woken the neighbourhood and the priests had gone out to help the victims. Abbé Finet found himself in a vaulted passageway and was nearly buried when the hill collapsed for a second time. He managed to extricate himself but nineteen firemen, who had been right next to him, all disappeared. Following this incident the priest in charge at the cathedral was awarded the Légion d'honneur and Georges himself received a bronze medal, 'for the heroic dedication shown on the tragic night of 13 November 1930'. That night Marthe offered and suffered so much for him that Père Faure had to be called to support her.

When, after nine years, Abbé Finet left the primatial Church, there were many who were sorry to see him go. The leader of the men's group said: 'You have made available to us your sacred knowledge which is extensive, your commitment which is tireless, your advice which is inspired by sound doctrine, your profoundly loving heart which asks only to give itself to each and everyone, your apostolic zeal which by means suggested to you by your experience more often than not manages to make God known and have him served.'

In 1934 Abbé Finet was given a completely different mission: he was appointed deputy director of Church-run education in the diocese of Lyon which at that time encompassed two *départements*: the Rhône and the Loire. He was in charge of no less than eight hundred Church schools, which he had to keep going and for which he had to recruit teachers. Because Church schools were then a prime means for the Church to evangelise, their position was an important one, even if taking on so sizeable an administrative job was somewhat disconcerting for a priest with such an apostolic orientation. Abbé Finet had a very good understanding with his superior, Canon Bornet, the future bishop of Saint-Etienne, a man of the heart in whom he had great faith. The experience was excellent formation for him.

His heart continued to lie with apostolic work. Struck by the unsatisfactory way in which faith was presented to children, in 1936 he compiled a programme of preparation for First Holy Communion. 'It seems to me,' he wrote, 'that an error often finds its way into the teaching of Catechism. Very little emphasis is placed on Christ.' Well, if we do not 'meet' Christ we may have an intellectual religion but we will not have a living faith. In 1948, together with Abbé Babolat, he published a manual of *Catholic Doctrine*. As parish priest in Montréal in L'Ain from 1919 to 1964, Abbé Babolat experimented with and developed methods of evangelisation. Ever since the 1925 retreat he had kept in touch with Abbé Finet whom he accompanied spiritually, together with Père Valensin. He too was concerned about poor methods of teaching Catechism and wanted to provide people with a life-giving doctrine. Abbé Finet shared his concern and the result was this innovative Catechism. This too would later be helpful for the Foyers' retreats on the fundamentals of faith.

Although he had little spare time, Abbé Finet remained very close to his family which became more extended through marriage. Abbé Finet was to become very attached to one of his brothers-in-law in particular, Doctor André Ricard, a surgeon, with whom he regularly spent his holidays, and to Robert Birot, his brother Robert's brother-in-law, a well-informed businessman, who was later to help him at Châteauneuf.

Special devotion to the Virgin Mary
It would be remiss not to mention here another, crucial dimension to Abbé Finet: his love for the Virgin Mary. Abbé Finet was a friend of the Virgin, one might even say an apostle of Mary, so heartfelt was his desire to make her known, loved and prayed to.

Following his discovery of the Marian spirituality of Saint Louis-Marie Grignion de Montfort, Abbé Finet had realised that Mary could be of great help to anyone wishing to advance in the spiritual life. It was even possible to go so far as to surrender the conduct of our human and spiritual life to her as a mother. In Lyon cathedral he started to give talks on this theme. A little higher up, in the Cénacle convent on the Fourvière hill, lay people were trying to organise a series of talks on the Virgin Mary and looking for a preacher, but it was important not to make the wrong choice. The Cénacle in Lyon was the centre of a devotional network which extended all over the city. Then, once the choice was made, how was a parish priest going to be persuaded to allow an already heavily committed assistant to give of his time? This is Père Finet's vivid description of what ensued. It was 1930:

Quite naturally, having heard what was happening at the cathedral and that a priest was giving talks on the Blessed Virgin, she said to herself: 'That's the man I need!' Without saying a word she promptly dispatched several (four) people on pilgrimage to Lourdes to ask Our Lady of Lourdes for the assistant priest at the Cathedral to take on the Marian talks. One fine day, looking all innocent, they sought me out at the vicariate office. I never suspected their pious plot. They asked me if I could give some Marian talks. But I said to them: 'I'm an assistant priest. I have a lot of work to do.' 'Oh yes but you know, it would be for five or six talks on the second Sunday in the month at four o'clock in the afternoon.' 'Oh, five or six talks, we'll have to see. After all, the parish priest will have to be consulted.' But my priest in charge answered: 'Oh well, as it's for the Blessed Virgin, I agree!' And there I was, committed to five or six talks, one talk a month on the second Sunday of every month. They actually had me give a hundred![5]

Abbé Finet began with a select group of only a dozen or so girls who, following a retreat in 1927, had founded a Montfort-inspired Marian Union, the purpose of which was to know and love Mary better. The success of his preaching was such, however, that the group of listeners grew dramatically. The number rose swiftly to 150 and then 300. On 8 September 1935 Cardinal Maurin, Archbishop of Lyon, elevated the Union to the status of a Fraternity of Mary Queen of Hearts, and by 1937 it had over 1,300 members. Its activities had extended to organising pilgrimages to places such as Notre-Dame d'Ay and La Louvesc in 1937 to celebrate the centenary of the founding of the Cénacle congregation by Saint Thérèse Couderc, or Notre-Dame de Fourvière. In 1937 the Fraternity organised its first diocesan pilgrimage. Between 1935 and 1937 the Fraternity also arranged silent retreats preached by Abbé Finet.

A sketched portrait

By the time Abbé Finet met Marthe Robin he already had a well-formed and developed personality. He had received much from his family. Through his priesthood and then as a Priest of the Sacred Heart he had opted for a radical life. His love of Mary had given him a fruitful spiritual path. He had benefited from the examples of remarkable men and women, and was beginning to have some experience of souls. Little by little he had elaborated a joyful and liberating theological doctrine in which God was presented as a Father and Christ as a brother, someone close to us, a friend. His responsibilities in the army and then in Church education had shown him how to exercise authority.

His was an enthusiastic, assured temperament, which had preserved and would maintain throughout his life something of a childlike spirit. He was a lively optimist who looked on the positive side of things and people, and was gifted with an excellent ability to adapt. He was an upright, sincere man with a clear mind that identified what was important. His will was unshakeable and most of the time he kept good control of himself. His faith, piety and sense of duty came from his family. From the Beaumonts he had received an openness to people of different social backgrounds. His head and heart were well balanced. Rejecting retrogression of any kind, he wanted to build and advance. He was just the man needed to be a founder. He would see it through to the very end.

His defects were the reverse side of his qualities. Throwing himself as he would with heart and mind into a particular enterprise, he could lack distance, a critical faculty in relation to himself and others. He had difficulty in questioning himself. If he was sure of something it was not open for debate. Marthe Robin who had more critical distance would on the whole be a good balance for him.

III. Marthe Robin and Abbé Georges Finet's first meeting

In the journal she was keeping, Marthe Robin wrote no account of her meeting with Père Finet. Nor did she say anything about it subsequently, at least not as far as we know. This was something very intimate, the memory of which she would keep in her heart. Thus our primary source remains Père Finet. What he recorded is, however, reiterated by Mother Scat in what she wrote in a private notebook we have, as well as by Mlle Jeanne Lavenant of Lyon, a friend both of Mother Scat and of Mlle Blanck. Père Finet referred to the meeting in his notes on Marthe's experiences of the Passion on 6 January and 3 June 1941. Then, on 11 February 1943, he wrote an actual account of it. Later he would talk about it at the end of the retreats at Châteauneuf. What he said about it can be confirmed to have remained consistent.

And so Abbé Finet entered Marthe's room, bearing the famous picture of Mary Mediatrix of all Graces that was the reason for their meeting. Later he would remark with humour that it was actually the Virgin Mary who brought him: 'I thought I was bringing the Blessed Virgin, whereas in fact she brought me.' Marthe recognised Abbé Finet because she had already 'seen' him twice, and was at once extremely moved. Such 'recognition' is not unique in the life of mystics. Père Finet described Marthe's reaction thus: 'It was at this point that he (Jesus) showed Marthe the priest he had chosen: she had seen me spiritually with a sick boy, little Lapicorey, who died while I was with him (this sick little boy had been commended to Marthe's prayers) ... Marthe had even seen my features because she would have picked me out from ten thousand others.' 'I had thought,' Marthe recounted, 'when the second time God showed me the priest he had chosen was at the Fourvière disaster, that it was a sign that this priest would be a builder ... Why was I so deeply upset by that disaster? It made me ill and I told M. le Curé and my mother about it before it appeared in the newspaper.'

Marthe had been given a mission to pray for this priest now standing before her and had in some way protected him with her prayer and her offering. Marthe Robin would later officially confirm this to one of the Foyer priests but she said nothing to Abbé Finet at the time. They started talking. The subject of the picture the Abbé was carrying was the first common ground between them. It is not difficult to imagine therefore how the conversation began: 'For over an hour Marthe and Abbé Finet talked about the Blessed Virgin. He was very surprised to hear Marthe explaining points of Marian theology he had expanded on in his Marian talks at the Cénacle and that he himself had discovered more through prayer than through books. So it was that they talked about Mary's intercessory role in Gethsemane. Gradually through the Blessed Virgin they were led on to talk about France. Marthe was overjoyed to find that the priest God had sent loved the Blessed Virgin, and was much reassured by this confirmation of God's choice.' Abbé Finet was later to say: 'I who gave Marian talks, was stunned by the way she spoke about the Blessed Virgin. She called her "maman chérie". So I took it that they knew each other well.'

Two things are worth noting. The first concerns Marian theology. At that time theological thinking relating to the Virgin

Mary was tending to become an autonomous entity. It was as if a body of 'Mariologists' were being created which functioned progressively more according to its own principles and distanced itself from other theologians. If, as a consequence, the Virgin Mary was not perceived as part of the whole plan of salvation, certain elements of understanding became obscure. Hence complicated, not to say pointless and even dangerous theological questions arose. Little by little a 'Marian question' was created, against which the Second Vatican Council would react soundly. Marthe's response to this situation was founded very simply on the experience-based knowledge she had of Mary. The intimate relationship she had with her made it possible to resituate questions outside the sterile debates that were going on at that time. She came back to what she actually experienced.

Ever since 1638, France had, moreover, been dedicated to the Virgin Mary. She was its queen and patron saint. France was not simply a piece of land with a population in Marthe's eyes, or those of the Abbé Finet, or of many other Catholics of that period. It was a spiritual entity too, a country with both a human and a spiritual mission. Later, in 1980, Pope John Paul II was to say as much at le Bourget when he asked: 'France, eldest daughter of the Church and educator of peoples, are you faithful to your Baptismal promises?' In 1936 France was still the mainstay of Catholicism. Over half the world's missionaries were French (two-thirds in 1914). There were still plenty of vocations and the cultural influence of French Catholicism was without equal. During the interim period, however, the country had undergone a series of trials. It had not recovered from the losses of the First World War and was internally divided and badly governed. At a time when Nazism was on its doorstep and preparing to take revenge, when Communism was on the ascendant, and the Anglo-Saxon countries were failing to recognise the threat that Nazism and Communism represented and allowing them to develop, France did not know where it was going. The legislative elections on 26 April and 3 May 1936 brought a left and an extreme left wing majority to the Chamber of Deputies, which introduced social reform but did not react to the mounting Nazi peril. These were the same members of parliament who, four years later, would vote in full powers for Marshal Pétain and allow the Vichy government to establish itself, in absolute contravention of their initial convictions. They were deeply turbulent times. It was not unreasonable therefore to go on from talking about the Virgin Mary to speak of the country consecrated to her, of which Marthe and the Abbé Finet were citizens, and about the direction of which people were wondering. Once again I shall leave it to Marthe to speak:

> France is going to descend to the very bottom of the abyss, to a point where it will be impossible to see any human solution for recovery. She will remain alone, abandoned by all the other nations who, after leading her to her undoing, will turn their backs on her. She will not remain in this extreme state for long. She will be saved but not by arms nor by the genius of men because there will be no human way out left … France will be saved because God will intervene through the Blessed Virgin. It is she who will save France and the world …
>
> God will intervene through the Blessed Virgin and the Holy Spirit: there will be a new Pentecost, a second 'advent' of the Holy Spirit. There will be a new era and from then on Isaiah's prophecy about the union of hearts and unity of peoples will be fulfilled … After the new 'advent' of the Holy Spirit, which will be more particularly manifest in France, she will really fulfil her mission as eldest daughter of the Church and the trial, by purifying her, will restore her lost title to her.

Firstly, it may be remarked, these words of Marthe say something about what she was experiencing deep within her. She was among a number of other holy souls in history who had been given a mission to offer and pray for their country. This was a dimension of their vocation. Then, her words are in a prophetic vein and are not alone in being so. Several holy figures, including some who were not French, made similar pronouncements about France, among them the Blessed Maryam Baoardy (1846–1878), a Lebanese woman, and the Vietnamese, Marcel Van (1928–1959). Thirdly, barely four years after this conversation, France whose army had been considered the best in the world, met with the greatest military defeat in its history. This came as a terrible shock. Finally, the idea of a 'new Pentecost' was precisely what the Blessed John XXIII was to ask of the Holy Spirit before the Council, and for which John Paul II expressed an ardent desire on many occasions. Note the importance afforded the action of the Spirit which was unusual at that time. The part of Marthe's prophecy that has not been fulfilled relates to the conversion of France following on from all these events, but a prophecy can remain valid in the long term, as may be seen for example with the third secret of Fatima.[6]

How was this new Pentecost of Love to come about?

'She told me,' Abbé Finet stated, 'that the Church would be totally rejuvenated through the apostolate of the laity. She talked a lot about that to me. She even said: 'Lay people will have a very important role to play in the Church ...' She added that there would be many ways of forming the laity, notably through Foyers of Light, Charity and Love. I did not really understand what she meant.

So then she said to me: 'It will be something quite new in the Church; it has never been done before. It will be made up of consecrated lay people, not a religious order. The Foyers of Charity will have a priest at their head, the Father, and they will be made up of committed lay persons.' And she said to me: 'These Foyers of Charity will radiate light throughout the world! They will be an answer from the Heart of Jesus to the world after the material defeat of people and their satanic errors.'

Marthe Robin's predictions were to be fulfilled. The Foyers, as they were to be born, would indeed be something without precedent in the Church. They were to be the first of the new communities, followed by many others.

After two hours of conversation, the talk suddenly took a different turn. Let us give the word back to the Abbé Finet:

During the third hour she turned to me:

'Monsieur l'Abbé, I have something to ask you on God's behalf.'

'What is it, Mademoiselle?'

'You are the one who must come here to Châteauneuf and found the first Foyer of Charity.'

'I, Mademoiselle? But I am not in this diocese. I am from Lyon!'

'What does that matter since this is what God wants?'

'Ah! I had not thought of it like that. But what would I do?'

'Mainly you would preach retreats.'

'Yes, three-day retreats would be a good thing.'

'No, five-day. In three you do not have the time to change a soul.'

'Indeed. But to whom will these retreats be given?'

'To ladies and older girls.'

'What shall we be doing during these retreats? Workshops? Discussion groups?'

'No, no, no. The Blessed Virgin wants complete silence.'

'You think I shall be able to keep ladies and girls silent for five days?'

'Since that is what the Blessed Virgin asks!'

'Ah! I did not know … But how shall we publicise these retreats?'

'The Blessed Virgin will take care of that. Jesus will grant extraordinary graces. You won't need to do much advertising!'

'But where will these retreats be held?'

'In the girls' school.'

'But we shall need beds, a kitchen. Who is going to take on this work?'

'You!'

'But with what money?'

'Don't worry … the Blessed Virgin will see to it.'

'When would the first retreat have to be held?'

'On 7 September.'

I was stunned. I told her I would talk to my superiors:

'I can't refuse but I shall still have to ask permission from my superiors.'

'Oh yes! You must remain under obedience.'

Abbé Finet's objection, 'I am not in this diocese' was not unfounded. A priest cannot exercise his ministry in a diocese other than his own without the agreement of the local bishop, especially if the ministry in question is an ongoing one. In 1936 the tie between a priest and his diocese was strong. It could not be taken for granted that Abbé Finet would be released to go elsewhere and, as we shall see, things would in fact take a long time to slot into place.

IV. The aftermath of the meeting

Abbé Finet left Marthe's room much moved. 'What have I been called to! What an undertaking!' he remarked to himself. When Père Faure was told about the conversation he 'could not contain himself for joy'. On the evening of 10 February Père Faure returned to Lyon with him. Next day Abbé Perrier, the parish priest at Saint-Uze, took Marthe Holy Communion for the feast of Our Lady of Lourdes in his stead. On the morning of the following day, both Père Faure and Abbé Finet offered their Mass at Fourvière for the Foyers of Light, Charity and Love, after which Abbé Finet lost no time in going to see his superior. 'On 11 February back in Lyon,' he said, 'I went to see Mgr Bornet, director of Church education, who listened to me carefully and responded, "My dear friend, you must accept".' He had the same reaction from the Vicar General, Mgr Rouche. Of course he also consulted his spiritual director, Père Albert Valensin, who stopped him as soon as he began to confide in him: 'I know Marthe Robin. Mgr Pic, Bishop of Valence, took me to see her recently and I was able to talk with her for three hours. Marthe Robin: Catherine of Siena, she is part of the Church. You must do everything she tells you. She will never lead you astray. I shall always be with you to help and support you and defend you when necessary. Go ahead!'

All the Abbé Finet had to do then was see the Bishop of Valence, Mgr Pic, who received him warmly: 'He welcomed me with open arms. We understood each other at once. He gave the project his blessing.'

In the months that followed, between February and September, Abbé Finet kept up his ministry in Lyon but went back several times to Châteauneuf at Marthe's request. Père Faure was still Marthe's spiritual director and the two priests kept in touch. On 24 July 1936 Abbé Finet, whose feelings can well be imagined, was present for the first time at Marthe's Passion. In his words:

'We went into Marthe's room where she was groaning constantly. She was unconscious. The Passion did not involve bleeding for I saw no trace of blood on her forehead or face.' Marthe interceded for particular sinners and prayed especially for priests. At 3.30 p.m. she said: 'I know, my God, that I do not deserve that you answer my prayers but there is your mother. You cannot refuse her. Mother, I ask you to beg for your child, grant everything for sinners, for priests.' At 3.37 p.m: 'Dear Mother, tell Jesus that I shall not be quiet, until he has granted my prayer'. At 4.01 p.m. Abbé Finet noted: 'Father into thy hands I commend my spirit'. At 4.02 p.m: 'Death. Death was preceded by a great sigh and her head fell gently onto her left shoulder. It would not move for two hours. All moaning and movement ceased completely. Marthe remained in a death-like state.'

NOTES

1. Charity sale.
2. Although this section is written in the third person, Georges Finet is still referring to himself and Alfred Ancel.
3. Saint Louis-Marie Grignion de Montfort (1673–1716) was a French priest, preacher and classical writer of Christian spirituality. His book, *True Devotion to Mary*, has been considered one of the most influential Marian works and his approach of 'total consecration to Jesus Christ through Mary' had a strong impact both in popular piety and in the spirituality of religious orders.
4. Henri Caffarel (1903–1996) founder of the 'Equipes Notre-Dame', a spiritual movement for married couples which has spread all over the world. His cause for beatification is under consideration.
5. In his memoirs, Père Finet attributes the initiative to Mother Scat although it in fact came from young ladies among the laiety. Mother Scat was, however, the only Cénacle nun to attend these talks.
6. The third secret of Fatima remained secret until Pope John Paul II made it public in 2000. It announced an era of persecution of the faith, and in particular an attempt on the life of the Pope, which John Paul II linked to the assassination attempt to which he himself was subject in 1981.

CHAPTER 7
The First Retreat (September 1936)

The first retreat at Châteauneuf from Monday 7 to Sunday 13 September 1936 was a major event in Marthe Robin's life and a decisive step towards the founding of the Foyers. It marked the beginning of a new kind of preaching and its spiritual fruits were apparent in many ways. The form the Foyer retreats would take was established at the very outset.

I. Preparing for the retreat

Much had to be done before the retreat could take place. For one thing there were practical arrangements to be made but the teaching had also to be prepared. Abbé Finet had already begun his preaching ministry, but what he had to do now was different. He must provide fundamental instruction to form the laity, in other words a kind of elementary theology course but at a higher level than Catechism and presented very differently. What was more, it must fit into the framework not of a study session but of a retreat. Combining theology with a prayer life was not easy. There was no formation of the kind at that time. For lay people there was at best a continuation of Catechism classes which followed on from their First Holy Communion. What was required here was on a higher level. It was an innovative idea, the success of which could not be guaranteed.

Materially, Mlle Blanck was the kingpin of the organisation, making herself and her money available, with the financial help of one of her Lyon friends, Mme Neyron de Champollion (of the Rassurel clothing manufacturers in Lyon). She saw to the arrangement of the rooms and the chapel, and provided the crockery, linen and furnishings. All this was done in close conjunction with Marthe who was kept abreast of everything, and with Père Faure. Hence numerous visits and much correspondence throughout the year 1936. As soon as the schoolchildren broke up for the long holidays in July, some of the parents and friends of Marthe transformed the orangery into a chapel in which the talks would be held. Kneelers were lent by the parish. The bedrooms were actually cubicles separated by sheets hung on lines with clothes pegs. In the kitchen there were not enough tables and the crockery was simply placed on planks supported on trestles.

Retreatants had also to be recruited. This was done by word of mouth via the personal network of Abbé Finet who had no small number of connections of all kinds. 'For several years,' said Marie-Ange Dumas, a philosophy teacher at a Catholic school in Lyon, 'I had been pursued by the desire to go on silent retreat. I had talked about it on several occasions to my "spiritual father", Père Finet.' Abbé Finet told her about the one he was due to preach and added: 'If the Good Lord nudges you in that direction, don't hesitate, follow his inspiration. For very specific reasons that you will understand when you get there, this retreat will be particularly interesting.' He said not a word about Marthe. Similarly, Hélène Fagot sought out Abbé Finet to tell him she would like to go on a serious retreat. 'I have everything you're looking for in Drôme, at Châteauneuf-de-Galaure,' he replied. She did not go without a struggle. Shortly before 7 September she wrote to Abbé Finet, telling him that she had three good reasons for not coming to Châteauneuf. He replied simply that none of them held water and so, much to her own surprise, she turned up at the gathering.

To Abbé Finet's efforts were added those of Mlle Blanck and Marthe herself who tried especially to get people from the valley. What would Mgr Pic say if all the women who came were from Lyon? 'I do not want to displease him with an almost complete absence of retreatants from Drôme.' Mlle Viricel, Abbé Finet's secretary at the director's office for Church education in the diocese, also took care of the secretarial work for the retreat. She was no more aware than the others of Marthe's existence.

The Bishop of Valence, Mgr Pic, followed the project's progress. He visited Marthe Robin in August 1936, together with Abbé Thellier de Poncheville, one of France's best-known priests. Charles Thellier de Poncheville (1875–1956) was a contributor to the French Catholic newspaper *La Croix*, one of the founders of the *Semaines Sociales*[1] and a much-prized orator in great demand, who preached a Salesian-inspired religion of love, hope and peace close to the spirit of Abbé Finet. Marthe asked the bishop to pay a visit to Châteauneuf during the retreat.

The political and social context within which the exercises were to be conducted was tense in the extreme. With the Popular Front holding the majority in the Chamber of Deputies, the front pages of the newspapers showed revolutionary demonstrations and the threat of strikes. The rise in the share of the vote for the Communist Party in Drôme from five per cent to nineteen per cent was even higher in the north of the *département* where Châteauneuf was, particularly in Saint-Uze and Saint-Vallier. It was there that Doctor Luc, president of the League of Rights of Man, joined the Communist Party after a visit to the USSR. To many, a Communist regime seemed the solution for the future, whatever the cost of establishing it.

II. Initial surprises
We have Marie-Ange Dumas and Hélène Fagot's recollections of the days they spent at Châteauneuf that were to have such a decisive impact on their lives. Quite by chance on Wednesday 2

September Marie-Ange heard talk in Lyon of a stigmatic who lived in Châteauneuf. Next day it was confirmed. 'I wonder,' she said to the friend who had mentioned it, 'whether you were right to tell me. It has removed any desire I had to go on this retreat .... From that moment on I couldn't think about the week ahead without dreading it.'

Hélène Fagot, for her part, arrived a day late after, that same morning, attending the ceremony at which her sister Gaby took the religious habit. She was met at the station by Marie-Antoinette Brocard who also did some secretarial work for Abbé Finet. 'Her welcome was a real let-down: "If you only knew what a wasps' nest we've let ourselves in for! Just imagine. There's a visionary in the area who is behind this retreat. Abbé Finet told us so yesterday evening." I climbed the mountainside that first time, deeply perplexed and with my thoughts racing.'

The composition of those attending was a disappointment to Hélène Fagot who was twenty-eight years old (Marie-Ange was twenty-three): 'I had expected to find myself amongst teachers, young people, but the people there were rather old: Marie-Ange and I were the youngest and the only teachers.' 'Stuck-up old cows,' was how she referred to these ladies in front of Marie-Ange, who was shocked. The dining-room was 'quite dilapidated'. In the kitchen she noticed 'a little stove, a small sink, table, store cupboard, everything was small'. She lost no time in locating Mlle Blanck and Mlle Viricel, whose 'rooms' were on either side of the one she shared with Marie-Ange: 'We were well surrounded!' It is clear that Mlle Blanck's temperament was not to Hélène Fagot's liking at all.

The cooking was seen to by Mme Neyron de Champollion who had brought her cook, her crockery and lots of provisions. No sooner had the retreat started, however, than she was called back to Lyon: her factory workers had gone on strike. She would return nonetheless for the conclusion of the retreat, bringing with her a hearty meal.

III. Discovering Marthe Robin

The retreat began on the Monday. On the Wednesday Abbé Finet spoke about visits to Marthe Robin and handed out a list. The first three on it were Marie-Antoinette Brocard, Hélène Fagot and Marie-Ange Dumas. 'I had no desire to see the woman, who had been given such a poor introduction on the previous day,' said Hélène, adding, 'In my heart of hearts I said to myself: "Wait and see the look on the faces of the people going up when they come back down."' Marie-Antoinette Brocard's visit went on for a long while. Hélène and Marie-Ange waited in the kitchen which at that time was only separated from Marthe's room by a door. 'They were speaking very loudly. We were worried, especially me.' When at 2.50 p.m. the first meeting was still not over, Hélène and Marie-Ange hurried back down in order not to miss the next talk which was due to start at 3 p.m. 'Which I did with a certain relief,' Hélène admitted.

Abbé Finet was not to be beaten. Next day, on the Thursday, 'After breakfast, Father had Marie-Ange and me get into his car. This time I couldn't get out of going. Marie-Ange went in first with me afterwards. It was a long visit during which Marthe talked a lot about my pupils in Lyon at the St Augustine school. She indicated to me how important it was to educate those completely fresh little souls entrusted to us by the Lord. From the first instant of that visit I was conquered. My heart was won over for ever more and the Lord saw to it that I never ever doubted Marthe. After so many years I realise that this was a very great grace.'

Marie-Ange too had an extremely meaningful meeting with Marthe. 'You teachers in Church schools have as much of a vocation as religious; and to make up for not being mothers you have immense spiritual maternity. Teaching is a form of priesthood! After the mission of a priest there is none greater. Make your retreat well, I beg you, do not let grace pass you by.'

IV. Abbé Finet's preaching

We have the programme for that first retreat written in Père Finet's own hand. It included no less than twenty-five talks. This then was a form of retreat in which instruction played a considerable role, and all the more so because Abbé Finet was not given to brevity when getting to grips with a subject. Great attention was therefore required of the retreatants. Yet experience was to show that the idea of providing plenty of substance corresponded with a need and despite various adaptations, it was to continue to inspire the preaching in the Foyers.

The retreat had a very Marian feel to it. It began with a talk on 'Mary, paradise of the word incarnate' and concluded with 'The Assumption of the Virgin into heaven'. It was not, however, a course of continuous Marian theology. In fact, personal involvement was immediately asked of the retreatants with instruction about the apostles' calling and God's plan in our lives. Next, teaching about the spiritual life and how to respond to God's call alternated with talks about Christ and his love for us to 'the very end', and about the Virgin Mary as a way to Christ. On the Saturday the retreat came to a climactic moment of consecration to Jesus through Mary according to the formula of Saint Louis-Marie Grignion de Montfort. The programme for the retreat was not the clearest. What was remarkable, however, was the intricacy of teaching about the Virgin Mary, Christ and each individual's spiritual life. They combined to make up something extremely powerful, by which it was difficult to remain unaffected. Prayer times and a night of adoration, during which people took it in relays, provided periods in which people could be more open to God speaking in the silence of their hearts.

To go back to Hélène Fagot's testimony, she was not thrilled by the consecration to Jesus through Mary: 'I can't remember anything about it. Devotion to the Blessed Virgin was not my strong point, thinking as I did that it was much simpler to address myself directly to the Lord. It was through contact with Marthe that I discovered Mary's maternal dimension that is so marvellous.' She did, on the other hand, receive a remarkable grace that was to be granted quite frequently thereafter in the Foyers: 'Through Père Finet's account of the Divine Family I discovered the love of our Father in heaven, made up of kindness, active goodness, of liberating protectiveness, of caring attention to straightening us out, devotion and mercy. This love – provided by God, gives us the grace – necessarily attracts total faith. We had a "small" reflection of it in front of us![2] This was a precious help to me in my spiritual life.'

On the whole the people who came to that retreat benefited from it greatly. 'It was marvellous in graces the retreatants would never forget,' Mother Scat was to write.

V. Further surprises

On the Saturday night there was such agitation in the dormitory on the floor above Marie-Ange Dumas and Hélène's cubicle that people hardly slept. The housekeeper to the priest at Saint-Uze had some sort of nightmare that woke everyone. Then one of the retreatants suffered an attack of hysteria. Next day, moreover, she tried to strangle Abbé Finet as he was taking her back to Lyon. Then a clap of thunder was heard, very dry and without lightning. After that came a motoring noise as if there were a car in the dormitory. 'I said to Marie-Ange,' Hélène Fagot testified, '"Whatever kind of car could get here at this time of night?" And Marie-Ange replied calmly with a slightly mischievous look: "In the Curé d'Ars' time the devil used to arrive in a horse-drawn carriage. He must have modernised his transport." 'This didn't do much to reassure me.'

Finally in the early hours a terrible crashing of crockery was heard on the ground floor. 'We remembered that all the crockery had been laid out on a trestle table and thought it must have collapsed. Well, in the morning all the crockery was in good order on the table! Yet everyone had heard the noise.'

What was going on? Were there natural causes for what appeared to be happening? Natural causes exploited by the devil? With the exception of the hysterical woman mentioned those who had heard the noises were not unduly perturbed.

VI. Final surprises

On the Sunday morning Abbé Finet asked each retreatant to take her prayer stool back down to the village church so that it could be used for parish Mass. He added with a laugh: 'You've been sanctifying them all week.' There followed 'the procession of the prayer stools'.

After a festive lunch at which people were at last able to speak again, nearly everyone was able to go back up to La Plaine to say goodbye to Marthe. Hélène and Marie-Ange were among them. Abbé Finet was afterwards to take them to the station. On Marthe's doorstep they saw Père Faure who 'in his distinctive slightly grumpy tone, said to us, "You should stay here and teach in my little school." – "But Monsieur le Curé, it's too late to think about that because we're both engaged to start in Lyon on 1 October. What's more, you have the two teachers from last year for when school starts back." He responded with a grimace, "Yes, they're coming back but I'm not happy about it."'

At the station Hélène Fagot 'turned round to look back at the château and said to Father: "It would be strange if I were to come back and teach here one day." He said nothing in response and it was time to go. In the train we were very quiet, rather meditative.'

Abbé Finet went back up to Marthe Robin who told him that the Lord had shown her that Hélène and Marie-Ange would return to take over the school in Châteauneuf. 'Father pointed out that she should have said so half an hour earlier when we were there. Marthe replied, "I didn't dare to."'

VII. Abbé Finet becomes Père Finet

Something important had happened during the retreat, something about which the retreatants knew nothing: Abbé Finet had become Marthe's spiritual father. From then on their destinies were to be truly bound together.

It is likely that Père Faure and Marthe had talked about the possibility. Marthe was a very sensitive person. She owed much to Père Faure and would not have just dismissed him abruptly. He was the one who had felt more and more that she was outreaching him. The arrival of Abbé Finet had presented him with the solution to his most difficult problem, that of the spiritual accompaniment of his parishioner. He must have been glad to hand over the baton. According to Père Finet, it happened symbolically on the evening of Monday 7 September:

> I was with Père Faure when he went up to take Holy Communion to Marthe. When he wanted to hear the victim of love's confession … she designated me for this apostolate of mercy. Then, when Abbé Faure wanted to give her Holy Communion, she said, 'No, not you, but Father,' pointing to me.
>
> And that day I received the marvellous title of 'Father' that I was subsequently to share with all my brothers leading our Foyers of Charity.

On the Friday 'Father was present during the Passion in Marthe's room for the second time. On the Saturday, in the late morning, we saw an extremely distressed Father come back from La Plaine, telling us with tears in his eyes that the Passion of the previous day had been offered very especially for his sins and his perseverance.' At the conclusion of the retreat Mgr Pic came to visit the retreatants and said to Father and to Marthe, 'I give you my blessing. For the time being, be content with mine.'[3]

※

From then on, the title of 'Abbé Finet' was more and more frequently abandoned in favour of 'Père Finet'. Abbé derives from the word *abba* meaning 'father'. The two words mean the same thing. In France in 1936 the word 'abbé' was used for secular priests and the word 'père' (father) for those belonging to religious orders. 'Père' should not therefore have been applied to the Abbé Finet. But the word 'père' has an affectionate sound and a sense of closeness which the word 'abbé' does not. It also has associations with the family. It establishes between two people a real bond of filiation which bespeaks something of the relationship between the Father and the Son in the Trinity. Thus a considerable step had been taken in the relationship between Marthe and her Father, Père Finet. Père Faure had been Marthe's Father for a while but that relationship had paved the way for another which was to last to the end of their days.

NOTES
1. Les Semaines sociales de France, created in 1904, is a congress which gathers each year to consider the social and economic life of the country from a Roman Catholic perspective.
2. She was no doubt referring to Père Finet.
3. Probably a reference to the future development of the Foyers which he was already envisaging.

CHAPTER 8
The Founding of the Foyer in Châteauneuf (1936–1947)

After the retreat in September 1936 everything was to fall into place very swiftly. The hour of God, so long and silently prepared for, had come. Not everything was done by Marthe or Père Finet, however. Others were to respond courageously to God's call for the new Work and many generous people would help them. It all began with Hélène Fagot and Marie-Ange Dumas' vocations, for which the first retreat had paved the way.

1. The first vocations to become members of the Foyer (September 1936)

To be a teacher in a Church school in France in 1936 was not a job, but a vocation. Stripped of all its possessions between 1901 and 1905, the Church in France was very poor. It paid its priests, many of whom lived in poverty, very badly and the lay people working for it, not much better. When the Church wanted to re-establish a network of schools to educate and evangelise children therefore, it was difficult to recruit teachers. In the absence of better, sometimes a school would take anyone on as a teacher, especially when the school was isolated, tucked away in the remote countryside. Yet many parents still preferred Church to lay schools which were often politicised. This was something of the story of the school in Châteauneuf. It had made do with what it had (the first two teachers had been expelled from the diocese of Lyon) to not very good effect. By contrast, Hélène Fagot and Marie-Ange Dumas represented what was best among Church school teachers. They had chosen this way because they believed in it; they were capable and they were teaching in excellent schools in Lyon. Having them come to Châteauneuf was to the good, but it was also a form of folly. It might well seem strange to take people of their calibre and exile them to so forsaken a place, a consideration which was further compounded by family problems. They were daughters with prospects. People were counting on them. Following their calling would involve an element of heroism. Yet that was precisely what was to bring about the birth of the Foyer community. Without heroism, without what might appear folly to human eyes, nothing would be founded.

Once again Hélène Fagot's memories are invaluable:

'On the Tuesday after (the retreat), 15 September I went in the morning to buy shoes and gloves for my cousin's wedding. When I got back at midday my mother said to me, "Abbé Finet sent a girl, Mlle Brocart, to ask you to go and see him as soon as possible at the diocesan education office." We had no telephone at home. I never for one moment suspected what it was about.'

Bear in mind that at this point Hélène Fagot did not yet know what Marthe had told Père Finet. She goes on:

'I said to my mother: "You'd better come with me because there will probably be some decision to make." [My father had died] two years previously. He was fifty-six. I was the eldest of six, the youngest being fifteen. I felt very responsible for the family and my mother, who was often ill, relied greatly on me.' As soon as she entered his office Père Finet told her what Marthe had said. Hélène replied that the school reopening was too soon (in a fortnight's time) for her to hand in her resignation. 'To which he said, "I'll be responsible for finding a replacement for you." Whereupon I said "Yes" without any hesitation … I went to find my mother who was sitting on a bench in the Avenue Adolphe-Max because she hadn't wanted to come up with me. She didn't say much in front of Father but that did not mean she was not thinking. The way back was painful. She wasn't very impressed. In fact seven years would go by before she set foot in the Foyer.' Thereafter things would sort themselves out but it took a good deal of courage on Hélène's mother's part to accept her daughter's calling. She did, however, come to realise that God had not abandoned her and that he was looking after her family.

'At the end of that visit on Tuesday 15 September, Father had directed me to go and see Marie-Ange and pass on Marthe's request. I went that same evening. I shall never forget being in the dining-room of the small apartment at 5, Rue Terme in Lyon. In front of Mme Dumas and her son Paul who was a seminarian, I repeated to Marie-Ange what Father had said to me. What I said shook them all. Then Mme Dumas started to cry and her son was vehemently against the idea which he considered to be unrealisable. I pitied Marie-Ange because I could see very well that she wanted to say yes but that, being the only breadwinner out of the four, she felt she could not abandon them. On the morning of Wednesday 16, I telephoned Father and told him about Marie-Ange's difficulties but said that I was willing to go alone. Father answered me: 'Write to M. le Curé in Châteauneuf this very day, telling him you accept but do not mention Marie-Ange.' I did so and that letter was to change my entire life. Later I discovered that Marie-Ange saw Father on the following day, Thursday 17 and that she too had accepted, despite what was going on in the family.'

The beginnings of the school at Châteauneuf
On Tuesday 22 September the son of Roudil, the printer, drove Hélène and Marie-Ange over to see Marthe: 'An excellent and very reassuring visit to La Plaine. At one point Marthe said to us, "Ah my little ones, if you only knew ... if you only knew..."' They

moved in definitively on 30 September. They found the school in a state of total poverty. In the dormitory were: 'Three cold water taps over a metal trough that was all rusty. There was no furniture. We discovered next day that the children stowed their things in a suitcase under the bed.' They had to go and ask the parish priest for sheets and blankets. Classes were held in the former orangery where the retreat had been preached. A wooden partition which came halfway to the ceiling divided it into two with a stove in the middle. They had to talk very quietly in order not to disturb the other teacher. When the school opened, beds had to be bought in Lyon for the fourteen boarders. A friend of the parish priest told them: 'We went into a "slum" area where the friend in question was surrounded by all kinds of bric-a-brac. Outside some ten rusty iron bedsteads, with bases that were sagging to say the least, were awaiting a possible purchaser. They must have been standing in the open air for some time because the rust was flaking off all over … It took a lot of time and elbow grease to strip them down and repaint them, first with red lead paint and then with a sea green paint of which the children were very proud.' Officially the school still had a headmistress but she was of little help. Hélène was obliged to step in as cook and then bursar. She had to work within a tight budget but they were in the country and the parents and Marthe gave much in kind.

On 1 October the little girls arrived. There were twenty-four of them. Marthe had asked that an additional course be started at once to prepare the children for the elementary exam. At the time this was like the culmination of primary schooling and passing it opened all kinds of doors. For the school it was a considerable plus. Marie-Ange bravely took on the older classes, which was quite a change for her from teaching philosophy! Hélène took the rest of the children. Marthe had also said that the school would later take pupils up to the baccalaureate. At that time very few girls reached that level. Only a few State schools and Church institutions prepared them for it.

Life for the two teachers was demanding. Every morning they went to Mass in the parish at 6.30 a.m. while the little girls were still asleep. Their day with the children ended with prayer in the church. Père Finet was very taken up in Lyon and with his commitments as a reserve military officer so in the beginning they did not see him. By contrast Marthe was very present and followed everything closely. Hélène and Marie-Ange were inseparable from her:

In the beginning, as Mlle Deleuze, the former headmistress was in the house, right next to the dormitory, we would go up to La Plaine. After dinner we would put the children to bed and almost every night Marie-Ange and I would spend the evening with Marthe and quite often with her mother. We would come back down quite late, around midnight.

We would keep the farm dogs we woke at bay by shining our torches straight into their eyes as we retreated. In the middle of winter when there was a lot of snow, any tracks across the fields would be lost. We used to hold hands …

Those enjoyable evenings made us so happy. We used to talk about everything, about the children, about our difficulties, about the Blessed Virgin, about where to put the furniture! I remember saying to her that we could put a small piece of furniture we'd been given to the left of the large cupboard in the east corner of the room in the old château and Marthe answering: 'Impossible, you're a few centimetres short.' When I got back I measured it and she was right.

We used to pray too. Marthe could still see at that time; she wore glasses for short sight and one of the first things we would do when we got there was clean them for her. Her mother would often stand at the head of her bed and plump up Marthe's pillow to prop her up. Marthe would talk and receive people as soon as Saturday afternoon and Sunday.[1] Those visits did us a lot of good because we were very much on our own.

It is important to note that Marthe formed the first members of the Foyers herself and that through them she transmitted a spirit to the girls' school. The first members of any work are the foundation stones. Even if they are not perfect, it is essential that they are sound and Marthe was very attentive to this.

On 8 December 1936, through Mary's hands, Marie-Ange Dumas and Hélène Fagot committed themselves to God for life with Père Finet. Their giving of themselves took the form of a consecration:

> On the afternoon of 8 December we had made our commitment in Marthe's room, with Father. We did it using Marthe's prayer of abandonment, the one of 15 October 1925. We were very naïve to dare recite words that were so plenary and which really went a long way towards the total gift of oneself; but the Lord must have accepted us, ignorant children that we were.

II. The second retreat (26 December 1936 – 1 January 1937)

Père Finet and Marthe had planned a second retreat for the end of December 1936. Difficulties had already started to arise with Mlle Blanck whose irrepressible love for unusual phenomena was proving awkward: 'She knew a lot of people who were mystics – or claimed to be mystics! – whom she had been to see personally. So when she stopped by the school she would tell us sensational stories!' Being somewhat overbearing too, she wanted to be directly in charge of organising the retreat that Père Finet had assigned to Hélène Fagot. She had to be kept at a distance. Naturally this was quite painful, especially as she had been generous to the Work.[2]

Good people from the valley came to help clear the classrooms, arrange the chapel and do the cooking. At the end of the retreat Steffie Hauslish, a medical student of Romanian origins, was baptised in the parish.

The exercises concluded on 31 December 1936 with the first night of adoration at Châteauneuf to mark the beginning of the New Year. This time in the early hours, the retreatants were treated to a real earthquake: 'Quite a big one because Father was thrown out of his bed and Mlle Viricel, who was resting in an armchair in the dining-room, was thrown onto the floor. Next day the event was reported in the press (*le Petit Dauphinois*) identifying the Châteauneuf region as the epicentre of the quake!'

According to witnesses another phenomenon occurred. 'At that retreat there was also an effusion of a marvellous perfume in the small chapel. Several retreatants remarked on it,' said Hélène Fagot. When Père Finet was told, he confided that the same thing had happened in Marthe's room.

III. The spiritual and material development of the Foyer

The Foyer was now in existence and was to be progressively consolidated, even if for a while the Foyer was just the school. At first life was exhausting. Rest meant exchanging looking after the children for looking after retreatants.

The increase in numbers

The first thing to note is the success of the school. The number of pupils increased from thirty-five when it opened in 1937 to 130 in 1946. Vocations to become Foyer members came in: by 1939 there were already six members; five people turned up for the start of school in 1946. By 1948 the Foyer had twenty-four members. They could cope. Every Sunday evening in Lent 1939, Père Finet gave a talk for men. Forty-two attended the first and the numbers increased week by week. On Palm Sunday there were 320, most of whom were not particularly practicing. The success of the retreats was similarly confirmed. They progressed from sixty-three retreatants in 1936 to 405 in 1947. By the summer of 1947 the sixty-fourth retreat was already being held. In November 1947 came the first retreat for priests.

At that time men and women went on retreat absolutely separately. A priest from le Mâconnais, Abbé Robert, asked Père Finet if he could take part in the retreats hitherto exclusively for women. Père Finet did not want him to do so without permission from Mgr Pic. Mgr Pic told him: 'You can sit at the back.' Then the retreatants objected that there was no reason why their husbands or sons should not attend. When Mgr Pic was consulted he again said: 'Let them sit at the back.' So, on 8 September 1942 began what were called retreats 'for the people of God'. People continued to behave very modestly. Initially husbands and wives had separate rooms but when the Grand Foyer was built, rooms were created with a communicating door between them. Husbands were put in one with wives in the other. Later, however, it was decided to honour the sacrament of Marriage and give them a double room. It was a revolutionary idea at the time and some neighbouring preachers of a slightly reactionary disposition thought it inspired by the devil.

Before and during the war Châteauneuf thus became increasingly well known as both a school exemplary for its education and the evangelisation of children who held the retreatants in their prayers, and a location for a completely new kind of retreat.

In 1937 the education inspector had come to visit the school. 'At the end of the usual kind of visit – pupils, mistresses, premises, qualifications had to be shown – there was a long silence. Having seen them, he looked at us, particularly Marie-Ange, and said: "What are you doing here? You can't have come here just to bury yourselves in a place like this. With these qualifications you must have some other idea at the back of your mind." Looking at the large central heating pipe waiting to be put in (the room adjoined the Paquien house[3] which didn't belong to us yet but which we were indeed hoping to buy): "You're going to expand, create a large school." Then pointing to the terrace which looked out over the countryside, he added: "In a few years time there will be a large sign over the valley, with the words, 'Boarding school for young ladies' on it." He was a real prophet. He had no idea how true his words would prove to be.'

The building work

In the existing premises, which were basic to say the least, it was impossible to take in both children and retreatants at the same time. Père Faure had already started some building work. In 1934 the east wing of the former château had actually collapsed at about 1 a.m. while a ball was going on. As soon as the château had been bought, the priest had started reconstruction work which was finished in 1937 but more still needed to be done, and it was no longer merely a matter of building but rather of fulfilling a mystical design for the house.

As early as 1933 we find in Marthe's notebooks precise instructions about future building work to create the Foyer of Charity:

> Jesus opened out his arms in a glorious gesture of benediction and love, looking down at the earth which he was covering majestically with his shadow and surveying it with ineffable tenderness and kindness. After a moment in this attitude, he indicated to me the precise place where he wanted his Work, a place that had to be acquired ...
>
> 'So let the building proceed without interruption, despite the difficulties of the time and mounting anxiety! ... This is my will! ... Have not great and wonderful flourishes of my divine works and my love come about in the most turbulent and troubled epochs, in the midst of battles, fires and ruins?'

Thus in theory Marthe knew what had to be done. The land was extremely fragmented and belonged to a series of owners but the purchases were gradually made. The Lord revealed his precise plan for the Foyer on 20 September 1940, in the very midst of disaster, at a time when France was crushed. On 23 September Père Finet wrote:

God showed Marthe the Foyer during the Passion of Friday 20 September. On the left as you go in, where Le Paquien is, a chapel with a crypt open to the east. On the other side, on the ravine, an extension to the school … the courtyard will need levelling on the ravine side. The Champion, Mondet houses etc. will be demolished.

In the inner courtyard between the school and the Foyer trees will be planted, pretty trees, not ordinary ones … Our Lady of Fourvière will have her statue in that courtyard in the middle of a cluster of trees.[4]

Over the door to the street a modern Virgin holding out her arms, but like the Miraculous Virgin who has them lowered, leaning forward slightly, without a crown. She is waiting for souls, welcoming them. With her crown she is the Queen of Heaven and that will not go with the gesture of outstretched arms.

The statue was ordered from Hartmann, an excellent Drôme artist, who sculpted it with the help of his wife out of a fifteen-ton block of Euville stone. It was a great success. The love and serenity it conveyed measured up to Marthe's requirements well. It was reproduced in photos and statuettes and distributed across the five continents.

To appreciate the extent of the building work you have to imagine the terrain. It was on a steep slope on the side of a hill so an artificial terrace had to be created. That involved substantial earth-moving which meant employing a large and expensive workforce. We should note too that the plans were for two main buildings: one for the Foyer proper with a chapel and the other for the school where the old premises would go on being rearranged and extended. They were to be separated, not just by some form of recreation area but by a landscaped garden for which Marthe supplied the details because they were symbolic. 'God is in the details' as Cardinal Eyt, then Archbishop of Bordeaux, used to say.

For a Virgin Mary, close to humanity, to hold out her arms to arriving retreatants was not insignificant. Keeping an old sundial familiar to the local people bespoke a readiness not to sever all connections with the past but to preserve what was beautiful and the fruit of the labours of previous generations.

For all that, embarking on construction work at such a time was, humanly speaking, folly. It was a case of rebuilding a Church and a country, however, so it went ahead. Houses went on being bought right up until 1943.

As early as May–June 1938, before the project was even definite, they had begun to talk about the building work. Charles Vial, Père Finet's cousin, had drawn up some preliminary plans. Mother Lautru had a friend in Saint-Etienne whose husband, M. Stribick, was an entrepreneur. He agreed to take on the job and a large digger was brought over from Privas to dig out the hillside. The village had never seen anything like it before. It caused quite a sensation and saved a considerable amount of time. In May 1939 when they set about the earth-moving, the entrepreneur could not 'find rock to support the foundations. It was Marthe who said to dig deeper. He did and the rock appeared.' These were the foundations for the Grand Foyer building. A new worksite for the school opened in October 1940 at what to all intents and purposes could not have been a worse time. Cardinal Gerlier, Archbishop of Lyon, thought the idea 'mad'. But, cardinal though he was, no one took any notice.

The building had to be financed. There was no lack of generous donations but effort had to be put into finding them. Marthe herself did not hesitate to ask a number of people for help. So it was that one lady sold a magnificent pearl necklace raising exactly the amount needed to meet one shortfall.

Mgr Pic pushed hard for the construction of buildings that were large enough. Later, in 1961, Père Finet was to say: 'No one could have missed him walking about our muddy building site in his ceremonial patent leather shoes and violet cassock, climbing ladders, crossing the jumble of planks, pushing the chapel walls out with a word, enlarging the conference room with an order, increasing the number of floors to our building which he thought was too small.'

During the war, when cement and building materials were in short supply, the Foyer still managed to get coupons. Mistakes even happened and lorries turned up unexpectedly. Afterwards it was realised that they were meant to have gone elsewhere but by then their contents had already been used.

On 28 February 1943, when the Foyer was still a long way from completion, Père Finet organised a ceremony to consecrate it to the Blessed Virgin. A picture of Mary Mediatrix of all Graces was placed in the chapel. Père Finet had the idea of compiling a text of consecration based on the 1933 text describing the mystical intuition relating to the Foyers, and also on notes taken during Marthe's Passion on the previous Friday. He had not said anything to Marthe when she announced: 'Father, you should take your inspiration from the Passion of the other Friday and from the little 1933 paper.'

IV. The Foyer during the war

The founding of the Foyer went on amidst all the events of the war that affected Châteauneuf along with the rest of France.

The beginning of the fighting brought with it renewed religious fervour throughout France. Marthe took advantage of this to launch a new evangelisation initiative in the parish, instituting the continuous saying of the Rosary, a Rosary crusade. All through the winter of 1939–40, which was a very cold one, people managed to keep the prayer going day and night. Père Faure himself was responsible for the Rosary between 3 a.m. and 6 a.m. The Foyer members did their bit every three nights. 'To start with we would go down to the church in the middle of the night but afterwards Marthe asked M. le Curé to let us say it in our chapel because the roads were too dangerous.[5] They were a long two hours! We would wrap ourselves up in a blanket we were so cold.' Père Finet took it upon himself to write and tell all the bishops of France about this crusade. Cardinal Gerlier, who had not been consulted, took it very badly and made his feelings known. Mgr Bornet, who had been made Bishop of Saint-Etienne, consoled Père Finet who was upset by the reprimand.

When war was declared Marthe Robin was extremely worried. She even advised hiding the sacred vessels despite the fact that Châteauneuf was a very long way from the front. 'Hitler is in the image of the antichrist,' she said, 'but he is not the antichrist … How the German Catholics must be suffering!'

When the collapse came, people fleeing the Germans passed through Châteauneuf. The Foyer fed anyone on demand. Hélène Fagot, who did the cooking outside, found herself saying, 'Whoever's going to eat all that today?' Food for the refugees always arrived as needed. Women and children from the town of Modane retreated to Châteauneuf and great solidarity was shown. The school gave shelter to families with children under two: 'House filled to bursting. Mattresses in all the rooms. Baby bottles. Laundry. Cooking with nothing very much except locally grown asparagus.' Any children old enough to understand were told about Marthe. They were subsequently reluctant to leave Châteauneuf because they felt protected by her.

The fighting of 1940 spared Châteauneuf and a German unit made up of older soldiers was beaten by the French at Romans: 'The wounded sprawled out on the grass were cared for in front of the house but not one German came inside.'

Support for prisoners of war went on all through the war. Marthe and the Foyer sent them parcels to keep them going. Children and the community also had to be provided for at a time when food was being requisitioned by the Germans. 'The shops emptied and supplies were reduced. We set off on bicycles to go round all the neighbourhood farms. Not one potato, only swedes and Jerusalem artichokes. The children complained! … So

Marthe, who received presents from old friends, sent down lots of goodies that were much appreciated.' Friends often went to great lengths to find food. The roads were controlled and sometimes the vehicle-loads of foodstuffs for Châteauneuf were illegal, but no one was ever caught.

Another more dangerous form of solidarity related to people on the run. Marthe was scandalised by the treatment of the Jews: 'By what right are they treated like that? Spiritually we are Jews. Our Holy Father the Pope has said so.[6] Without them there would have been no Christ and no Redemption. This is something crucial which prevails over time and eternity. Jesus was Jewish, Mary was a Jewess.' So Châteauneuf, like many other places in France, hid Jews in trouble: 'In 1941 or 1942 we saw a taxi arrive at five in the morning with a Jewish family looking for somewhere to hide. We gave them shelter for a while, but the house was well and truly full of refugees so we advised them to take lodgings at Marron, the local hotelier's[7] place. Which they did. And I found one of the girls from that family in our register, enrolled with us as a boarder in 1943–1944, in class two, under the name of Mila Ferrier. Her real name was Ellia Friedmann of 6 Rond-Point Faventines, Valence. It was only later that we found out her real name. We also took in two young men (possibly Jews) who taught mathematics for a year ... I can't remember their names which weren't their real ones anyway.'

The summer months of 1944 were marked by the Liberation fighting which was very fierce in the region. The Americans landed in Provence in the August and went up the Rhône valley. The Maquis[8] prepared the way for them by attacking the Germans who were having none of it. The front line was fluid, moving backwards and forwards. Danger came from several quarters: bombing, the sometimes hasty actions of the French Resistance fighters and German reprisals. The Foyer lived according to the rhythm of events under a threat that was very real. Additional support was provided for refugees and the wounded from the different camps.

On 9 June 1944 Père Finet wrote: 'Last Friday Lyon was bombed:[9] 900 killed. Greatly upset. We can feel events gaining pace.' 'The Maquis are on the move and are starting local battles. Yesterday[10] they attacked Saint-Rambert-d'Albon. Pushed back by the Germans, during the night they commandeered my small Simca to go – so they told me – and pick up their wounded in Anneyron: sixty killed or injured.' On 14 July there was a tense encounter with the French Freedom Fighters of Communist tendency, who turned up at the Foyer at one o'clock in the morning: 'They accused me of having concealed weapons since the Cagoulards[11] days of 1936! I was angry at having to answer such a gross accusation. They accused me of political involvement. I gave them a heated answer. There were eight of them round me, all of them armed. I thought at one point they were going to take me away. They asked me for petrol and finally my Citroën … They went down into the cellar etc. In the end they apologised and said they approved of my anger at their accusations, as a priest and former officer. At 4.30 a.m. they left with my car. "May the Blessed Virgin watch over you," I said to them as they left. They thanked me very much. I strongly affirmed my independence as a priest and my mission to souls. In the end they behaved as they should.' That same day a German plane came down near the Foyer. The Freedom Fighters took the two crew members who had parachuted clear, prisoner. The Germans were furious when they looked for them and did not find them. They killed several people in the village and announced that they would torch Châteauneuf on Sunday 16 July at 10 p.m. One can imagine how anxious the people of the Foyer must have been, but on 16 July at 9.30 a.m. came a counter-order and Châteauneuf was spared.

In the month of August the bombing in the Rhône valley and its environs intensified before the advance of the American troops who had landed in Provence. Saint-Vallier, a checkpoint for the Rhône, was severely bombarded. Refugees flocked to Châteauneuf where the Foyer took them in. It was holiday time.

Retreats had been planned for and they were maintained. A retreat was held with about twenty people. It went on as if nothing was wrong, with explosions from the munitions depots blown up by the retreating Germans going on in the background. The Foyer shook with them. 'We did not lose faith. The atmosphere of war was harrowing.' A liberation committee dominated by extreme leftwing elements was formed at the town hall. People in the Foyer were woken at night 'by the most revolutionary and anti-religious songs' but the Foyer was an important centre for taking in the wounded brought from round about by the Freedom Fighters. Vehicles 'with machine guns mounted on them' were constantly parked outside the building: 'Our courtyard is not lacking in the unusual. All the wounded feel well looked after at the Foyer.' Military doctors came and stayed there. Thus the Foyer became a hospital and a meeting place where much heated conversation went on and yet 'the retreat went on as usual in an atmosphere of contemplation despite all the comings and goings in the north courtyard.'

The situation worsened abruptly on 27 August when the German army launched a counter-attack. It retook Romans by surprise – 'The town is on fire' – then proceeded towards Châteauneuf where the Freedom Fighters were encamped. 'The local people left the area en masse to go and sleep in outlying farms. In the Foyer we kept up a state of calm and peace with many men and women on retreat.' When Père Finet went up to see Marthe on 28 August, he ran into the Communist leader of the Freedom Fighters who had visited him on the night of 14 July. He had the Communist insignia tattooed on his forearm. 'I thanked him for getting the Citroën back to me. For all his hard, coarse appearance, the man spoke to me pleasantly … He parted from me civilly with a handshake and not without having seen Marthe, with whom he had had a "long and excellent visit"'. The Maquis were in the Mantaille woods near Marthe's home, a good position on top of the hillside overlooking two valleys, but the

Germans were in the immediate vicinity, between Saint-Sorlin and Châteauneuf. They had taken hostages and set fire to farms. The sound of gunfire could be heard all the time behind Marthe's house but it did not stop Père Finet: 'Coming back from Marthe's house at night we would walk with a certain caution.'

Transformed into a hospital, the Foyer continued to take in the wounded. On the evening of 29 August 'Some wounded were brought to the Foyer, among them two of the little Communists who had taken my Citroën. They had been injured by American aircraft fire ... Two Mongols in German uniforms were also brought in. They had killed their German officers in Anneyron but had been wounded in the process. We gave these men who had been sowing terror in the region for two months a charitable welcome. They were the ones who had raped fifty-seven women and little girls in Saint-Donat. Also, I was fearful about their presence because of possible reprisals by the Germans who were in the immediate environs of Châteauneuf. During the night the Russian, the Mongols and some of the other wounded were evacuated to Voiron. We kept only a few others with minor wounds who would be able to conceal themselves if the Germans turned up.

On 31 August there were sudden developments. At breakfast time someone arrived, saying, 'The Americans are in the square.' They were referring to five reconnaissance jeeps looking to make contact with the Germans. They were shown where they were and the jeeps went off, handing out cigarettes and sweets. 'We were very excited and happy.' Other jeeps arrived. 'We could already smell freedom in the air.' At about 10 p.m. at Marthe's house we heard a 'tremendous distant and muted throbbing'. It was a tank division on the move in the distance. On their way down at 11.25 p.m. Père Finet and Germaine, a friend of the Foyer, passed close to armoured vehicles without knowing whether they were German or American. Had they been German, Châteauneuf would have been directly in their line of fire! The two made it to the Foyer under cover through the back streets. They found it full of Americans of the 367th division. The Foyer became the American troops' HQ. 'Our north courtyard harboured at least forty vehicles in various strange guises.' Tanks and pieces of artillery had taken up position and there were trucks everywhere. The Americans left the next day. 'Intensive aircraft activity went on throughout the days that followed. Little by little the sound of the cannon and the bombing by the aircraft became more distant and Monday 4 September was a day on which we heard nothing any more except the sound of aircraft engines. The silence made a deep impression on us.'

The hospital continued to function in the Foyer with a dozen wounded people. Châteauneuf was full of refugees from Saint-Vallier. But there was no question of interrupting the retreats. On Monday 4 September 'the fourth retreat of the summer began with thirty retreatants who had not previously booked, and on 18 September there was another retreat with over sixty men and women who had managed to get there from fifteen dioceses 'despite the complete absence of any post, newspapers or means of transport'. 'Gradually the men of the Maquis disappeared and calm was restored to Châteauneuf.'

The war was over for Châteauneuf. The months of July and August 1944 had been fraught with all kinds of dangers. Several times there could have been tragedies of the kind that occurred in many other parts of France, but the village and the Foyer had been protected. The Foyer's mission would be able to continue in a France that must rebuild itself, and then spread all over the world.

V. The discernment of the Church

Two enquiries (1942)
As far as the Church was concerned wartime was also a time in which to come to a decision about Marthe. True, Mgr Pic,

Bishop of Valence, had shown his support for her and for Père Finet but in the light of the success of the retreats and Marthe's growing influence, the matter had to be taken further.

Several types of discernment were therefore set in motion. On their own initiative, it would seem, three priests from the diocese of Lyon were brought by Canon Bérardier to Châteauneuf from 26–28 August. Père Finet and Marthe cooperated without any problem and a report was compiled in September 1942. It was very favourable. The three priests had been won over. 'On the way back,' Canon Bérardier wrote, 'the three pilgrims' hearts were all beating to the same rhythm of joy and gratitude to Providence.' He added for Père Finet's benefit: 'I have understood your role: it is burdensome but so beautiful! ... I found you to be in a state of physical and moral equilibrium that is almost disconcerting when one thinks of the life imposed upon you.' These few words provide a very valuable insight into Père Finet at that time.

A short while previously, on 14 April 1942, at the request of Mgr Pic, Marthe had received a medical visit from two well known doctors in Lyon: Doctor Jean Dechaume, professor at the faculty of medicine and André Ricard, the surgeon and brother-in-law to Père Finet. Mgr Pic and Père Finet were present at the beginning of the visit.

The outcome was a medical report which is all the more useful for the fact that it is the only one we have for Marthe. It was also studied closely during the cause for beatification. The examination went on from 9 a.m. to 2 p.m. with only one break between 11.40 a.m. and 12 p.m. It has been suggested that the doctors had previously received favourable reports and that their diagnosis was thereby distorted, but this is not true. They did their job as well as was then possible. Their descriptions are flawless. Like true professionals they relied on medical facts and came to an appropriate diagnosis of Marthe's illness. They found themselves confronted, however, with phenomena such as the stigmata which they could not deny but which could not have natural causes. It was their view therefore that it was impossible to 'provide a plausible explanation for them in terms of the causes current scientific knowledge would usually invoke'.

The conclusion of the bishops in 1943
In this context on 7 August 1943 Mgr Pic published a ruling in the *Semaine religieuse de Valence*[12] which, as was pointed out, is the opposite of a warning. Its purpose was to show the Church's esteem for Marthe and protect her so that she could carry on with her mission without being subject to idle curiosity. It is important to quote the original text:

> For eleven years our attention as a bishop has been drawn to the person and activities of a woman in our diocese, Mlle Marthe Robin. We have made a point of not publishing anything about her or naming her in any of our writings.
>
> This reserve imposed by prudence and in conformity with the prescriptions of the Church corresponded fully with the constantly manifested desire of a soul who wishes to distance from her person all misplaced curiosity and, through suffering, to consecrate herself solely to the good of those souls who come to her.
>
> Circulars of varying content and provenance, with no author's or printer's name and without the imprimatur that is nevertheless required for publications of this kind, have vulgarised her name, adding numerous fanciful details to the precise facts, sometimes most imprudently calling into question the most respectable theologians, bishops and even cardinals ...
>
> We ask our priests and members of our diocese to have recourse in the present case to this same reserve, that it is necessary strictly to observe, if we do not wish to open the way to controversy in which incompetence is given free rein, and which will ultimately cast discredit on what is most respectable in the life of souls and on the Church herself.

❦

Marthe and Père Finet were certainly satisfied with this statement which gave her a form of 'ecclesial status' and allowed her to carry on acting in accordance with her mission. Indeed, all through this period Marthe had remained faithful to her call to prayer and intercession.

NOTES

1. Just after her experience of the Passion.
2. The break with Mlle Blanck was not complete. For some time she went on coming to retreats.
3. A house in the village which the Châteauneuf Foyer subsequently bought.
4. For reasons we do not know, this statue was never put in place.
5. Because of the ice.
6. Pius XI: 'Spiritually we are Semites.'
7. And a great friend of Marthe Robin.
8. During the Second World War French resistance took two forms: on the one hand a network to gather and pass on information and rescue persecuted Jews and allied airmen who had been shot down; on the other, groups of armed fighters known as 'Maquis' which increased in number particularly from 1943–44 on, to include tens of thousands of combatants provided with weapons by the Allies.
9. By Allied aircraft.
10. 8 June 1944.
11. A right-wing political group between the two World Wars.
12. Valence Religious Weekly.

CHAPTER 9
Marthe's Personal Development (1936–1947)

Wartime was a significant period in Marthe Robin's spiritual development. It was also a difficult time, during which she was tested in various ways. It was a time of foundation but no foundations are solid unless they are sunk deep.

I. Relations between Marthe and Père Finet

The advent of Père Finet in Marthe's life changed her completely. In the beginning they saw relatively little of each other. Then the priest was appointed to Châteauneuf by his superior, Mgr Bornet, who was very understanding. Cardinal Maurin, Archbishop of Lyon, however, was less convinced than Mgr Bornet of the usefulness of Père Finet making his home in Châteauneuf. He was sceptical about Marthe so asked Père Finet to spend at least two days a week in Lyon. Even during the war when travel was dangerous, the Archbishop's successor as of 1937, Cardinal Gerlier, refused to revoke this measure. It was no doubt also a test of Père Finet's obedience and thus, indirectly, of the authenticity of the life Marthe was leading. Only in 1944–45 would Père Finet be able to be at the disposal of the Foyers on a full-time basis. The situation cannot have been easy from this point of view.

Marthe and Père Finet got on well. In character and experience they complemented one another. It must not be thought that any influence Marthe had on Père Finet was unilateral. It was true that the priest found in Marthe the presence of God, proximity to Mary, a spirit of sacrifice, great intuition, and a thousand useful and practical pieces of advice which gave him direction and courage and were a constant source of nourishment to his spiritual life. In particular, he was present during her experiences of the Passion and took notes. He could not help but be moved in the very depths of his being. For this reason he was at the disposal of the Work with all his fervour and generosity. It was the Work that gave more and more meaning to his life and enabled him to marshal his energies.

He also had a great feeling of paternity towards Marthe. He was not just an auxiliary. It was he who through the Eucharist and the sacrament of Reconciliation gave her the life of God. He was at the service of that life in his child. This paternity shaped his interior formation more and more, and especially so because he exercised it, albeit in a different form, in relation to the members of the Foyer who gradually appeared, and also in a way that was different again, in relation to the retreatants. It was a paternity made up of goodness, indulgence and hope vested in people, but also of exigency and desire for the truth. It knew how to tinge itself with humour or, by contrast, with authority. Marthe was constantly calling him back to this paternity.

Thus an ever greater intimacy was created. Nor did they conceal their affection for one another even though the manner in which it was shown continued to be very discreet. Did that mean that they always understood one another perfectly? Marthe probably saw into the priest more effectively than he was able to fathom her. But she had no authority over him and did not permit herself to control him. He could take initiatives that she could not. On the other hand Père Finet was given to a mystical theology which though well established lacked critical distance and nuancing. He therefore interpreted everything that Marthe was living in a theologico-spiritual light which sometimes forgot about other people's reactions. They could then find themselves confronted with shortcuts, which could have negative consequences later. Fortunately he was also a man of good sense and for the time being he tried as best he could to do what Marthe suggested.

Marthe's mother, who continued to look after her until her death in 1940, seems readily to have accepted Père Finet's role in relation to her daughter. By contrast, Père Faure's position became more delicate. He was also very conscious of the fact and so gradually withdrew until in 1955, he left the parish. No doubt it was a source of suffering to him: how could it be otherwise? To his dying day he was to treasure the text of a prayer by Marthe that he kept in his breviary and that we only know thanks to him. On the other hand, Père Finet's arrival was a relief to him and unburdened him of a spiritual load he had had difficulty carrying.

But Marthe too had needs. Close to God and Mary as she was, she was still an ordinary woman, a bed-ridden peasant. Even though her vision was to grow increasingly with time and with the people she met, she did not have Père Finet's horizons. For the time being she had much to learn. The mystical life is in no way disconnected from the most ordinary human life and like anyone else, spiritual people need information in order to work out where they stand. So she talked to Père Finet but she also listened to him. He had studied. He came from a wide social circle in Lyon. He had knowledge. Marthe was impressed by the quality and distinction of his family, which she was quick to get to know and appreciate. But in times of suffering she would sometimes say, 'By comparison with his [Père Finet's] family I am a slob'. Sometimes Marthe would espouse Père Finet's assessment of this or that social problem. She remained very discreet with visitors and did not assert her views, but there were times when they came out in her prayers and even in what she said during her experiences of the Passion. Père Finet's characteristic tones were identifiable in some of Marthe's words. It was only natural after all. Things would sort themselves out with time.

For all that, as Marthe was to remark one day to the person in charge of the Foyer in Mexico, 'love makes us suffer', and the relationship between Marthe and Père Finet was to engender suffering on several perfectly understandable counts.

The first related to friends and family. Little by little Père Finet instituted a procedure for people wanting to see Marthe. They could no longer just go in and see her when they wanted without the agreement of the Foyer. Also, in order to give Marthe a little more peace, Père Finet had the house extended at the back. A new room was created for her that no longer gave onto the courtyard but onto fields. A corridor separated it from the kitchen. On 18 September 1942 Marthe was moved into what she humorously described with deliberate exaggeration as 'Père Finet's château'. She was never to leave that room and would end her days in it. She was a little further removed from the life of the farm and the kitchen where visitors waited.

Those, however, who were quite naturally used to seeing Marthe whenever they wanted, felt alienated by this priest from Lyon. They started to come less frequently. Marthe quickly noticed and suffered as a result. She had a deep love for her family members whom she saw regularly, and for her friends. She needed them. She had neither a glorious body nor an angelic psyche. She needed affection, even consolation, and was afraid of finding herself abandoned by them. But she had very little autonomy or authority in her own home. She did not want to contradict Père Finet. Her loyalties were therefore divided and doubtless she suffered as a result. It should, however, be pointed out that Père Finet did nothing to alienate family members and that he always tried to find meeting times compatible with their commitments.

Bishops and priests, although not hostile to the Work, were also raising questions in good faith about the connection between the Work and the presence of a mystic, and about the balance of relations between Père Finet and Marthe Robin. Were their respective positions right? Was Marthe not in fact playing the role of spiritual director? Was Père Finet not being indiscreet by giving the public who came to the retreats information about her life about which he should be more reserved? The same people were, however, to see an improvement in this respect and had the goodness to say so. Père Finet himself would honestly acknowledge that he had at first lacked prudence.

In order to exercise his role as Father, Père Finet had to be there, but the distance involved was still considerable. Hélène Fagot wrote of the beginnings of the Foyer: 'It is generally believed that Père Finet was with us but he was still in Lyon in the office for Church education until the war when, from 1939 to 1940, he was mobilised.' Having been an officer in the reserve artillery at the start of the war, Père Finet fulfilled his regulation duties but he was already forty-one – no age at which to go off to the front. Mgr Pic saw to it that he remained posted in the region. He was demobilised at the end of July 1940 and in principle was resident in Châteauneuf. But the archbishopric still required him to go backwards and forwards to Lyon. The to-ing and fro-ing could be very trying and Père Finet had at times to finish his journey on foot. Thus in January 1941 he wrote: 'I arrived in snow and cold. Yesterday evening, coming back from Lyon, I got stuck in a snowdrift on my way out of La Motte-de-Galaure. Some farm people got my car to cover and I arrived walking through the snowdrifts on the route.' The whole of the railway line from Lyon to Saint-Vallier ran through the Rhône valley which was a strategic axis. At the end of the war transport became dangerous. The depots had been bombed so some of the carriages had no windows and in winter they were bitterly cold.

Marthe suffered as a result of Père Finet's inability to be permanently there, divided as he was between two ministries. No doubt she also suffered because of Cardinal Gerlier's lack of trust. For a while, rightly or wrongly, Père Finet thought he was being considered for the episcopate which would mean his having to leave Châteauneuf. His relationship with Marthe was not then quite as definitive as one might think. There was consequently a doubt in her mind, which was to assume new proportions after her mother's death.

II. The deaths of Monsieur and Madame Robin and the aftermath

Marthe's father had been 'very sick for some time' and died at the age of sixty-three on 23 June 1936, shortly after Père Finet's first visit. In his illness he had undergone a great spiritual change: 'He spent his days and nights in prayer, his hands constantly crossed over his poor chest,' wrote Marthe to a friend. 'Then in his last days, when he could no longer cross his hands or pray for any length of time, he kept saying, "Lord, have mercy on us" over and over again.' She believed he had 'really died a saintly death'. Marthe's parents were also respectfully present when she received Holy Communion every week. However, the health of Marthe's mother – Célestine Robin – was very precarious.

The demise of Marthe's mother (November 1940)
Marthe had a great affection for her mother who looked after her and saw to her intimate needs. They slept in the same room and Mme Robin witnessed all that her daughter went through. In 1937 she had a blockage of the bowel and was thought to be lost but Marthe prayed fervently to the Virgin Mary and something both astonishing and amusing happened: 'A few days later Doctor Sallier came back. Sitting on a chair in between Marthe's bed and the head of her mother's, he palpated the patient's stomach with his left hand, with his right on the foot of Marthe's bed, and looked at her. Several times he repeated what he was doing to the patient, each time looking at Marthe and drumming the wood of her bed in irritation. Finally, after one last examination, he said brusquely: "Well! There's nothing there anymore." Then more loudly and almost angrily: "There's nothing there anymore!"' Marthe, of course, saw this sudden cure as a miracle brought

about by Mary and sent her mother to Lourdes on pilgrimage to give thanks.

In November 1940, however, Marthe's mother suddenly fell very ill. Everything was set in motion to have her treated: Père Finet had Doctor Ricard come from Lyon. She was transferred to Lyon to the Sainte-Anne clinic accompanied by Hélène Fagot who never left her side. Mme Robin was given every care. She underwent an operation and from a distance Marthe followed the details of it and was able to describe them. On 22 November Mme Robin was brought Holy Communion. She took it 'with a calmness that greatly impressed Hélène and Mme Devaux'. A little later that morning she was given extreme unction. 'She realised herself that there was no hope.' Père Faure wanted her to be brought back to die with her daughter in her room at Châteauneuf, and that was in fact what happened. Père Faure, Marthe's sister Mme Serve, and Henri went to Lyon to arrange it, and Mme Robin was brought home in an ambulance attended by Mother Lautru. Marthe was in the throes of reliving the Passion at the time. Her mother was placed on her bed in the room she shared with Marthe. 'At my request,' wrote Père Finet, 'the nurse took Mme Robin and helped her to lean over Marthe who was unconscious. I raised Marthe's head to her mother's lips. She kissed her and said: "Little one." She often used to call her: "My little one."' This was to be her last gesture of affection. She died shortly afterwards: 'She went to sleep peacefully in God, without any anguish. Marthe was to tell me that the devil left her mother completely in peace. The child had no doubt taken all his onslaughts on her behalf.'

When Marthe emerged from her Passion, she found her mother dead. 'Marthe's grief was painful to see.'

The consequences (November 1940–November 1941)
The death of a mother, even when we are adult, often brings with it a feeling of having been abandoned and difficulty in knowing

where we are in relation to our family, our community or even the Church. Marthe experienced a terrible feeling of solitude. It might even be suggested that for about a year she went through a form of depression. There was also a spiritual dimension, however, which suggested an alternative interpretation. 'Marthe had taken her mother's purgatory upon herself in order that her mother might go directly to Heaven,' wrote Père Finet. A real crisis arose in her relations with Père Finet, a crisis which was to be hurtful to them both. It is simplest to allow him to describe this period:

Marthe suffered more and more from loneliness, often asking, even whilst accepting God's will, why her mother had left her, and calling constantly for an end to her trial and for Heaven. How many times did Marthe tell me that she was going to leave us to be with her little mother! Usually she would inform me of her departure on Sunday mornings when she started to speak[1] ... Marthe was afraid I would leave for good. Nearly every time I left for Lyon on Tuesday she would say to me:

'Father, don't be cross with me but I have something to ask you.'

'What is it, my child?'

'Will you be coming back on Thursday? Are you going to stay in Lyon? Is the Cardinal going to keep you?'

Only with difficulty could I allay her fears. Marthe also became more and more convinced that I would not be able to get used to Châteauneuf, that I would miss Lyon, that my family was suffering because of my absence etc. The devil had also made her believe on one occasion that I had called her a devil. She had concluded that I despised her and that she deserved it. For all that, she remained very trusting towards her father and continued to rely totally on obedience to him.

Here we are no doubt dealing with what is known as heroic virtue. In this already difficult context there was to be an additional trial: Père Finet's illness. He had a very serious attack of jaundice. 'I myself,' he wrote, 'underwent a purification of the heart during my illness. Going through ninety hours in which I slept for only six, I thought during one of those sleepless nights that my last hour had come. I called out but no one heard and I quietly prepared for death ... I made a sacrifice of the Work, accepting not to see it through to the end, and a sacrifice of everything I loved. I united myself with Marthe and quietly said my Rosary with inner joy. I was in a state of great peace and eventually slept from one to five in the morning. Then I prepared myself for Holy Communion. This sacrifice of everything left me peaceful. God gave everything back to me.'

While Père Finet was ill, Marthe had little company, particularly during her Passions. Père Faure had to stay at home because of a leg injury. Two other priest friends on whom she might have been able to call had, in one case, diabetes and in the other a kidney stone. 'In short, Marthe was left alone and wasn't able to receive Holy Communion once. On the Friday before his recovery on 15 November,[2] Marthe was left completely on her own; even her brother Henri had gone out into the fields.'

On Thursday 20 November 1941, Père Finet came back to Châteauneuf but he was still very tired and asked Abbé Petit, parish priest at Saint-Martin-d'Août, to attend to Marthe during her Passion instead of him. This was the lowest point in her crisis and, spiritually, the moment when she felt most abandoned:

It was then at about 6.30 p.m. that an excessively painful agony began. Marthe first asked for her father,[3] then began to groan in utter solitude and pain (it was her mother's birthday). Very sorrowfully Marthe, convinced that I despised her, accepted the loss of her father for ever. Abbé Petit asked that she make this sacrifice for her entire life. She made it. She thought that the Work of the Foyer was now over, that she had been wrong to ask for it, that she had deceived everyone. She wanted (though she did not actually do it) to destroy the Foyer documents, notably page forty of Gethsemane about the future Foyer.[4] In short she agreed to renounce everything, accepting total abandonment, complete solitude, the end of her mission, of the Work, and contempt. She renounced all God's promises about the Work. She could go no further from the point of view of abandonment, abandonment by people, by her mother, by the Blessed Virgin, by God and of course by her father. She had not been able to take Holy Communion, which was yet another sacrifice. And it was in this state that she began the Passion.

That evening after twice calling me, 'Canon Finet' she then called me 'M. Finet'. I was no longer her father.

From a spiritual point of view, she was reliving the mystery of Jesus' agony on the cross: 'Father, why have you abandoned me?' The spiritual life involves extreme and profound joy, but God only grants it to hearts that have been totally purified. There also comes a time when that joy in itself has to be given up. It is generally when the lowest point has been reached that God gives everything back. That was in fact what happened with Marthe. On Friday 21 and Saturday 22, she experienced several 'Marian ecstasies'. The Virgin Mary came to bless and console her. On Sunday 23, emerging from her Passion, it was as if Marthe were beginning a new life 'and timidly, not daring to believe her good fortune, found her father again. "Father, Father," she repeated. "I dare to call you Father again."'

Later, doubtless because of temptations from the Evil One, Marthe's relationship with her spiritual father came under attack again. In her Passion of Friday 30 March 1945 Père Finet found her in 'a state of utter spiritual desolation, believing she had failed completely and thinking only of leaving Châteauneuf. Immense separation from her father during those two days'. Note the fear that she was wrong, of having failed.

This trial of Marthe's is understandable. It came on top of, or rather as part of a spiritual experience that gave her direction and steered her from within. It is an experience that remains extremely mysterious but perhaps it is good that something be said about it.

III. Marthe's spiritual states

The purely physical context of Marthe's health formed the backdrop against which her mystical experience was played out. Like anyone else Marthe needed security. She had no income and could not have any, which meant that she lived off her parents' charity. Now, in 1934 M. and Mme Robin had arranged their estate in such a way that on the death of the last of them, everything would go to Henri. Marthe would only receive part of Mme Robin's property in Saint-Sorlin and a two-and-a-half-hectare plot of land. So she could live in her room for as long as her relatives were happy for her to do so but then what would become of her? One of her uncles, her father's brother, who was eighty-two, offered to have her in his house, but Marthe did not want to leave the place where the Foyer was to be.

Thanks to Père Finet these circumstances changed. When he realised that Marthe's mother might be close to death, on 5 November 1940 he drew up a legal agreement with her and Henri. The latter agreed to hand the house and lands over to Doctor Ricard, Père Finet's brother-in-law, for a payment of 15,000 francs in cash. He would still, however, have the use of it until his death. Henri was not being short-changed. Thanks to Doctor Ricard's generosity, he was relatively well off and could move elsewhere if he so wished. Alternatively, if he liked he could also stay. Marthe was assured of being able to remain where she was but, though she was in friendly hands, her home was no longer really her own. Not to have anything of her own, even a room, was a sacrifice even for a saint, but Marthe is not known ever to have complained about it.

The death of Marthe's mother raised another question, however: who was going to look after her? Marie-Ange Dumas and Hélène Fagot used to come and see her but they could not be there all the time. A Mlle Maurer was prevailed upon but she was not there permanently and would be absent herself even at times when her presence was indispensable. Henri was often alone at the farm with his sister. They got on well. Their niece Mme Danthony (Célina's daughter) said: 'Henri was very fond of Marthe and used to ask her advice … They talked easily together. Marthe loved him very much.' But Henri would drink at times when he had money coming in and lose his self-control. On occasions he would hit Marthe, move her bed, pour water over her in winter when she had a cold, light a piece of paper in front of her and threaten to burn her alive. One can imagine how frightened Marthe must have been. It was only gradually with the arrival of new members of the Foyer that a constant eye could be kept on her.

Marthe's illness worsened: in 1940 she went blind. She offered up this great source of suffering to God. At times she could see shadows and she remained extremely sensitive to light. 'I heard her cry out one day,' said her niece Simone Gaillard, 'when I carelessly bumped into the lamp and sent a ray of light into her eyes … Marthe also confided to me that a ray of morning sunshine through a poorly closed shutter made her eyes and head hurt for several days.'

For all the reasons just mentioned Marthe was thus even more vulnerable to what she underwent in her Passions.

Marthe's experiences of the Passion

Marthe's entire spiritual life was given direction by her weekly union with the Passion of Christ. There are so many testimonies from people who saw it that there can be absolutely no doubt about its reality. On Thursday evenings during the Rosary, Marthe would start to relive what Christ experienced. More often than not on Friday afternoons she would speak and Père Finet would take notes. It was very important to Marthe to feel someone with her even if she did not speak to him. The Passion would increase in intensity to the point of resembling actual death on Fridays at 3 p.m. Marthe would come to the end of this Passion 'broken'. Père Finet would then have the very delicate and difficult task of gently straightening out her body and raising her head. She would often next experience Marian ecstasies on Friday and Saturday and would recover her speech on Saturday, then on Sunday, and finally, from 1969 onwards, on Monday.

Many things occurred during the Passions. Marthe was actually completely 'in touch' with the world about her. She carried it all in her prayer, suffering and offering. She was especially concerned about the Work of the Foyers which was in its initial stages. She thought about its members and she supported Père Finet in particular because the whole project depended on him. Marthe's prayers for the Foyer were numerous. One she used on 1 January 1937 was a good summary of the core of her thinking:

Oh God bless my father, bless those he loves, bless his works; sanctify all his words. Bless his Foyer of Charity, bless all the souls in that Foyer, sanctify them in your love, fill them with your divine virtues, that they may no longer be inclined to destructive talk, divided, rebellious, nor unfaithful to grace, but may the humility, charity, kindness, goodwill, joy and peace of Heaven reign in and radiate through them and the light of faith illuminate their minds.

On 5 January she announced:

God wants this house to be his garden of delights and each soul that lives in it to be a Paradise plant. Souls are God's delight, not walls. Jesus finds his joy there, his heaven of love, his repose on earth, not in extraordinary things but in everyday things done with love.

Marthe's prayer and offering during the war

Her other concern before and during the war was world peace, and connected to it the evangelisation and conversion of nations. As a French woman, she had received a particular mission in relation to her own country which was to be a prime concern throughout the war. Marthe echoed some of Père Finet's analyses and intuitions in a way that might be construed as nationalistic but should not be so. She prayed like the children of Fatima, in the conviction that God had a plan for each nation, that each must recognise God and undergo a conversion, and that only prayer could definitively hasten that conversion. She committed herself wholeheartedly to this ministry of offering because this was the role allotted to her. 'Let us arrange to have prayer everywhere,' she said as soon as the conflict began. She was acutely conscious of the gravity of the situation: 'Oh God, do not wait any longer. Oh God, do not delay. If you delay any longer, will we not die, oh Lord?' (1 September 1939).

In fact Marthe thought that France was engaged in a combat that was not just military but had a religious dimension to it. The forces involved were not just human. There was something inhuman about Hitler, something that was connected to hell. The battle could not therefore be fought with arms alone. It too must have another dimension. And in that struggle she could join. History has plenty of examples of others who have done the same: the Blessed Anne-Marie Taïgi for example or the Blessed Anne-Catherine Emmerich.

On 5 January 1940 Père Finet found her undergoing the Passion with 'much blood'. She said:

My God, may my blood, which is Jesus', cover all the earth, flood especially your beloved France with it, oh my God, and assure men's victory[5] ... over the devil, over hell in its entirety, not with weapons but with the gift of your heart. Your Divine Grace, give us your light, Lord, give us your peace, that total, complete, definitive peace for which we never cease imploring, but that we have not received, that you have not granted us. Yes, Father, it is divine and lasting peace that I ask of you, the peace that you alone can bring about in all souls, that only you can give this world.

In this combat she felt very much at one with Pius XII. She even thought that he would have a role in bringing about peace. From God she hoped for what she called 'the miracle of love' which formed part of all her prayer even after the war. This was an intervention by God for peace. Did she foresee, as was predicted at Fatima, the fall of Communism and the period of peace that would later be granted in Europe? Be that as it may, this 'miracle of love' was linked to the new Pentecost, the new evangelisation that was to be brought about by the Holy Spirit: 'Marthe asked Mary for her miracle of love. She was assured of it but we have to pray.' (15 September 1939) 'Mornings and evenings I continue to offer myself[6] in order to bring about the end of the war, the miracle of love and the new Pentecost' (13 October 1939).

In these circumstances one can imagine how upset Marthe was when, in 1940, France was defeated. She seemed to be expecting it. From then on she implored God to spare her country and give it back its true face, praying much to this end. But her prayer expanded to encompass all the countries of the world. Thus on 29 January 1943 she said during one of her experiences of the Passion: 'My God, I have said "Yes". Again I say: "Yes, Father", until the supreme consummation of your divine will, I offer myself completely for every nation. "Yes, Father", for all your children on this earth ...' She prayed to 'the angels of the nations' that God's grace might reach the whole world. 'Oh God, keep them in your love, keep France in your love, win over all nations and souls to your love.'

It was not easy to see events from a spiritual point of view. On the subject of the British attack on Syria in 1941 Père Finet noted: 'Where are we headed? Nothing is comprehensible any more.' Sometimes Marthe would have flashes of insight which turned out to be true. In May 1940 she announced that the ships carrying soldiers destined for Norway would not go. And sure enough next day a resident of Châteauneuf who had been due to sail was seen unexpectedly home on leave. His regiment had been disembarked.

It is clear that Marthe had always hoped that in the end some good would come of the fighting. Her sights remained firmly set on the announcement of the Good News of salvation and the conversion of the world. She did not militate for any particular political organisation or any particular ideology. That is why, as the end of the conflict gradually came into sight, her prayer remained unchanged. On 8 December 1944 she said: 'Oh Father, oh my God, give back to France the divine life that she no longer knows, the life of charity and love, the life of union in your truth. Oh Father, oh my God, grant her all your divine life, grant her your compassion and forgiveness, grant her your peace ...'

Marthe went further. She considered it her duty to intervene, as other saints have done at times, with the government. In March 1940, on the advice of Père Finet, she asked Mgr Pic her bishop, and Doctor Banssillon, professor in the faculty of medicine in Lyon, to meet the Secretary of State for Foreign Affairs, August Champetier de Ribes, who was possibly the only practicing Roman Catholic in the government. Later he would tell his son that 'a stigmatic residing in the South-East had informed him that the French army should not enter Belgium but hold its positions. My father took the matter seriously.' Pope Pius XII had warned the allied command through the intermediary of the British, of a trap set by the Germans who had invaded Belgium and the Netherlands. Champetier de Ribes had just been told of the Pope's intervention which was not taken into account.

Later, in 1941–1942 she sent word to Marshal Pétain that he was surrounded by people who were ill disposed towards him and that he would be betrayed.

Marthe had views on political matters and she had preferences. She appreciated Daladier for example and mistrusted Paul Reynaud. She considered Laval a traitor.[7] That was her prerogative. But she did not fight to assert her own ideas. She was not seeking to promote an ideology of any kind. Her battle lay elsewhere. It was mysterious in nature. And to that conflict she gave all her energy. By doing so she was seeking to protect her country, the Foyer, Châteauneuf and the whole world as much as she could. She emerged from the war without having given up hope but one can appreciate to what extent she must have been tried by it.

Attacks by the devil
In her struggle Marthe was attacked by the devil on numerous occasions. She was beaten and banged against the chest of drawers next to her bed. Her ribs were even broken as a result. This is not unusual with some mystics. Such episodes can be put down to convulsions or hysteria. To do so was and still is fashionable but it does not take into account certain objective situations.

There were times when Marthe seemed prey to an extraordinary force that gripped her, a force that was completely beyond anything her sick body could muster. When, during the Passions, the devil wanted to throw her out of her bed, Mgr Pic was unable to hold her down. Only Père Finet could do so.

Marthe's spiritual accompaniment
How did Père Finet react? He was a witness to phenomena totally beyond his understanding. Not only was he present during her experiences of the Passion, seeing blood flow from Marthe's eyes and his spiritual daughter sometimes tossed about in all directions, not only did he see, along with several other witnesses, the stigmata on Marthe's forehead, but he was also party to her

receiving Holy Communion in an extraordinary way. Marthe was incapable of swallowing. She was unable to make the necessary movements. There were times when the host escaped from the priest's hands and entered her mouth. And even when it was placed on her lips, it would enter without any movement. Several priests, among them Canon Bérardier of Lyon and Abbé Talvas, founder of the Le Nid refuge for prostitutes, witnessed this when they were giving Marthe the Blessed Sacrament.

It should be said to Père Finet's credit that he remained calm. He kept his nerve commendably in circumstances in which anyone else might have lost it. But what was the quality of his spiritual accompaniment in this initial stage of their relationship? Canon Babolat, his own spiritual director, was concerned about it and sent him a number of letters of advice.

It would seem that Père Finet intervened actively to give precise meaning to Marthe's Passions. Almost certainly he entrusted her with a number of missions that corresponded with his personal view of things. Marthe, obedient and therefore influenced by the priest, took on board what he said. It is likely that this increased Marthe's inner tension. We are certainly dealing here with a situation where spiritual accompaniment may have restricted and even caused regression. Instead of encouraging Marthe to go beyond what was perceived by the senses, her spiritual father may have brought her back to them because of his own experiences and prejudices.

But that did not affect Marthe's spiritual experience at the deepest level. She remained given up to the love of God. She offered herself for her brothers and sisters. She had a familiarity with the Virgin Mary which was undoubtedly a great support to her. It was thanks to the love of Mary that she was able to live, and the Virgin Mary was such a source of wisdom to her that even theologians came to draw from it.

IV. Marthe Robin, 'the theologian'

With the passage of the years Marthe's influence and reputation spread. Her world of relationships extended and was enriched. We have numerous testimonies about people with whom she established sometimes very strong links, whose lives she helped to change or whose thinking she shaped. In particular she had an effect, albeit indirectly, on certain aspects of theological development.

Père Garrigou-Lagrange

At the end of 1940 a Dominican priest by the name of Réginald Garrigou-Lagrange entered Marthe's room. Considered one of the Church's greatest thinkers, he was to have a very beautiful friendship with Marthe.

Réginald Garrigou-Lagrange (1877–1964) was so important a figure that he warranted a detailed entry in the *Dictionnaire de spiritualité*, the reference book in this field.[8] Renowned for the soundness of his doctrine, he had made the link between the theological thinking of Saint Thomas Aquinas and the mystical experience of Teresa of Avila and John of the Cross. A professor at the pontifical Angelicum University since its foundation in 1909, between 1909 and 1941 he published some fifteen books – a considerable accumulation of spiritual theology – which had been swiftly translated and republished. In 1938–1939 he had just published *Les trois âges de la vie intérieure*,[9] a work in two large volumes providing the best summary of the mystical life in the entire Catholic world. Père Garrigou-Lagrange was taking a strong stance against authors such as the well-known Sulpicien, Albert Farges (1848–1926) who did not think that all Christians were called to a life of sanctity. He, by contrast, believed that the mystical life was open to all. He also thought that the Virgin Mary was a sure guide along this path and had great regard for the doctrine of Saint Louis-Marie Grignion de Montfort in this respect. Later it was to be said of Père Garrigou-Lagrange: 'the first to arrive in the choir, austere and poor, refusing all comfort, given to mortification, with simple piety and the obedience of a child, careful with his time, concerned about and even haunted by the poor, for whom he made himself a beggar, R. Garrigou-Lagrange was a prestigious teacher. He exercised a profound intellectual and spiritual influence on generations of students both secular and regular of diverse orders and from several countries. A preacher, confessor and director, he enlightened and guided many priests, nuns and lay people.'[10]

When Italy declared war on France he was obliged to leave Rome. He taught then at the study convent for Dominicans of the French province who had retreated to Coublevie in Isère. He was not, therefore, very far from Marthe Robin.

For all his learning, Père Garrigou-Lagrange was preoccupied with one extremely sensitive problem of Marian theology, which had grown more complex with time and had detached itself from dogmatic theology. Since the fifteenth century what were known as the 'privileges of Mary', which is to say those elements about her that were different from those of other Christians, such as the Immaculate Conception and Divine Motherhood, had gradually become the starting point for reflection on the Blessed Virgin. By separating them from dogmatic theology their very *raison d'être* was being overlooked. People had reached the point of asking which was the greatest of her privileges and whether they should not always be looking for new ones. But this intellectual game was making people lose sight of the real Virgin Mary. She was becoming a figure apart, removed from Christians, and more and more difficult to understand. Later, in 1963, Abbé Laurentin would write a courageous book about what had become 'the Marian question',[11] and the Second Vatican Council would put things back in their proper perspective. In 1940, however, that stage had not yet been reached and many theologians were in a state of confusion, which was not helpful to popular devotion which remained generally sound.

Père Garrigou-Lagrange was well known to and particularly appreciated by Pope Pius XII who in 1957 said of him: 'We have often had evidence of the talent and zeal with which, by your words and writings, you have defended and safeguarded the integrity of dogma.' So why did he go and see Marthe? He himself provided the answer to this question in confidence to his Dominican students at Coublevie in 1941: 'I am in a position to tell you right now, without giving any secrets away, that in Drôme there is a saintly woman leading a contemplative life as a victim of love, Marthe Robin. I went to see her at the personal request of the Pope to judge the theological expression of her faith. I came away amazed and I have written as much to the Pope.'

We have several accounts of various meetings Père Garigou-Lagrange had with Marthe. The first encounter, which was decisive, was definitely the one to which the priest himself was referring when he spoke to his students: 'He told us about his meeting with Marthe in the presence of Père Finet,' one of them said. 'He had asked the latter to ask her two questions so that he, Père Garrigou, who was in the shadows, could hear her answer. The first question was as follows: "What is greater in Mary, her personal grace or her divine motherhood?" "Her immediate response," he told us, was: "If Mary is full of grace it is because she is the Mother of God." And in my corner I felt small but full of joy because I thought the same, but I could see theologians drawing such a distinction between Mary's grace and her motherhood that they were saying that if the Mother of God had not been faithful to supernatural grace she would not have been saved and glorified because her motherhood, though called divine, did not in itself sanctify her.'

'The second question was not put to her because Père Garrigou "thanked Marthe at once for her first answer which sounded so right, despite the contrary opinion of the majority of theologians over the last centuries". Marthe then said to Père Garrigou-Lagrange, "Why don't you write something on the subject?"'

It was probably on the same day, after this conversation, that Marthe asked Hélène Fagot to take Père Garrigou to the Foyer or rather to the school. 'We took the steep path that ran alongside M. Cheval's field. As I walked behind the priest, I was surprised to hear him remark: "Poor Garrigou, poor Garrigou, you thought you knew it all!"' Abbé Joseph Petit, parish priest at Saint-Martin-d'Aoôt recounted the same anecdote without, however, having been a first hand witness: 'On the way back from paying her a visit the learned man looked stunned. He was talking to himself along the way saying: "If only you could talk as well about the Blessed Virgin!" Later, shortly before his death, he was heard to say: "What am I by comparison with that humble girl?"'[12]

This meeting calls for comment. Père Garrigou-Lagrange believed totally in the possibility of a mystical life. He was also aware, however, that illusions were not uncommon in this domain. How was he to know whether what Marthe Robin was experiencing was authentic? He had a very serious theological concern, so serious that after the Council the subject was to lead to a real crisis. Good theologian though he was, he was not part of the 'confraternity' of specialist Marian theologians who knew each other and formed a very particular circle. He had not published anything on Mary. He was, however, well aware that there was a problem. So he passed on the question to Marthe. She was not a theologian but lived with Mary. She was not capable of formulating arguments but knew very well who she was talking about. With a single statement she put things back in perspective: Mary's life was entirely relative to that of her son. She existed only for Jesus. Her 'privileges', especially her fullness of grace, to which the angel of the Annunciation referred, existed only in relation to Jesus, in connection with her role as the Mother of Christ. To envisage her 'in her own right', independently of her mission, was a mistake. Everything must be restored to its proper axis. In this way, by implicitly taking a stance against the majority of Marian theologians, Marthe without realising it was paving the way for Vatican II. She was well aware, however, that things must be justified, rendered explicit, which is why she suggested to Père

Garrigou-Lagrange that he write a book, even if it was outside his specialist field and he would be treading on his colleagues' toes.

Père Garrigou came to see Marthe again after that. Once, when Père Finet could not be there, he asked a friend, Doctor Banssillon, to drive him to Marthe's house, who has given an account of that meeting. The conversation began in a jocular manner: 'Père Garrigou said: "Forgive me, Mademoiselle, for coming and disturbing you despite all your suffering but I have been told that you are willing to talk theology with priests, even if theology is rather boring." Marthe immediately retorted: "Theology is a magnificent field of knowledge. It is the theologians who are boring."' The priest burst out laughing at this answer and readily agreed. 'The ice was broken and I withdrew to a room next door. Over an hour later Père Garrigou came to find me and said: "Our conversation was very stimulating but now she won't say any more." I responded: "Father, this is Thursday and it is eleven o'clock at night. Marthe is starting the Passion. She is in Gethsemane."'

The remark about the boredom brought on by theologians was not just a joke. It touched on another sensitive point for Père Garrigou-Lagrange. He had reacted against a theology so technical that it was turning in on itself. He had put a great deal of effort into linking theology to the spiritual life. He was one of the advocates of what Urs von Balthasar was later to call 'kneeling theology'. In declaring her regard for theology but her doubts about theologians, Marthe was once again spot on.

Père Garrigou-Lagrange's relationship with Marthe and Père Finet was to continue. He came back to Châteauneuf with Mgr Pic and he kept up an affectionate correspondence with them that we still have, which is how we know that Marthe prayed for the book he was writing on Mary. He must have set about it at once because it was published in 1941 by Editions de l'Abeille in Lyon under the title, *La Mère du Sauveur et notre Vie Intérieure*.[13] Apparently the first part of the book picked up on the conversation with Marthe and developed it. It was an innovative work and nothing clearer had been written on the subject for a long time, but Marthe was not entirely satisfied with it. It did not altogether resolve the basic question of restoring Marian theology to its proper axis. So Marthe said to him or had word sent to him: 'You need to go back to this book. It does not answer adequately the problem preoccupying you.'

Père Garrigou-Lagrange reacted positively to her assessment. He asked one of his students, Henri-Marie Manteau-Bonamy, a young Dominican, to write a thesis on precisely the topic of his first conversation with Marthe.

Père Manteau-Bonamy

On 31 December 1945 it was that same young Dominican's turn to enter Marthe's room. Since 1941 he had been hearing about Marthe from his teacher Garrigou-Lagrange. 'I had been a priest for three years and had gone to ask her to pray for my young priesthood. But I had no sooner entered her room when immediately after responding to my greeting, Marthe said to me: "Aren't you doing a doctoral thesis on the Blessed Virgin?" (There was nothing mysterious about that. I discovered afterwards that Père Finet had told her ...) "Yes, Mademoiselle, and I have nearly finished it. Its title will be: *Maternité Divine et Incarnation*."[14] After a pause Marthe went on: "Have you noticed that our Lady of Lourdes didn't just say as in the Rue du Bac, Paris, that she had been 'conceived without sin', but 'I am the Immaculate Conception!' She waited for the Church to proclaim the dogma of her holy and immaculate conception to present her personal identity before God..."[15] Marthe continued: "In the same way Mary is not just a human mother like any other, better of course because she was conceived without sin, but she is above all the Mother of God; she is the 'Divine Motherhood' just as she is the 'Immaculate Conception'. That is her name which she revealed to the Church through Bernadette. That is very important for your work.'"[16]

In relation to this conversation, which may appear technical and which is indeed difficult to understand, it is important to bear in mind that in the Bible it is said that each person has a name that nobody knows which in some way expresses his mission and the depths of his being.[17] What then is Mary's hidden name, the name bound up with her mission? In Lourdes she did not say: 'I am the one whose conception was immaculate', but 'I am the Immaculate Conception'. Her very being is linked to her conception and her Immaculate Conception is in relationship to her being the Mother of God. Mary's hidden name is thus 'Divine Motherhood'. Naturally she is a human creature. She is absolutely not God. She is a sister to humankind. But she has a specific mission and everything that she is arises out of that mission. This intuition of Marthe's was shared in part by Saint Maximilian Kolbe, whom she did not know.

Impressed and interested, Père Manteau-Bonamy went on to become an esteemed Mariologist. In his thesis published in 1949, he took Marthe's intuitions into account.[18] Later, struck by how the Council had put Mariology back into perspective in the dogmatic constitution *Lumen gentium*, no. 56, he went on to extend his reflection by studying the life of the Holy Spirit in Mary.[19] This was to give him a good understanding of the Charismatic renewal movement where he would once again come across Marthe's intuitions. Finally he was to become one of the experts in the diocesan stage of her cause for beatification. Thus his entire life was to be marked and oriented by his 'theological' meeting with Marthe.[20]

Père Paul Philippe

In that same year, 1945, another Dominican came into contact with Marthe. The man in question was Père Paul Philippe, a professor at the Angelicum. He had heard about Marthe through Père Garrigou-Lagrange while they were both at Coublevie. Père Paul Philippe extended his stay in France for three years at the request of the Holy Office. The Holy See was in fact worried about certain aspects of the development of the Church in France and of the Dominicans in particular. Père Paul Philippe was there to assess the situation. He was a demanding theologian and not unduly soft-hearted. He asked to see Marthe. In his letter to Père Finet expressing this desire, he specified that he was not in the habit of 'seeking contact, even for my own instruction, with those souls favoured by God. Yet it seems to me,' he added, 'that the time has come because I have a very serious personal motive for asking for the prayers and illumination of your saintly child. If you see fit to respond favourably to my request, could you tell me if I might be present at a reliving of the Passion? I would be pleased to do so because I have attended two similar cases, one of them as a delegate of the bishop, and I would like to compare my observations on so sensitive a matter, because I am confident about Mlle Robin's case, whereas I am not sure about mine.'

Père Philippe was very pleased with his visit and unable to 'express [his] gratitude'. Such was his faith in Marthe that he had her read the manuscript of a work he was about to publish, and asked her to make any necessary corrections or additions. A delegate of the Holy Office having a theological work corrected by a mystic was not something that happened every day.

V. Marthe's meetings

During this period Marthe began to receive and help people who were to have an important role in the future of the Church in France. Abbé Talvas has already been mentioned. 'I was struck,' he was to say, 'by her common sense and perspicacity. She sensed how those women had suffered from being reduced to prostituting themselves.' When he told her that his intention was to centre his entire work on Mary, she responded: 'Oh yes, the Blessed Virgin! Those women, who have not been loved, have such a need of a mother's tenderness. She is the one who will lead them to Jesus.' In 1943 Little Sister Magdeleine, foundress of the

Little Sisters of Jesus, came to see her for the first time: 'Marthe occupied a prominent place in my life … Whenever there was a problem in the Fraternity, I would go and confide in her or write to her. She offered much of her suffering for the Fraternity.' In 1944 Père Épagneul, founder of the Frères missionaires des campagnes, visited her and told her that a branch for women was being founded: ' I consider it a great grace to have been able to spend some time with Marthe Robin. It did me good to be fully immersed in the supernatural.' A young Sulpicien priest, André Feuillet, came to confide in her: 'I too am linked to Marthe but in a way known only to Our Lord. I met Marthe for the first time in circumstances that were very difficult for me in July–August 1947. Immediately afterwards (still in 1947) the Lord gave me a doctrinal mission to fulfil in the Church as a whole with a view to restoring the meaning of and respect for the Word of God as a whole.' He was to become a great Biblicist.

Other people Marthe received were to enter more closely into her life. Jean Colon, a twenty-two-year-old medical student, came to meet Marthe on 10 July 1944 at Mother Lautru's suggestion. '"I would like to become a good Christian doctor like Professor Dechaume,"[21] he told her. "That's not enough," she replied and she talked to me about the priesthood. With my family background … The interview lasted about twenty minutes. It was calm, not anxiety-inducing, not tense. I felt very peaceful and joyful talking to her… It was not an order but it was clear, declaratory, obvious: "The Lord is asking more of you."' Sure enough, after being a doctor in Châteauneuf from 1947 to 1950, Jean Colon entered the French seminary in Rome. He was later to become one of Père Finet's most valued collaborators and one of those closest to Marthe.

NOTES

1. After her experience of the Passion.
2. The recovery in question is that of Père Finet who is talking about himself in the third person.

3. Père Finet.

4. Marthe Robin wrote about her experiences of the Passion and when she referred to Gethsemane, talked of the future Foyer.

5. The Allies.

6. The original says: 'I continue to offer Marthe'.

7. Edouard Daladier, Paul Reynaud and Pierre Laval: French politicians of the period between the wars. Laval collaborated with the Germans and was tried and shot after the liberation of France.

8. B. Lavaud, art. 'Garrigou-Lagrange', *Dictionnaire de spiritualité* (Dictionary of spirituality), Paris: Beauchesne, t.VI, 1965, co.128–134 and Tables, 1995, col. 248.

9. The three ages of the interior life.

10. Ibid. t. VI, col. 129.

11. René Laurentin, *La question mariale* (The Marian question), Paris: Éditions du Seuil, 1963.

12. Père Garrigou-Lagrange died in 1964. He had given up his chair in 1960. His last years were marked by a diminishing of his faculties, of which he was aware and which he bore in a saintly fashion.

13. The Mother of the Saviour and our interior life.

14. Divine Motherhood and Incarnation.

15. The apparitions in the Rue du Bac, Paris date from 1830, the proclamation of the dogma of the Immaculate Conception was in 1854, the apparitions occurred in Lourdes in 1858.

16. Henri-Marie Manteau-Bonamy, *Prier 15 jours avec Marthe Robin* (Two weeks of prayer with Marthe Robin), Paris: Nouvelle Cité, 1999.

17. Revelation 2:17.

18. Henri-Marie Manteau-Bonamy, *Matenité divine et incarnation* (Divine Motherhood and Incarnation), Paris: Vrin, 1949.

19. Henri-Marie Manteau-Bonamy, *La Vierge Marie et le Saint Esprit* (The Virgin Mary and the Holy Spirit – A commentary on chapter VIII of *Lumen gentium*), Paris: P. Lethielleux, 1971, republished 1975.

20. About whom he would write, in addition to the book cited above: *Marthe Robin sous la conduite de Marie* (1925–1932) (Marthe Robin under the guidance of Mary), Paris: Éditions Saint-Paul, 1995.

21. Catholic doctor and Professor in the faculty of medicine in Lyon, and friend of Père Finet.

— PART THREE —

A Time of Fruitfulness

CHAPTER 10
Marthe's Interior Life (1948–1978)

The years 1947 and 1948 show a clear turning point in Marthe Robin's life, after which she came to a new personal, spiritual and social 'status'. The following thirty years were a period of great fulfilment.

I. A period of accomplishment

All the foundations had been laid. God's plan for her was now clear. She had understood what her spiritual calling was, accepted it and integrated it. She knew what her mission in the world was to be and she knew what the role of the Foyers of Charity was to be. In Georges Finet Providence had given her the spiritual father and co-worker she needed and she now had a stable and fruitful relationship with him. Helpers were beginning to appear and she knew there would be no shortage of them. Marthe had also surmounted a number of hurdles and come through trials: trials that had given a solid basis to her being, trials during which she had felt completely abandoned even by the very graces Jesus had given her. She had nothing left to defend. She lived simply according to what God gradually gave her.[1] Free, Marthe could give herself wholeheartedly to her mission. This then was a period of remarkable fruitfulness in every respect, which stemmed entirely from the quality of her interior life.

During this time Marthe became much more silent about herself. She had long ago given up her journal. No longer did she talk during her experiences of the Passion and rarely did she confide anything about herself. It was not that she set out to dissimulate but the king's secret had become simpler, more transparent. It was enough to live it out without analysing it. Marthe was also aware that she was becoming more widely known. She did not try directly to control what was said about her. She had no hold, for example, on how Père Finet presented her and she trusted him. But she did at least want to avoid distortion and was mistrustful, therefore, of journalists and publicists. She asked to be protected from indiscretion, knowing very well that things were attributed to her that she would never have dreamt of saying: 'Dear God, what nonsense they have me talk!' she confided one day to Père Bonnafous. All this reinforced her natural reserve. Even to her friends she said little about herself.

Fortunately we have a few precious testimonies which have a bearing on various aspects of her inner life. They at least shed light on her interior state. Someone who knew her throughout this period provided the following general assessment: 'In a way things remained the same between 1948 and 1981 because by 1948 she had already reached this state of sanctification and surrender. In any case, I myself noticed a growth in compassion at the same time as in her inner solitude with the Lord, in the cross, in difficulties. She was alone, facing the mystery of the cross and of Easter … As I see it, there was greater serenity. She went, I believe, to the furthest extremities of suffering.' We shall see later precisely what these words mean.

II. Intimations of an inner journey

The friendship between the philosopher and academician Jean Guitton and Marthe Robin, of which more later, has afforded some valuable notes about their meetings and then a book about

Marthe.[2] She trusted Guitton, and so agreed – and this was a unique instance – to answer some of his questions. She did not go into detail but what has been passed on to us gives some idea of Marthe's itinerary in the years we are now considering.

Jean Guitton was interested in mystical phenomenology but had not studied theology nor, it seems, spirituality in any depth. He had, however, a fine, observant mind, and asked good questions. Marthe did not shy away from answering them.

Jean Guitton's questions

One subject that preoccupied Guitton was the nature of Marthe's 'visions'. She was in touch with the next world: of that he was sure. But how did this contact come about? Were the visions within or outside her? Without probably realising it very precisely – because he does not use the vocabulary of spiritual theology which he seems not to know – Guitton asked an important question. Marthe answered him very specifically: 'I have had image visions when I saw something outside myself, but then there is a sort of anguish, you are not absolutely sure, but ... there was one instance when there was evidence and I was quite sure: when God does what is said, then he is doing everything.'[3]

'I asked her if there had been any development,' Jean Guitton went on: "Yes and no. In the beginning there was more doubt because she was still in the images, and one always has to go beyond, to traverse. Now she is in the attributes of God; and has even left the attributes and immersed herself in the essence; and there, there is deepening in this essence."'

Jean Guitton was very interested and tried to get her to be more specific about certain points. We can draw some conclusions from their exchange.

Marthe did not in any way deny having had visions perceptible to the eye, with normal sight. But this vision remained external and was not accompanied by absolute certainty. It would be possible to stop at this but that would serve little purpose. 'Once upon a time I think I was held up by colours, appearances.' So the soul is called 'to go beyond … to surrender itself through and with her.' 'Inner visions' (known in spiritual theology as imaginative and intellectual visions) were more profound. In any case what demonstrates the authenticity of a vision is that God immediately accomplishes in the person what the vision announces. Grace is given at the same time as what is seen: 'The real proof,' she said, 'is not so much evidence, nor even certainty, but efficacy, the fact that God does what he says; this is evidence in the form of creativity … this is divine action substituted for all states of the soul.' But, Marthe emphasised, 'I have given that up. Now I am in the attributes of God and I am even sinking in … to the essence of the divinity.'

Jean Guitton also questioned Marthe about her relationship with the saints. She told him: 'I don't like reading the lives of the saints because each one has his own particular emphasis. I prefer doctrine to imitation.' He asked her more specifically about Catherine Emmerich and her 'travels' in the Holy Land. She replied: 'Yes, I experienced that at one time, but I've forgotten about it. It is not important. It is not the main thing. And what is annoying about it is precisely the risk of making it the important thing.' 'At one time I used to have very distinct views of a particular scene in the Passion. I would see it. I could recognise individual faces. I would hear the yelling of the crowd, for example. But now I am much more within. I no longer see anything. I am in communion with the very depths.'

A spiritual state
These last words of Marthe's are a perfect expression of the spiritual state she had reached. She was to go on to say in conclusion: 'I have passed into the interior, the essence, the substance; my heart has been filled. It is within. I can't explain it to you. It is much more certain than things, much surer.'

How are we to understand this? Christian spiritual tradition makes it possible to decode the language. The spiritual life commences with God taking over the exterior part of a human being. It is as if God somehow moves from the exterior to the interior. When there are mystical phenomena in which God renders himself present in a more perceptible fashion, they involve part of the senses. That is what happened to Marthe and she confessed that at times she was too attached to them. It should be said that phenomena discernible by the senses are extremely attractive: God appeals to people by means that he knows will reach them.

Then God goes further. He purifies, removes the extraneous and keeps only that which is essential, which is to say himself. After all, the spiritual life does not exist for the satisfaction of the self but in order to achieve union with God. That is the purpose of the trials traditionally known as the dark night of the senses and the dark night of the spirit. The first disengages and purifies the whole domain of the senses and action; the second reaches more deeply into a person's very being. If that person is generous and accepts these trials, everything is eventually simplified. Images are no longer important, one has moved beyond sensation, even spiritual sensation: one is in God, or rather God is in one: 'After all the passive purification, all the stripping away of reason, imagination and memory, after the death of the self – or rather intimately bound up with the death of the self – there is really a new birth which brings about the rediscovery, in complete faith and absolute surrender, of a very small baby's attitude of love for its mother.'[4] One then leads a life of union with God which defies description. That is what Marthe was explaining when she said 'in the essence'. One saintly Mexican soul, Conchita Cabrera, referred to it as 'mystical incarnation'.

What happens in this state? Everything becomes simple. The relationship with God is that of a child in its father's arms, allowing everything to happen because it trusts. The paternity of

God and filiation is lived out to the full. It is as if one is 'identified' with Jesus who lives within one. One is entirely compliant with the slightest inspiration of the Holy Spirit. One is not absolutely perfect because humanity remains weak and sinful to the last. One still remains fragile and vulnerable to temptation but one senses fully that God is master: 'It is no longer I, but Christ living in me,' says Saint Paul.[5]

If God wishes, various mystical phenomena may still occur in this state. But one is no longer attached to them as such. One is beyond satisfaction and curiosity. These phenomena are therefore placed at the service of a mission which is facilitated and deepened because of them. This was true of the Passion with which Marthe continued to be united.

III. Marthe's experiences of the Passion

At the core of Marthe's personal vocation was identification with Jesus in his Passion. On the cross Jesus gave everything to humankind. It was as if he emptied himself completely of self. He could not have done more. This was what Marthe relived each week and because the Mass is the memorial of Christ's sacrifice she saw her whole life as a Eucharist: 'My life is a continual Mass. I never feel that my bed is a bed. It is an altar, the cross'. Each time God asked her to engage herself as much as possible. Of course she could not go as far as Christ in generosity but she certainly went a very long way within the parameters of human capacity for giving.

The experiences of the Passion were, however, situated at the heart of suffering that was continuous. 'I suffer constantly, day and night,' said Marthe. Her body was always in pain and in an awkward position. Her illness made itself greatly felt and never gave her any respite. But there was also moral and psychological suffering. She heard a multitude of things that stirred her compassion. She was at the heart of the Church's problems. And finally there was the spiritual suffering about which she was consistently discreet.

Suffering then was Marthe's daily lot. In her journal she wrote: 'Suffering teaches us charity, surrender to God, detachment. Suffering teaches us to see and understand. Suffering teaches us to relieve, sympathise with and console those who suffer.'

The sequence of the Passion

When the time came for the Passion to start Marthe would invariably recoil from it. It was never natural for her to go through with it and she never got used to it. She was afraid she would be unable to consent to it and told Père Finet so. He had to find the words to encourage her. Marthe would then surrender herself to God's Work and the Passion would begin. Père Finet would help her during the most painful times, especially on Fridays. Let us note in passing how much courage he must have had to hold out all through those Passions, watching the person he loved most suffering, but unable really to do anything. There were times when he would allow a few select witnesses into the room. They would be deeply upset. They noticed too Père Finet's sometimes considerable emotion: he never really got used to what was going on in front of him.

The testimony of Mgr Elchinger, Bishop of Strasbourg, is that of a man who described himself as having a 'fairly critical mind', but who was never uneasy about what he experienced with Marthe because it seemed so authentic to him:

On the Thursday, at night, she shared in the Lord's agony. I heard her groaning: raucous shouts then a very harmonious weeping. The devil flung her head against the wall with terrifying violence. We prayed the Rosary (fervently). On Friday at about mid-day when I returned to Marthe's room (which had been locked all night) I was surprised by a sweet smell in the room, when Marthe had sweated blood, wept blood, lost blood all that time. Père Finet showed me two trickles of blood running down either side of her head (from the place where Marthe felt the imprints of the crown of thorns). Her eyes were covered with coagulated blood, her forehead covered with sizeable bloodstains. Père Finet allowed me to look very closely. What an expression of pain there was in her drawn features and lips. It was not the same face that I had seen three to four days previously. The devil's attacks resumed in our presence (they had gone on throughout the night). Père Finet told me to try and hold on to Marthe's head. And I felt the considerable force with which she was flung against the wall by 'Satan'. Marthe's head was wrested from my hands. Being paralysed, Marthe could not get back onto the bed herself. The movements of her body and head could have no normal, rational explanation … It was painful for me to experience. I put great fervour into praying the Rosary. But on the Thursday night especially I could do it no more, I was so moved. I thought I was going to vomit or collapse.

The progress of the Passion and of Marthe's reactions was clearly identifiable. On Thursday evening, the time of the agony in the Garden of Gethsemane, 'what struck me most,' said Père Finet, 'was the feeling of fear'. On the Friday towards the end of the afternoon, she would pronounce these words: 'Father, thy will be done.'

During her experiences of the Passion Marthe would bleed profusely. Doctor Alain Assailly, a Parisian neuro-psychiatrist, was in her room one day and able to examine the wound in her side by the light of an electric lamp. It was clearly discernable in the left sub-mammary area and was six or seven centimetres long. The blood flowed 'red, very red. Her gown was embedded in the wound … It was fresh blood. It had not clotted at all.' What also struck the doctor was the heat coming off the wound. The rest of the body was distinctly colder.

The moment of Jesus' death, which Marthe relived – or which Jesus relived in her – was totally realistic. Here is what one of the Foyer members witnessed on Good Friday 15 April 1960:

The Châteauneuf-de-Galaure countryside
(with the Vercors plateau in the background).

The village of Châteauneuf seen from the Galaure valley.

Marthe's farm in around 1936.

The facade of Marthe's farm shortly before her death.

The kitchen at Marthe's farm.

Marthe's parents.

Henri Robin, Marthe's brother.

Marthe Robin in 1926.

Marthe Robin around 1932.

Marthe's room from 1942 to 1981.

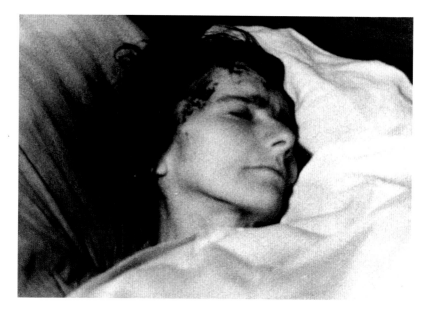

Marthe after Holy Communion.

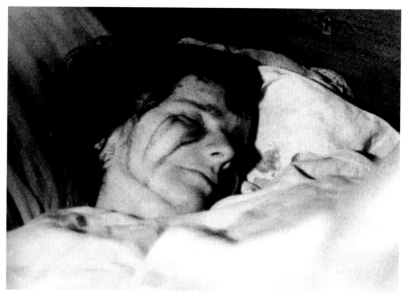

Marthe during one of her experiences of the Passion.

The picture of Mary Mediatrix of all graces that Abbé Finet brought with him on 10 February 1936.

Père Finet
in the early years of the Foyer.

Père Finet
outside the door to Marthe's farm.

Père Finet with Père Faure
at La Plaine.

From left to right: Père Babolat, Père Péchoud,
Mgr Pic, Père Beton and Père Finet.

Père Finet with his parents (1948).

Doctor André Ricard, Père Finet's brother-in-law.

Marie-Ange Dumas and Hélène Fagot
on 22 September 1936 in front of the
window of Marthe's farm.

Sister Marguerite Lautru.

Père Garrigou-Lagrange OP.

Paul-Louis Couchoud kissing Marthe, a drawing by Jean Guitton.

The former château when the girls' school was founded (1934).

The first eleven pupils at the girls' school.

The picture of Mary, Queen of the universe in the chapel of the Grand Foyer.

The chapel at the Grand Foyer.

The statue of Our Lady of the Foyer
by Hartmann, outside reception at the
Grand Foyer at Châteauneuf in 2006.

Père Finet in the Foyer
in Japan in 1981.

Laetitia Van Hissenhoven and
Father Santamaria in Colombia around 1965.

Père Michon
preaching in the
lecture hall of the
Grand Foyer (2006)

The Châteauneuf community and members of various Foyers
at the June 2005 Assembly.

Children from the Châteauneuf Foyer schools.

Mass to mark the return to school in Châteauneuf in 2005.

Père Wouters, Père Finet, Mgr Marchand, Pope John Paul II
and Mgr Dziwisz, Annecy, 7 October 1986.

Père Jacques Ravanel,
founder of the La Flatière Foyer,
Père Finet's first successor.

Père Bernard Michon,
Père Finet's second successor.

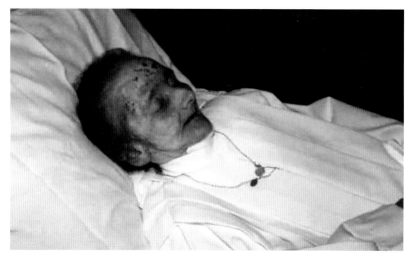

Marthe on her deathbed.

Marthe's funeral Mass
in the great sanctuary at
Châteauneuf, 12 February 1981.

Marthe's tomb in the
Saint-Bonnet-de-Galaure cemetery.

I wanted to go with Father. I waited alone in the kitchen. Father went in to Marthe. He came out saying: 'If you want to hear Marthe's last gasps, come' … In total darkness with the window open and the curtains closed, Marthe was quietly breathing her last, very slowly, each breath coming at less frequent intervals. On my knees I said to myself: 'When will this be over?' But it went on for a quarter of an hour that seemed interminable to me. At the end of that time, Father said to me: 'It's finished!' He said to me: 'You can come close and put your hand under her nostrils.' I did. I could feel absolutely no breath. I had my hand so close that one of my fingers touched Marthe. She was not cold but motionless, as if lifeless. She did not stir: just as if she were dead.

Marthe's face during her Passion was poignant to see. 'I was able to gaze at the blood seeping from her forehead,' said another witness. 'There were patches of dried blood with drops of fresh blood on top of them. From the corners of her pupils flowed on either side of her cheek a trickle of blood mixed with a watery liquid … over a face that was absolutely white.'

In her Passion Marthe was totally alone. She knew what it was to feel abandoned as Christ had done:

During my experiences of the Passion I receive no earthly consolation. Father is there, there may be ten priests there, supporting me with their prayers. They help me like that but I must have no consolation. I am the sin rejected by Heaven.

Like Christ, Marthe undertook to 'take upon herself' the sins of the world. This was probably one of her most intimate and greatest sufferings. When the Passion was over, Marthe remained in total silence. It was if she were no longer there. Père Finet himself had to help her emerge from this state. Then she would 'come back' and was able to resume her everyday life.

Marthe's experiences of the Passion continued to be part of a range of other sufferings. The devil, for example, would attack her head on at other, sometimes unexpected junctures. One day Doctor Assailly was in her room with Père Finet:

> We had all three been talking at the head of her divan for a few minutes when suddenly she gave something like a rattle and was projected brutally to her left as if an invisible hand were holding her by the neck. Her head came crashing with extraordinary violence and with redoubled blows against a small piece of furniture there.
>
> Instinctively I did what many others would have done in my place. I lunged forward, trying to grab hold of her shoulders, saying: 'Father, it'll kill her!'
>
> Père Finet stood up and said to me: 'No, Doctor, let go of her!' Then he immediately declared firmly: 'In the name of Christ, of his Blessed Mother the Virgin Mary, and of the Holy Church, I order you to leave Marthe at once!'
>
> Calm was immediately restored and after making sure that our friend's skull or neck had not been broken, I left her with Father and went out to get some air.[6]

The meaning of suffering: an offering of love

It is impossible to understand the above without entering a dimension which completely transcends suffering: that of an offering made out of love. Marthe did not go through her Passion for her own ends, any more than Christ did. Marthe was affected by the sin of the world. All day long, when she was receiving people, she was hearing difficult things. They did not spare her their problems, confidences, sources of anguish or questions. Her experience of pain and sin went far beyond that of the average person. She knew too that she had a mission as large as the Church and the world. She was not untouched by all the failures, pain and digressions of humanity, and indeed the Church. How was she to react to them, bedridden as she was and unable to take direct action?

Marthe took them all upon herself and offered herself to bring them before God. She was like a shield, a living sacrifice for humanity, a sacrifice made out of love, a sacrifice the innermost constituent of which was not suffering, but love. When she told someone that she would take them or a situation on, these were not mere words. She wanted to go to the farthest reaches of love for that person or for a particular situation that needed resolving. She wanted to substitute herself for those who were not doing as they should. To go to the extremities of love, she offered herself, gave herself completely, and since she could not give her hands, her mobility or physical abilities, she gave her body and consented to its being 'destroyed' each week. And this, as has been said, was accompanied by the gift of inner suffering in proportions that we cannot in any way measure. What is therefore most extraordinary about Marthe is the quality of her love for humanity, and the strength of her commitment to serving humanity out of love. She used to say: 'Jesus did not promise that he would take the cross away from us. He said he would place it on our shoulders. But with Jesus the cross becomes wholly love.' She could also say: 'To expiate, make good, console, love! To give myself, spend myself without reserve and with my entire being for God, for everyone, for souls. To transform all my actions into supernatural and divine action, that is the most beautiful truth, that is the greatest and the last word in love.'

We should note too the extraordinary extent to which she abandoned herself into the hands of God. Marthe could not have entered into his Passion without absolute faith in God. If her suffering was extreme, her trust was even more so. Had she not believed that God would support her, she would have protected herself, refused to face a trial that endangered her body to the point of a form of death. But with each Passion, as was shown above in relation to Gethsemane, her faith had to be renewed.

Self-abandonment was not something achieved once and for all. The choice had to be made freely each week with the most extreme consequences. 'Father,' she said, 'today's Thursday.' – 'Yes, my child.' – 'Father, I can't do it.' – 'Yes, you can, my child.' – 'Father, help me to offer.'

The integration of times of sorrow

Like any other human being, Marthe was also affected by bereavements which became in some way part of her offering and her Passion. Cruellest of these was probably the suicide of her brother Henri on 8 August 1951.

Henri had decided to remain on the farm. It was his lawful right and he would most likely not have been able to live anywhere else. Because of his temperament it would probably not have been easy for him to find a wife either. But the Foyer, now the proprietor, sent two young women members to live at the farm. This was vital both to help with the farm itself – to see to the house-keeping and to the welcoming of people who came – and for the protection of Marthe, who must not be left alone with Henri who could be dangerous. Marthe loved Henri, prayed for him and protected him from a distance. One day when Père Finet arrived, she sent him urgently to Henri's room: 'The Virgin has just warned me … He's suffocating, poisoned by fumes from chemicals used to fertilise the land.' Père Finet rescued him.

Henri was fond of some of the people who used to visit Marthe and demonstratively so, but Marthe was becoming more widely known, and there were more retreats and more and more visitors. The farm was small so they were made to wait in the kitchen. Henri used to eat his meals in front of them, which was not a happy arrangement. In this sensitive context he also suffered from facial neuralgia which eventually became unbearable. He took his gun and committed suicide. Marthe did not hear the shot. 'I never suspected a thing' she said. 'There were three priests waiting in the kitchen. They did not hear anything either.'[7]

As soon as Henri was found, someone went to inform Père Finet who was preaching a retreat at the Foyer. He immediately made his way up to La Plaine.

Marthe's reaction was one of extreme and unconcealed sorrow. A fortnight later when Marcel Clément came to visit her, when mention was made of what had happened she burst into tears: 'Marthe was sobbing. She sobbed so loudly that I picked up the rhythm of a pain that nothing seemed able to stop.' She was primarily concerned for his soul: 'In the first instance I had only one thought: Where is he? Where is he? Where is he?' People invariably ask themselves questions about a life curtailed. It would seem, however, that she immediately – or at least very swiftly – received inner assurance of his eternal salvation, which was important for her to be able to get through the crisis. If Henri was in Heaven his life had not been lost. She also understood that Henri's responsibility had been diminished by the severity of his pain: 'Facial neuralgia you know is dreadfully painful. He suffered for a long time. His nerves were exhausted from lack of sleep. So ...'

Marthe had also to deal with her own impotence in the affair: 'My poor little one! I didn't know how to protect him.' Like anyone close to someone who commits suicide she had to go through all the stages of bereavement. Fortunately she was helped and consoled by those close to her and received some very heart-warming letters, including one from Mgr Suenens, the future Cardinal Archbishop of Malines-Brussels.

The incident gave Marthe great compassion for those tempted to commit suicide: 'Do not put poisons on the night tables of some patients,'[8] she told Guitton who thought she herself must have known this kind of temptation. She found the words to console those close to people who had taken their own lives. 'She may be closer to God than we might think,' she dictated in 1952, referring to a woman who had committed suicide, 'because it was not her days that she wanted to end but the evil that was tormenting her...' In 1967 she had one young woman told: 'We pray in union with you for the two people mentioned in your letter who died so tragically, but we believe in the infinite mercy of God, for deaths like theirs denote illness and serious illness, in which there is minimal responsibility, and I would add that by doing what they did, these sick people were not wanting to make an attempt on their life, but were attacking the terrible evil that was tormenting and obsessing them, and from which they could not escape. I do not see how that can be an assault on our faith. On the contrary it is an invitation to even greater trust and abandonment, with limitless hope in the mercy and forgiveness of our Father.' To write this, Marthe herself must have gradually progressed further along the way of trust.

IV. The Eucharist

Marthe Robin did not eat. She lost blood every night and each time she went through the Passion. Yet she did not die. From where did she derive her strength? From the Blessed Sacrament she received each week. Christ said: 'My flesh is real food and my blood is real drink.'[9] That was her actual experience. She expressed it very well on 16 August 1945 during an episode of the Passion: 'I would like to cry out to those who ask me if I eat, that I eat more than they do because I am nourished through the Eucharist on the blood and flesh of Jesus. I would like to tell them that it is they who prevent the effects of this nourishment in themselves, they obstruct the effects.' In 1958 she told Jean Guitton: 'I feed myself on that alone. People moisten my mouth. But I cannot swallow. The host provides me with a physical impression of food: Jesus is in my whole body. It is he who nourishes me. It is like a resurrection!'

Marthe thus tested out in a very specific way the idea that Christ received in the host gives life to the soul and even affects that of the body. For Père Finet the blood she lost was therefore the blood of Jesus himself. Marthe sometimes used similar expressions but she probably did not mean them quite so literally.

She probably saw it as the life, the blood that was given by Jesus. She confided as much to Jean Guitton in 1968: 'The blood. The Eucharist! It is the power of God that brings about this blood in me, through Communion but not necessarily so. It can be done by other means. We forget the power of God. Sometimes when I take Communion I feel this renewal of the body in me, but not necessarily. And sometimes other than through Communion too.'

For her the most important thing was God's taking possession of the soul, the spiritual process. She said as much to Jean Guitton: 'It is God who from within takes us wholly and fortifies, changes, renews and permeates us.' In 1947 she had confided: 'The taking possession is such, so invasive, so strong, so all powerful that I lose all human contact. Carried away by him in light and love and in the beatific light, the union is so complete that it is as if I am totally liquefied in Jesus, no longer anything but one with him in love and contemplation. My whole being is delighted in God, which goes much further than ecstasy.'

If the Christian life is ever stronger union with Christ, if, as the Fathers of the Church maintained, 'God was made man in order that man might become God', then Marthe lived out this union in a remarkable way, especially – but not exclusively – because of Communion.

Finally, attention should be drawn to her sensitivity to the real Presence. A priest friend had come to be present at her Holy Communion. Another priest had been due to give her the Blessed Sacrament in Père Finet's absence. Before he opened the custodial, Marthe said to him, 'Jesus isn't there!' The priest looked in the custodial. It was empty. He had to go back down to the Foyer to fetch the host.

V. The presence of the Virgin Mary

What was it that kept Marthe going? When we look at her life and reactions we see that Marthe Robin was well and truly human.

She needed support and consolation just like anyone else. But in the spiritual world in which she lived human consolation was not enough. Her offering could not have been made and renewed without a very particular complicity with Heaven. In her life, Heaven overlapped a little with earth and for Marthe this meant very specifically the constant attentive, loving, considerate presence of the Virgin Mary.

Marthe Robin was definitely one of the great Marian souls in the history of the Church. To those closest to her she did not deny that Mary visited her. Thus Jean Guitton wrote: 'Mary appears frequently to her as the Mediatrix. "You do not feel the urge to kneel but to throw yourself into her arms."' In 1942 she had given the following description: 'Her face is one of incomparable beauty (the Virgin Mary's features cannot be described because they are all perfect). It is softly luminous yet with nothing dazzling about it, which is all the more beautiful. The Virgin fills me with wonder at her beauty, her attitude, her movement, but she attracts and carries me away. I don't think of kneeling, falling to my knees when she appears but of flying towards her, not to ask anything of her but out of a feeling of gratitude and love. It is as if one were saying: "Maman chérie, we, your children, know very well that you love us and that you want to fill us with joy (May our hearts be your place of repose, Maman chérie)."' 'Yes,' she also told him, 'several times I have seen and been touched by the Blessed Virgin (I am not saying that I have touched her). As to the manner in which she makes herself seen, it varies according to the occasion: young or old, in a state of joy or of sorrow as at La Salette. Sometimes she has picked me up, helped me with her hands.'

During Marthe's Passion, the Virgin Mary would come to her aid, especially when the devil was attacking her: 'When "la Maman" appears, he can do absolutely nothing to her. Nothing. She is so beautiful, not only facially … He has no power over her. None whatsoever. When she appears, if you could only see all those demons clashing with one another, hating one another, fleeing, tumbling down. What a sight, pushing and shoving!'

Marthe had no hesitation therefore in writing: 'I love this tender, good Mother so much. She is my star and my dwelling place. I live in her light, completely hidden in the impregnable refuge of her Immaculate Heart.'

She did not, however, 'keep' Mary to herself in some way. She wanted to give her to those she met. Her attitude was in itself a sermon to that end. Visitors were often struck by the way in which she talked about or prayed to the Virgin Mary. 'It was very easy to tell that Mary had a very important place,' said one of her nephews. 'You had the impression that the two of them knew each other very well,' remarked someone else. In private she would refer to 'la Maman' or her 'Maman chérie' with a tenderness that was striking because it was the unadulterated voice of experience. It was as if the Virgin Mary were in the room: 'Sometimes I had the impression that she had almost forgotten I was there while she talked to the Blessed Virgin or said what the Blessed Virgin was for her. The tone of her voice would change a little. I remember the tone more than the actual words,' said one Foyer member. At the end of the conversation there would often be a 'Hail Mary', or even a decade of the Rosary or some other prayer.

Consistent with the Marian doctrine of Saint Louis-Marie Grignion de Montfort, Marthe believed that in the Christian life the simplest and safest thing was to give oneself to Mary like a child declaring its trust in its mother. The maternity of the Virgin Mary for each person was in fact a reflection of God the Father. She would say quite audaciously to M: 'See in her face the maternity of the Father. It is very beautiful … Don't you think?' If we consecrate ourselves to Mary she becomes the guide and mistress of our spiritual life. She forms Jesus in us: 'She wants to find Jesus in his entirety again in us … she who was the great former of the apostles.' She takes us into the very bosom of the

Trinity where she herself is: 'In order to live in the Heart of Christ, at the heart of the Trinity, you have to live in Mary.' She really looks after us: 'Keep on saying yes to her every day of your life. Keep your hand in hers, your eyes on hers and let her guide you day by day without ever questioning her.'

In her eyes, relationship with the Virgin Mary was thus essential, and it should not be dry, purely intellectual or restricted to a kind of duty. 'The Blessed Virgin holds you by the hand but also by the heart – but also by the heart,' she would repeat.

She saw Mary's involvement even in the detail: 'She told me,' wrote Jean Guitton, 'that the Virgin Mary's role was to concern herself with details, all the details, and that that was something her maternal function required.' She also used to say that Mary watched over each individual even in his or her work and helped if it was done for God. 'Through me,' she informed Guitton endearingly, 'the Virgin has invaded the Sorbonne.' Of a member of one of the New Communities she enquired: 'Do you really have faith in the fact that your work is prayed for in the Heart of Mary and [that], even when you are unfaithful in prayer or deed, Mary herself will still be faithful and present to the Work?' Several times she told people that they had been specially protected by the Virgin in difficult circumstances, among them a priest in one of the Foyers who had escaped an accident.

She knew that no one was a better comforter in times of great trial than the Virgin Mary. Mme E had come to see her with her two children. Strangely, Marthe talked of how Mary's heart had been pierced with a sword and told her that she always came to the aid of women going through such pain, insisting on the necessity to keep the faith at such times. Just as Mme E was on the threshold, about to leave, Marthe added: 'You must pray to the Blessed Virgin. She can do anything. She knows best how to dress wounds.' A year later the woman's two children were killed in a car accident. She informed Marthe who sent her one of the last letters she dictated.

She prayed to the Virgin Mary particularly for priests and recommended that they have a good relationship with her. When Père C asked her to, 'Pray that I may be a priest according to the Heart of Jesus,' she immediately exclaimed passionately, 'and of the Blessed Virgin'. He had come through a formidable test of his vocation during which she had supported him. Taking stock of what had happened, she said to him: 'Whatever would have become of you? The Virgin is faithful.'

She also urged teachers to talk about Mary to their children: 'Help them to know the Blessed Virgin, make her loved … give her to souls, because her grace as the Virgin is to help souls to become pure … [With her one senses] the need to purify one's heart. With her the soul has a radiance it would not otherwise have.'

VI. Extraordinary spiritual phenomena

Marthe's stigmatisation, her ecstasies, experiences of union with the Passion, visions – particularly of Mary – her ability to read people's hearts, her foreseeing of events, and her capacity to live without eating or drinking have all been mentioned. There were other instances of extraordinary spiritual phenomena, however, which, without affording them undue emphasis should perhaps be referred to. They are phenomena found elsewhere in the history of the saints and may have had importance for the people who witnessed them, forming a kind of visible sign of grace.

Sightings of Marthe in a luminous state

At least one person during the period we are looking at saw Marthe perfectly lit up as if by a sun, for about twenty minutes, when her room was in total darkness.

Receiving the host without contact

There were much more frequent witnessed instances of the host escaping from the priest's hand as he was giving it to Marthe and moving directly towards her mouth. An assistant priest from the neighbourhood gave the following account: 'When the time came for Communion, Father [Père Finet] said to me, "Go and stand on the footstool next to Marthe's bed, take the host and hold the host in front of her face. You will find her tongue." Easily said but difficult actually to do in the darkness. So I lent over her, trying to make out the features of her face and all at once I saw her head flop onto the pillow and noticed that the host I had been holding in my hand had suddenly disappeared. It had escaped from my fingers without my realising it. I am absolutely sure that I never placed the host on her tongue. Other priests have confided that they have had similar experiences. It had such an impact on me – I had really come up against the supernatural – that I never asked to do it again. And I regret that a little now.' Père A said: 'I was very moved to see it leave my fingers and enter Marthe's mouth of its own accord. Père Finet then shone a light on Marthe's face which I saw in a state of ecstasy. I had never seen anything so beautiful!' A Jesuit, Père F, claimed that it had happened to him several times.

Some lay people standing close to Marthe's face witnessed the same thing, among them C B who saw 'the host escape from the priest's fingers as he was bringing it close to Marthe Robin's mouth and disappear into her without any movement of her face.'

Seeing into people's hearts

No one ever managed to make Marthe admit to seeing, at least in part, what was going on in people's hearts but on 26 May 1947 at Pentecost, Père Finet had a conversation with her which he immediately committed to writing and which is reproduced here extensively because it sheds a light that is both profound and colourful on the subject:

> – Does the Holy Spirit often show you souls when you have visitors?

– Yes, with varying degrees of light and varying degrees of completeness. It is by the light of the Holy Spirit that God shows me souls who are in a state of sin, in a manner that may be more or less precise. Sometimes he has even shown me very clearly former sins not admitted or inadequately admitted. At other times God shows me a soul in sin without showing me each sin precisely, in detail. For example God shows me a soul that has lied or received Communion in a state of sin. I see that, without seeing what it has lied about, or the number etc. But this is not a day for you to give me a hard time. Today is Pentecost, a day off![10] On other occasions God shows me one sin very clearly and precisely among others.

– When he shows you that what do you do?

– I think I have to use a lot of sensitivity. I have two ways of dealing with souls: often I will say something general; at other times I put my finger on one thing, on a really serious sin that has remained forgotten, unacknowledged or poorly acknowledged. There is one thing I think, Father. You yourself question souls more than you used to. It seems to me I should say less: we should see to that. Why torment them twice without lightening your load? In the beginning I used to do more of it. Now the souls know that it is you, they trust you. Well, I'm not the one responsible for your renown! In the beginning souls often used to say to me: 'Why say that to that priest, to your Father?' Not any more because people know you, who you are.

– When you send me a soul without giving me any details about his conscience, what are you doing?

– I have pointed him in the direction of his sins. It seems to me he wants to put them behind him. When I tell him that God is giving him the opportunity to rid himself of them, he understands. Often I say: 'I shall pray hard for you and shall be with you.' Souls are often overwhelmed. The devil sometimes stops them on the way.[11] When I have said such harsh truths to a soul, I suffer with it and perhaps more than it, and I promise to be with it to help it in the admission of its sins. I promise that admission will be easier than it thinks.

– When it has admitted its sins, do you sense it?

– Yes, sometimes. At times I have said that souls have not said everything and I've seen them again for that reason. Some ask me to talk to you about them, which I only do with their permission because they want me to.

– Are there some visitors whose souls God does not show you at all?

– Very few, I think. I couldn't really say. Sometimes I remain outside.

– Why?

– To avoid trampling on their secret garden. I pray for them. I give in a different way.

– How does a soul appear to you?

– I can't find the words to tell you. It is something so beautiful, a soul in the state of grace, a soul ascending to God, for example … The soul of a saint is so beautiful that you might think you were looking at God himself, but it is his reflection.

There was nothing excessive about what Marthe used to say to people. There was one rather lax young woman who came to visit Marthe because she wanted to 'see a stigmatic'. She was about to leave when Marthe motioned her to sit down again. 'After a few minutes' silence which seemed like a century to me, she said to me: "I've just seen your case very clearly … Why do you offend God so much?" From that moment on she read my soul like an open book. Nothing was hidden from her. She reproached me for my laxity, my lack of faith, of piety, had me make a general confession and asked me several times: "Is that true?" After I nodded my agreement, she said: "Why do you offend God so much? Our Lord loves you very much. He loves you more particularly than some others but he is weary of waiting for you. You are making Our Lord impatient. He wants you."' That young girl was converted and later joined the Little Sisters of the Assumption. She often came back to see Marthe to ask for her support and her friendship.

Marthe's 'travels'

Sometimes people had the impression that Marthe knew particular places or had seen things that happened elsewhere as if she had actually been there. She talked about the pilgrimage church of L'Ile-Bouchard in Touraine, for example, as if she had been inside it. One day a child from Saint-Bonnet asked her a direct question: 'We've been told you came to see us in Saint-Bonnet. Is it true?' – 'Little rascal!' she replied. 'What if God did make it possible … he is after all the master of the impossible.'

Jean Guitton was not afraid to talk to her about it:

'You travel?'

    …

'You travel'?

'If one can call it "travelling". It's like Gagarine but Gagarine was still in this world. I "travel" in God, who takes me wherever he wishes.'

'To Asia, Rome, Constantinople?'

'Yes, that's it: to Rome, Constantinople (smile). But *in* Jesus and also *with* the Virgin Mary. Sometimes more with one; sometimes more with the other. I am in my state of suffering for the sinner.' (Père Finet specified that during these journeys she would weep blood.)

Marthe Robin did not conceal from him that this was how she had been present at the death agony of Pius XII to pray for him, as she had been present at that of her own mother. She was also at the Foyer with Marie-Ange Dumas when she was dying in 1970. How many other 'travels' did she embark on, about which we have no information from her? We do by contrast have some quite specific testimonies from others.

One of them is from Père Renirkens who later became a Foyer Father in Switzerland. In 1954 he came back from China where he had been a missionary. He had spent fourteen months in prison under the Communist regime where he was subjected to terrible brain washing. He went to see Marthe who had him tell her about what he and the persecuted Chinese Christians had been through. 'Here's what's important: Marthe very gently interrupted me, often apologising as she did so, and proceeded to add certain details to my account and specify episodes that I had personally experienced in Shanghai prisons but had never before revealed to anyone. They were things I had been through that were too painful and that I had not talked about even to those closest to me. No one could have known about them. Yet Marthe knew. I was astounded and said to her several times: "But Marthe you weren't there with me in prison and I haven't revealed this or that to anyone." Then Marthe would keep quiet and very humbly ask me to go on with my account of "my prisons."' What astonished him most was hearing Marthe describe landscapes, churches and hospitals that no one in Europe could have known with such precision. In the end he insisted on asking how she knew all this. 'Marthe gave me an answer I had not expected. Very simply and humbly she said to me: "Oh! You know, Jesus goes to China so often."'

҈

Why all these spiritual phenomena? Without attempting to provide an exhaustive answer here, we should note that they derive from the freedom of God. People expect God to act in a particular way, which more often than not serves and does not inconvenience them. But God is master of the universe. He does exactly what he wants, where and how he wants. Spiritual phenomena are a reminder of this sovereign liberty. For people of good faith who approach them wisely they are also an indication of the close proximity of the supernatural. God is not far from our world. Our eyes may not be able to see him but sometimes he shows us he is there. In this way Marthe Robin was a sign for our times. She had no desire to act as a demonstrator of the supernatural but it was nonetheless visible through her.

As she herself maintained, these phenomena were not what was most important, however: they were merely signs. What was most important was the love she lived out beyond sensible phenomena, the presence of God in her, the love of Mary, the ultimate gift of herself for humanity. This was the very heart of her life. All the spiritual phenomena were in support of Marthe's mission, particularly of the founding of the Foyers of Charity.

NOTES

1. These words of Patriarch Athenagoras are a good description of this time in her life: 'The hardest fight is the fight against oneself. You have to reach the point of disarmament. I conducted that particular fight for years. It was terrible but I am disarmed. I am no longer afraid of anything because love drives out fear. I am disarmed of the desire to be right, to justify myself by disqualifying others. I am no longer on my guard, jealously clutching my riches to me. I have given up comparisons. If we disarm ourselves, if we dispossess ourselves, if we open ourselves to the God-Man who makes all things new, then he

wipes out the ills of the past and grants us a new time in which everything is possible.'

2. Jean Guitton, *Portrait de Marthe Robin* (A portrait of Marthe Robin), Paris: Grasset, 1985. Although this book is generally faithful to the author's conversations with Marthe, here we have used his personal notes, made after their meetings, which are more accurate and closer to Marthe's exact words.

3. Literally 'He accomplishes what he does'.

4. Thomas Philippe OP, *La vie cachée de Marie* (The hidden life of Mary), Trosly-Breuil: La Ferme-Diffusion, s.d., p. 31.

5. Galatians 2:20.

6. Dr Alain Assailly, *Marthe Robin: témoignage d'un psychiatre* (Marthe Robin: the testimony of a psychiatrist), Paris: Éditons De l'Emmanuel, 1996, p. 104.

7. Marcel Clément, *Pour entrer chez Marthe* (In order to see Marthe), Paris: Fayard, 1993, pp. 171–5.

8. Marthe means: 'Do not leave dangerous medicines within reach of the seriously ill.'

9. John 6:55.

10. In other words: 'Pentecost is a holiday. You're bothering me, making me talk today.'

11. The way from the farm back to the Foyer.

CHAPTER II

The Spread of the Work of the Foyers

After the Second World War, Europe had to be rebuilt in a number of respects, and the Catholic Church was to be part of this reconstruction. It was not, however, a case of reproducing something identical. People sensed vaguely that the old order had gone and that they were moving towards a new one. But what would this new world be like? Opinions varied dramatically. For some it would see the triumph of Marxism; for others that of liberal capitalism. But the most profound question was that of how hearts and minds were to be reconstructed. For Christians this could no longer mean simply reproducing the Catechism of their grandparents and living as they had done. Things had to be done differently. The years 1945–1965 were thus marked, particularly in France, by much searching and experimentation that fed into the Second Vatican Council. Marthe Robin entered fully into this perspective. She had great hope for the future. Beyond all the political problems and even the ecclesiastical tensions, for her it was a case of preparing for the great Pentecost of love. The very depths of people's hearts must be worked upon. It was important that hearts be transfigured for if a person was converted in the depths of their being the rest would follow. This was the objective of the Foyers of Charity which were to develop considerably during this period. To do so, however, they needed the backing of the Church. They must not be left on the margins. The solemn blessing of the Grand Foyer in 1948 thus opened a new phase in the history of the recognition of Marthe's Work.

I. The blessing of the Foyer at Châteauneuf

On 17 May 1948, the Monday of Pentecost, the Foyer of Charity in Châteauneuf was officially inaugurated and blessed. Mgr Pic had wanted to come himself and was keen to give the celebration maximum impact by presiding over a Pontifical High Mass in the morning, at which twenty-two children from the school made their First Holy Communion. The diocesan weekly gave a very favourable report of the ceremony: 'Crowds came flocking from all directions, from Drôme, from the Lyon area, from Dauphiné and Savoie and from twenty dioceses further away. Over 1,500 people were estimated to be there that morning. There were many priests from our diocese and elsewhere, and far more in the evening.' As the statue of Our Lady of the Foyers was blessed, the crowd sang a canticle 'expressing the spirituality of this house': 'Lord, unite our minds in truth and our hearts in charity.'

The Foyers were already beginning to spread and when the time came for toasts, Père Beton founder of the La Léchère Foyer, was notably among those who spoke. As a gesture of gratitude to Père Faure for all that he had done to support the Work, Mgr Pic appointed him a canon of Valence cathedral, a much-prized honorific title at that time. When he installed the newly-appointed canon at the cathedral on 12 July 1948, 'he was to shower him with praise'.

Despite the fact that the Foyer had only just been built, Mgr Pic already felt it was too small. The chapel would only hold three hundred people so in his estimation a sanctuary dedicated to Holy Mary Mother of God would have to be built one day. 'We never think large enough,' he said, 'in the same way that we never see ourselves small enough.'

Marthe Robin for her part had prepared for the celebration with prayer. During the Passion of the preceding Friday, 14 May, in the course of a 'Marian ecstasy' she had prayed much 'to commend to the Blessed Virgin the Foyer and all our undertakings, present, past and future ... "Oh Father, oh my God, bless our Foyer with your wholly divine benediction ... Oh yes, Maman chérie, let it be yours, let it be totally yours, let it be only yours ... Act each day and at every hour as Queen and Mother. Take it entirely under your spiritual, moral and material guidance in all its life and activities, in all its intentions and works"'. During the next Passion, on 21 May, she was to tell God earnestly how grateful she was.

A deeper understanding of the Work

In the thinking of the time it was impossible to have lay men and women and priests living in the same community under the same roof. To do so was really revolutionary. The inauguration of the Foyer had led Père Finet to specify on 20 February 1948 the precise, radical nature of the Work:

> The Foyer of Charity is a Christian working community under the leadership of a priest. Members of the Foyer are lay people wishing to follow the example of the first Christians and form a community together, a small assembly of Christians. The community is directed by a priest. He is its leader and Father. Under his direction, the Foyer will become a spiritual centre of light, charity and love. Following, as it does, a form of spirituality for lay people living in the midst of the world, the community does not require vows ... Members of the Foyer undertake to give themselves totally to Jesus through Mary according to the formula of consecration of Saint Louis-Marie Grignion de Montfort ... They renew their baptismal and confirmation promises through the hands of Mary.

Shortly afterwards, on 8 July 1948, Père Finet celebrated the twenty-fifth anniversary of his priesthood. There was a public dimension to this celebration: not only was Mgr Pic there, but the ceremony was presided over by the Archbishop of Avignon, Mgr de Llobet. The Work of the Foyers was really finding its place in the Church and by then a growing number were already living according to the charism.

II. The founding of new Foyers

During Marthe's lifetime over fifty Foyers of Charity were founded throughout the world. By the time she died the Work would have some six hundred members. A glance at a chronological list of foundations is perhaps the simplest way of grasping the scope of the movement:[1]

1936	Châteauneuf-de-Galaure
1941	La Léchère-les-Bains (Savoie) (moved to Naves in 2001)
1943	La Gavotte (Bouches-du-Rhône) (became Sufferchoix in 1976)
1950	Roquefort-les-Pins (Alpes-Maritimes)
1950	La Roche d'Or (Doubs)[2]
1952	Notre-Dame des Ondes (Rhône)
1957	Poissy (Yvelines)
1957	La Flatière (Haute-Savoie)
1957	Spa (Belgium). The first of the European Foyers outside France
1958	Ecce Homo (Colombia, transferred in 1969 to Paipa). The first of the Latin American Foyers
1959	Baye (Marne)
1960	Rochefort-du-Gard (Gard)
1961	Aledjo (Togo). The first Foyer in Africa
1962	Bonheiden (Belgium)
1963	Souillac (Mauritius)
1963	Cuernavaca (Mexico)
1965	Ottrott (Bas-Rhin)

1965   Saint-Denis (Aude) (moved to Lacépède in
             Lot-et-Garonne at the end of 1997)

1965   Martinique

1966   Tressaint (Côtes-d'Armor)

1968   Mendès (Brazil)

1968   Dakar (Senegal)

1968   Saigon (Binh-Trieu, Vietnam). First of the Foyers
             in Asia

1968   Remera (Rwanda)

1969   Bex (Switzerland)

1969   Kampala (Uganda)

1970   Dilinh which became Thu-Duc (Vietnam)

1970   Bangui (Central African Republic)

1970   Branguier (Bouches-du-Rhône)

1970   Courset (Pas-de-Calais)

1971   Sutton (Canada). First of the North American
             Foyers

1971   Kotobi (Ivory Coast)

1972   *Guzenbach* (Germany)

1972   Tomé (Chile)

1973   Port-au-Prince (Haïti)

1973   Tampon (La Réunion)

1973   La Ferté-Imbault (Loir-et-Cher)

1973   *Gatagara* (Rwanda)

1974   Mugera transferred to Giheta (Burundi)

1975   Libreville (Gabon)

1975   Luxembourg

1975   Ngaoundéré (Cameroon)

1975   Agen (Lot-et-Garonne)
             (closed in 1995 and reopened in January 1998)

1976   Moresnet (Belgium)

1976   Thorn (Netherlands)

1976   Zipaquira (Colombia)

1976   *Korhogo* (Ivory Coast)

1976	Santa Marta (Colombia)
1976	Sufferchoix (Bouches-du-Rhône)
	(to which the la Gavotte Foyer was transferred)
1977	Boston (USA)
1977	Bucaramanga (Colombia)
1977	Lesotho (Southern Africa)
1977	*Bangalore* (India)
1977	*Madrid* (Spain)
1978	Medrano (Argentina)
1978	Japan
1979	Salera (Italy)
1980	Latacunga (Equador)
1981	Daloa (Ivory Coast)
	(closed then reopened in 2003)[3]

Some remarks[4]

First, let us note that the chronology of the foundations accelerates with time: three foundations between 1936 and 1949; eight between 1950 and 1959; fifteen between 1960 and 1969; thirty between 1970 and 1979. Clearly the work was flourishing, a sure sign that it was meeting a need. Six Foyers were not able to get off the ground and had to be closed. There is nothing surprising about that to anyone with any knowledge of religious foundations. One Foyer distanced itself from the Work. That too is quite common.

More surprising, over and above the speed of their creation, is their geographical location. Eighteen of the Foyers are in France so the work is rooted and has its base in a specific country. There are nine others in Europe, which is not all that many. True, Europe was already a continent well-provided for. It does, however, beg a question especially since Northern Europe, which is Protestant but where there are some Catholics, is not represented among the foundations. The same could be said of North America, with only one Foyer in the United States and one in Canada. By contrast there are thirteen in Africa, eight in South America (four of which are in Colombia), and four in Asia. This shows that the Foyers are largely a missionary Work. Indeed it was often missionaries or leaders of young local Churches who asked for Foyers. We should note too that expansion outside France was extremely rapid: as early as 1957 there were foundations in European countries other than France, from 1958 in Latin America, from 1961 in Africa, from 1968 in Asia, reaching North America in 1971.

The origins of the Foyers are many and various: they began as a result of different initiatives because priests wanted them. Often it was bishops themselves who asked for them. On Easter Monday 1966 the Archbishop of Rennes and future Cardinal, Mgr Paul Gouyon, came to Châteauneuf. 'I have come on behalf of twelve bishops in western France,' he informed Père Finet, 'to ask for a Foyer of Charity to be set up in Brittany to form a select number of lay Christians before it is too late, if possible in my episcopal city but at least in my diocese.' This was how the Foyer in Tressaint started. Mgr Ligondé, Bishop of Haiti, had come on retreat and wondered whether a Foyer could be founded there. Marthe realised that he did not have much understanding of what he was asking for. 'She explained to me,' he said, 'that a Foyer is a community of laypersons who do not take vows, who have everything in common and lead the life of the early Church, a simple, joyful family life in community. The Father of the Foyer must be a priest of great doctrinal maturity.' Cardinal Thiandoum, Archbishop of Dakar, who had come to Châteauneuf for the same reason, met Père Pagnoux who was helping Père Finet at the time, and immediately asked for him. So began the Foyer in the Cap des Biches.

Beyond the sterility of the figures and geographical locations we may glimpse an intense life worthy of slightly closer consideration.

III. Some examples of foundations

The story of the foundation of the Foyers is an important one, a story of love, effort, hope and sacrifice, and a page in the contemporary history of the Church which I hope will be looked at properly one day. It is impossible in a book about Marthe Robin to describe the full saga of the Foyers but it is important at least to provide a few examples. We might otherwise in some way be confining Marthe Robin to Châteauneuf or to France, when in fact she lived and breathed more and more on the scale of the Church and the whole world.

La Léchère-les-Bains (1941)

The first Foyer after Châteauneuf began not very far away in La Léchère, in Savoie. More recently it was transferred to Naves and is known as the 'Tarentaise Foyer' after the alpine valley in which it is located. Its foundation goes back a little chronologically to a Père Beton, who, during the Second World War, was divisional chaplain to the Rhône defence section. He enjoyed his apostolate among the soldiers very much and must have been well thought of too because the War Ministry invited him to become chaplain, either to the special military school of Saint-Cyr which trained officers, or to Saint-Maixent which trained non-commissioned officers, whichever he preferred. Then, in 1939 in the Tarentaise Valley, in the parish where in peacetime he had been the priest, Père Beton had bought a disreputable café-restaurant business and transformed it into a sanctuary where the work he did brought about genuine conversions. Becoming a military chaplain on a permanent basis would mean giving up this project. Not totally convinced that the appointment was right, Père Beton made a novena to Our Lady of Fourvière. On the last day he celebrated Mass in the basilica, then went to see a chaplain who advised him to get in touch with Père Finet. Père Finet gave him a 'big-hearted' welcome, told him about Marthe and invited him to come and see her ten days later. What follows is Père Beton's account of their conversation:

At the time Marthe was in the room that gave out onto the courtyard of her small farm. She was sitting up in bed with her head against the pillow. She had glasses on. Light was coming in through the window but Marthe was already blind. 'It was Satan,' she told me, 'who had the offer of remaining military chaplain until your retirement presented to you on a golden salver. He thought the game was won, he was already grinning, because with you out of the way, he would have come back seven times more powerfully.[5] Fortunately, you prayed as you usually do, at length to the Blessed Virgin. It is she who has brought you here from Fourvière.' Then she added: 'In the place where you bought the disreputable café-restaurant, God wants you to create a Foyer of Charity.' 'If that is what God wants, then I want it too,' I answered at once. 'It's very small,' she said to me then, 'but we will pray to the Blessed Virgin to make its walls grow. The day will come when it will be very large.'

Marthe was immediately concerned with the practicalities of the kind of ministry Père Beton was to have. She was not convinced he would make the right decisions of his own accord and she let him know straight away. In the words of the principal witness:

Then Marthe talked to me about the spa at La Léchère-les-Bains. 'Do you look after it?' – 'No,' I replied, 'the spa isn't in my parish.' 'I can quite understand that you must not tread on your neighbour's toes, but people taking the waters could come to you. If you were to put a small notice on the door to the former café-restaurant that is to be turned into the Sacred Heart sanctuary, showing the times when you will be there: Masses, Adoration, Confession, provided it were every day, souls might well come: lay people, religious, priests?' I said to her: 'It's not very likely because during the summer when my ministry in the parish is not so heavy, I arrange walks up to the peaks for the children of the parish, young men, young girls and married couples.' – 'Another priest can do that ministry for you,' she said. 'You must be in the sanctuary'. So following Marthe's words to the letter, I went down to the sanctuary every day, morning and evening. I stayed there for hours on end, even though my legs were straining to take me up to the mountain tops because I was completely smitten by the mountains and I was forty years old.

Souls began gradually to come to the sanctuary in ever greater numbers. It was in the following year, 1942, that the talks began every evening for those taking the cure, and they have been going on almost without interruption for forty years. The retreats for the people of God began later. The former café-restaurant was too small to house the retreatants: a large house was needed. Building work on the Foyer of Charity began on 15 November 1943 'despite the German occupation and the difficulties of the times'. These were Marthe's instructions.

We can see to what extent Marthe was involved in the discernment process in this foundation, which was unusual for her. But the future was to prove her right. It is also clear to what extent she considered the Foyers centres of evangelisation and how she did not shy away from unusual methods. In the case of La Léchère she did not immediately ask for the preaching of retreats. She wanted the Foyer to begin in a low-key way as a place of welcome. It was only afterwards that the retreats came about. This was the mark of a supple mind, open to reality and in no way rigid or dogmatic.

Spa, Belgium (1957)

The Foyers' vocation was a universal one so Marthe and Père Finet wanted foundations outside France as soon as possible. The founding of the Foyer in Spa, Belgium in 1957 was thus the fulfilment of a deeply held desire.

By the 1950s the Grand Foyer in Châteauneuf had a list of some six hundred former retreatants from Belgium. There was, therefore, an excellent basis for a Foyer. Gradually the idea germinated. Vocations appeared from two sources: the Legion of Mary and a group from Auxilia, a movement concerned with disabled people. The preparations were done systematically and, once a property, a former château, had been purchased, the Foyer officially began on 3 October 1957, the feast of St Thérèse of the Child Jesus. The house had stood empty for a long time and was in a bad state. Everything had still to be done when the members of the Foyer arrived, but there on a table set up in the inhospitable building site was an excellent lunch cooked for them by a caterer, a welcoming gift from a couple who were friends of theirs.

The Foyer began at a time when it was thought that some members could go to work outside the community. Père Finet was not against it so several founder members in Spa opted to do so. It became apparent, however, that working outside the community was difficult to reconcile with life in a house intended for preaching and retreats. These last were given priority and, under the direction of Père Oury, the community matured. Marthe was very present because members met with her several times a year and important decisions were not made without her. The Foyer also maintained its vocation to welcome people with disabilities, who were, and still are, central to the foundations of the charity. It maintained an ecumenical dimension in the holding of meetings and prayer to promote Christian unity and had a missionary one too in that several of its members were sent out to Foyers being founded in young Churches.

The Ecce Homo Foyer in Paipa, Colombia (1958–1963)
The story of the first Latin American Foyer is completely different. It owed its foundation to Laetitia Van Hissenhoven (d.1968), a young Colombian woman who had worked for

UNESCO in Paris since 1952 and been close to Mgr Roncalli, then nuncio in France and the future Pope John XXIII. He told her that her country now needed a different form of evangelisation from that to which it had been subjected at the time of the Spanish conquest. He suggested that Colombia be made aware of the teaching provided in the Foyers of Charity because it was profound and gave souls an understanding of divine filiation and the paternity of God.

In 1954, before Laetitia returned to South America, she went to a Belgian parish where Père José Van Hissenhoven was pastor. This parish had been completely renewed and reorganised. The priest told her he had been to a retreat at Châteauneuf-de-Galaure, that extraordinary things had happened to him and that his parish had been transformed. He told her about Père Finet and Marthe Robin but his reference to a stigmatic left Laetitia sceptical. Realising this, Père Van Hissenhoven talked to Mgr (later Cardinal) Suenens, Archbishop of Malines-Brussels. When the Archbishop met Laetitia he said to her: 'You belong to the Legion of Mary. So do I. You cannot go back to Colombia without first going to the Foyer of Charity. While you are here in my diocese I am your bishop and you must do as I say. You must go to the Foyer.' Next day he sent her a train ticket and a booking form for a retreat.

Another surprise was in store for her on her very first day at Châteauneuf. During Mass when it came to the consecration, Père Finet, who was the celebrant, declared: 'I cannot proceed with the consecration because there are people here who do not wish to forgive. I ask them to leave the chapel.' Several people went out and the priest went on with the celebration. When later the time came for testimonies, one young man said: 'When I got there I realised I was not worthy to be present at the Holy Sacrifice because I felt hatred for a fellow student. So I left the chapel and Father was able to go on with Mass. I have understood love, I have understood that this companion is my brother and now I shall go and ask his forgiveness.' How did Père Finet know that? He would never have made public mention of a confidence, and neither would Marthe Robin. Perhaps Marthe had learned it from Heaven and had told him ... Be that as it may, this 'infused knowledge' had led to a conversion.

By the end of the retreat, after meeting Marthe and Père Finet, Laetitia was convinced she was being called to found a Foyer in Colombia, but it proved very difficult. It took several years to find premises. In the meantime she started day retreats in a gym, then in a palace, then in convents and in a theatre, with all kinds of tragicomic incidents. In the end the abandoned Dominican convent of Ecce Homo presented itself. Her first visit was eventful. The house had fallen into ruin, scorpions scurried about the corridors, bats flew overhead making a terrible noise, there were rats in their hundreds and enormous poisonous spiders had filled the house with their webs. On the first night gunshots were heard. This was a way of alerting the local peasants that there was danger abroad. Laetitia remained there alone. Heedless of the cost, she gave up her job and devoted herself to God's work, achieving extraordinary things, visiting the peasants, caring for them, setting up a school, appeasing the criticisms of the neighbouring Church people, and spreading love for the Virgin Mary. One day a group of boys and girls came to her. She made them as welcome as she could, giving them biscuits and sweets. Night started to fall. When she drew their attention to the fact so that they could get home, one of them spoke up for them all: 'Miss, you told us the Virgin was calling us, so here we are to serve her.' So it was that the Legion of Mary began in the village. Without a priest for the Foyer, Laetitia led a life dependent entirely on Divine Providence. Humanly speaking, there was no future.

Finally, in 1959 Adalberto Gomez, a young, newly-ordained priest from the Medellin diocese, who had been to Châteauneuf, preached the first retreat. In 1963 the local authority for the nearby village of Paipa donated a six-hectare plot of land. Laetitia lived there at first in a sheep shed, on the bare earth. Several vocations presented themselves. They started building, still without a priest living there. A support committee was formed in Bogotá but it did not know the Work and did more to cause major problems. One day Laetitia, who was passing through France and knew nothing of what was going on, found herself in Marthe's room. 'I can see the devil on the committee in Bogotá,' Marthe declared. As if she were looking at a map of Colombia she said: 'The Foyer in Colombia will be a beacon illuminating Latin America.' This encouraged Laetitia greatly. 'It's clear what we have to do,' she said. 'We just have to keep on struggling. It doesn't frighten me. God will help us and see that his will is done.' With the help of Père Florin Callerand of the Roche d'Or Foyer, she managed little by little to move things along. She died in 1968 in a plane crash in Guadaloupe on her way to France, after God had mysteriously warned her she would be leaving for Heaven. But she had sown the seed and the Work continued. Marthe's prophecy enabled members of the Foyer to overcome their difficulties and devote themselves entirely to a Work which did indeed radiate great light thereafter.

Aledjo, the first African Foyer (1961)

The founding of the first Foyer in Africa was not easy either. Abbé Marcel was a priest in the diocese of Viviers, near Châteauneuf. Ever since his seminarian days he had wanted to join the missions but for twenty years his bishop had opposed the idea. He had come to know Marthe and Châteauneuf but, although drawn to the spiritual family of the Foyers, did not feel cut out to be a Foyer Father and had no plans in that direction. One day in 1958 he took someone to see Marthe and was discreetly waiting in the farm courtyard for the meeting to finish. The weather was fine and Père Finet, learning of his presence, went out to greet him. Abbé Marcel told him his good news. He had at last found a way of joining a mission. He would apply to join the Jesuits. The bishop could not refuse him and the Jesuits were willing to let him go. Much to his surprise, Père Finet informed him without hesitation and with conviction: 'That is not where you belong. You have something else to do!' Then, after they had walked for a bit, he said: 'Would you like to see Marthe?' So they went into her room and, after talking for a while, Marthe asked Abbé Marcel if he would like to come to Châteauneuf to preach a retreat for the boys from Saint-Bonnet School. This he did. At the end of that retreat Marthe went on to inform Abbé Marcel that a bishop from the Ivory Coast had just asked for the first African Foyer to be founded. Would he like to do it? If so he would have first to spend a period of two years at Châteauneuf to absorb the spirit of the Foyers by being a 'Father with Father'.

The suggestion was an answer to Abbé Marcel's most secret wishes but he had first to obtain permission from the bishop, who did not want to change his position. What was more, Père Finet wanted Abbé Marcel to do his formation period as a 'Father' at the Saint-Bonnet School and everything would have to be arranged before the return to school three months later in September. Abbé Marcel was in charge of a parish. He had numerous commitments and making all the necessary arrangements in so short a time seemed impossible. On the following 15 August he met his bishop in La Louvesc, the sanctuary where Saint Francis Regis is buried. Their meeting was apparently quite by chance but Mgr Couderc had just read the encyclical *Fidei donum*, in which Pius XII recommended that bishops lend secular priests to the missions. He immediately agreed to Abbé Marcel's request. Twenty years of obstruction fell away at a stroke.

The foundation, a short while later, was not devoid of problems. Where should it be? In which country? Where was the money to come from? Who would be community members? Père Marcel left at the end of 1959 without the answers to any of these questions but he went with the encouragement of Marthe and Père Finet. 'If God wants you in Africa,' Père Finet had said, 'he will give you what you need.' Marthe helped him to turn down a tempting proposal which might subsequently have been dangerous. After Père Marcel had looked in several African countries with discouraging results, the General Superior of the African Missions in Cotonou mentioned to him that there had been a plan for a retreat house which had failed to come to anything in Aledjo, Togo. It had a good climate and water but it was in a Muslim area. When he went there the village chief gathered the elders together and said to him after a lengthy palaver: 'Since you have left your country, your father was not able to give you a plot of land to bring with you. It is therefore right that we give you some land.' The chief concluded with an authority that surprised Père Marcel: 'I forbid you to continue looking elsewhere. You will choose a piece of land here. You will make it your home.' He also explained that local custom prevented him from selling the land. He could only give it to him.

Back in Europe Père Marcel quickly found himself at the head of a very small group of lay volunteers ready to start the foundation. He left Châteauneuf with a statue of the Virgin Mary which had stood in Marthe's room. 'You may think you are taking her,' she said to him, 'but she is the one who is taking you.' They had next to overcome opposition from the local Church, sceptical about mixed communities of men and women and about the choice of location far from the Christian bases in Togo. Little by little, with the encouragement of Châteauneuf these obstacles too were surmounted and the Foyers began on African soil.

Saigon, Vietnam (1968)

The first foundation in Asia was in Saigon. Its distant origins went back to 1948. A priest of the Missions étrangères de Paris, Père Boutani, told one of his Vietnamese colleagues, Father Paul Vo Van Bo, how before leaving for a mission in Vietnam, he had been on an extraordinary retreat at Châteauneuf-de-Galaure, France. Later, in 1954, Father Bo was invited to preach a week long retreat during Holy Week and started to learn more about this ministry.

A few years after that, the diocese of Saigon wanted a Foyer of Charity and Father Bo came to mind. In 1967 therefore he came to Europe and was sent by Père Finet to undergo formation at the Foyer in Spa where with Père Oury there was another Belgian priest, a Chinese from Formosa and an African. This was followed by a stay at the 'Central Foyer' of Châteauneuf where Father Bo was fortunate enough to have a meeting with Marthe every week.

In 1968 the Foyer began on a plot of land providentially purchased two years previously. Twenty-one people were involved in the first retreat and out of them came no less than four vocations to be Foyer members. There was a French priest, Père de Reyniès of the Missions étrangères de Paris, among those present. The Foyer, dedicated to Our Lady of Fatima, was officially inaugurated on 1 June 1969. A few months later, with Father Bo's help, Père de Reyniès opened a second Foyer in Vietnam near Dalat. The Vietnamese Foyers had no sooner been founded than they came up against obvious problems. Members often had the opportunity to renew the unconditional offering of their lives. But the flame did not go out and was passed on from there to other Asian countries.

IV. The expansion of the Châteauneuf Foyer

The spread of the Foyers would have been precarious had Châteauneuf not played its part as Central Foyer. It too evolved considerably in every respect.

The growth of the retreats

The number of retreatants was growing all the time. Between twenty-two and twenty-four retreats were preached each year. Until 1950 they were all conducted by Père Finet. After that other preachers came to help him. Until 1981 he preached an average of nine to a dozen retreats a year. Between 1936 and

1947, 3,124 retreatants were booked in. Between 1948 and 1978 there were no less than 68,076 (15,084 between 1948 and 1957; 18,330 between 1958 and 1967; 34,662 between 1967 and 1978). This escalation in attendance was due as much to Marthe's prayer and offering, as to Père Finet's talents as a speaker and his capacity to present Christianity in a positive and joyous light. It was also thanks to the prayer and offering of Foyer members. One retreatant described Père Finet's way of speaking as follows: 'The first thing that struck me, from the very opening talk – caught in passing – was the extraordinary freedom with which the preacher spoke. I had been expecting a "religious" style, characterised by unction and solemnity. I was taken aback by the simplicity of vocabulary, the familiarity of the examples used and the wisdom of insights that rooted us – or rather kept us rooted – in everyday life. Père Finet's gifts of oratory had their role to play. But more than that it was the absence of artifice, the absence of tremolos, the absence of emotional effects that made one forget where one was and that the chair was hard. Seriousness, humour, sadness, admiration – every human feeling was reflected in the rhythm of his speech and the intonation of his voice. It was absolutely spontaneous.'[6]

Père Finet evolved with the passage of time. He had been impressed by a retreat preached by a Jesuit friend of Marthe and the Foyers, Père Prosper Monier (1886–1977) who died with a reputation for sanctity. Many priests were to say, 'He changed my religion,' after they had heard him speak. As a consequence, in 1952 Père Finet decided to adopt the plan of salvation as the framework for his own retreats. Prosper Monier helped him to deepen his understanding of Saint Paul. Marthe used to say: 'The spirituality of the Foyers will be John illuminated by Paul and Paul illuminated by John.' Père Finet was also influenced by Père Gilbert Livragne, an Oratorian, especially with regard to the Trinity and the priesthood of the faithful. When it came to prayer, the Jesuit Père Jean Fournier was his inspiration. After hearing him in 1963 Père Finet placed much emphasis on introducing people to prayer.

Later, on Sunday mornings, he gave instruction on the affective and sexual life of adolescents and adults, which was one of his triumphs. He talked about these difficult issues with such geniality and humour that people could not stop laughing.

Foyer members, new foundations and new buildings
The number of Foyer members followed the general movement and new vocations came. In 1961 the Châteauneuf Foyer had seventy members, thirty-four of whom were at the girls' school. By 1975 the school had produced fifty-three. In 1978 there were 140 people in the five Châteauneuf communities. Priests like Père Colon in the Grand Foyer, Père Bondallaz in the girls' school, and Père Marcel and then Père Pagnoux at the boys' school came and lived in the Foyer to help Père Finet.

The children were a source of delight to Marthe: 'The Châteauneuf Foyer started with the school. I am always touched by this fact,' she confided one day to a class of third-year girls. Marthe was also concerned about boys' education. So on 3 October 1953 a school was opened for them in Saint-Bonnet with twenty-one day-boys. In the following year it took in the first six boarders. After that the school developed greatly. Marthe wanted to shape the whole person and insisted that it concern itself with the affective and sexual education of young people. She also gave thought to their families: 'We should educate the parents at the same time as the children. What we're doing is almost pointless if they are not involved.' Saint-Bonnet produced some thirty vocations to the priesthood and the religious life.

For local teenagers who did not go to secondary school but needed practical training, at the request of a parish priest, the Mandailles technical college came into being on the way out of the village of Châteauneuf. It began modestly in 1953 not without difficulties but it answered a need and, thanks once more to Marthe's support, it developed and went on to provide the region with an important service.

By 1961 there were nearly 300 children at the girls' school from primary through to upper sixth, 170 boys at Saint-Bonnet and sixty students at the Mandailles rural technical centre. The numbers would subsequently rise to over a thousand.

Buildings had to follow suit. At the Grand Foyer it became necessary to build a new kitchen and a large dining hall, and refurbish Foyer members' premises, workshops and offices. When plans were made for a large lecture hall, Marthe insisted that the seats should be comfortable 'because people are tired, they take time out of their holidays to come and Father speaks for a long time'. And so remarkably comfortable seating was provided.

The land on which the new buildings were to be sited was on the hill slope and not, as we have seen, easy. When it came to building the kitchen, the first thought was to have it on a level above the dining-room. Marthe was against this. She wanted everything to be on the same level to avoid tiring people. She also thought that the kitchen was the hub of the house, which people passed through to eat or drink or meet others. It was important to the communal life of a family. Her wishes had to be complied with and major earth removals were begun. The earth was deposited in a 'combe' (ravine) a little further on. When the new dining-room, with its very modern design, was inaugurated, the Archbishop of Tokyo, who was passing through, remarked: 'Now you're ready to come to Japan'. A little later, in 1978–9, a house for the elderly was built, linked to the Grand Foyer and dedicated to Saint Joseph.

There remained the question of the chapel. As anticipated, the one inaugurated in 1948 was becoming too small for large retreats so it was decided to build a more spacious one dedicated to Holy Mary Mother of God. Then it was thought best to put it in the former combe now filled with the moved earth. Marthe gave precise instructions for this building. She wanted the altar to be large and imposing: 'It is the sacrificial stone'. She wanted the tabernacle to be placed to one side so that people could pray in peace. She wanted the choir to be all on the same level for the sake of elderly priests. She was not averse to having an original design and modern structure. The architect researched and drew up, in agreement with the Foyer, several different plans. They were submitted to Marthe who did not say no, but did not approve them either. Clearly the right formula had not yet been found. One day the architect had the idea of building an immense concrete veil behind the altar and developing the church from there. He jumped in his car and drove to Châteauneuf. This time Marthe gave her agreement and building began. The sanctuary, inaugurated in 1979 by the Bishop of Valence, is one of the great constructions of post-war French religious art. Because of the terrain the initial position of the building had to be moved slightly. When it was finished, it was noticed one day that a straight line drawn through the axis of the relocated sanctuary and extended, would end up precisely in Marthe's room, situated two kilometres away and totally invisible from below.

Not surprisingly these buildings caused Marthe and Père Finet financial worries. More than once paying off the loans verged on the miraculous, but there were numerous small gifts and sizeable donations. Châteauneuf was built through the love of thousands of people who often put something very personal into their offering. Many a tale could be told. Suffice it here to relate one recorded by Jean Guitton: 'They needed to pay the bill ... They were 170,000 francs short. The architect said to Père Finet: "Father, we shall end up in prison." Father smiled. He tore open his post. He opened the first letters accumulated during a long absence, and found 170,000 francs, and more.'[7]

V. Marthe's involvement in the expansion of the Foyers

Problems and challenges

The examples above give only a faint impression of the 'Acts of the Apostles' that were – and still are – the beginnings of the Foyers. There was a challenge to be met. The Foyers were scattered all over the world. The Foyer Fathers and members came from completely different backgrounds and cultures. How was unity to be created? How was the charism to be transmitted without suffering from any particular individual's personal interpretation? Often the missionary Foyers lacked or had only limited resources. How could they be helped, for example, when it came to the major question of construction work? How were they to be provided with genuine vocations to support them? Each Foyer was a family with its own identity. How was this identity to be helped to find and gradually express itself? None of this could have been done if Marthe had not been at the centre of it all and if Père Finet had not been so totally dedicated that no amount of travelling deterred him. He had frequently to cover long distances, although he kept his journey times to a minimum in order not to be away from Marthe when she was going through the Passion.

Marthe followed the Foyers closely. 'Nothing escaped the eyes of her heart. She was interested in everything.' She did not regard herself as a foundress: 'Only Mary is Mother of the Foyer,' she would say. 'It is not our Work. It is the Lord's Work. Let us be very small.' Until the middle of the 1970s her relationship with Père Finet was remarkable. As far as discretion permitted they would share ideas about everything they heard, referring anything they did not feel duty bound to sort out themselves to the other, according to their particular roles and reciprocal gifts. Marthe kept abreast of any projects and commented on them. She knew the Foyer Fathers and watched over their formation. She was very attentive to individuals in the missionary Foyers who would come to see her at Châteauneuf while they were staying in Europe. She also kept an eye on members of European Foyers leaving for the missions.

The challenge consisted of enabling people who were completely different to live together. After a while religious from different congregations actually asked to become Foyer Fathers. Marthe's response to such ideas was astonishing. Her heart was completely open to possibilities that would have seemed impossible to anyone else. She relied not on a functional type of discernment but a spiritual one. Her desire was not to make a system work but rather to help souls. The important question was therefore whether the call came from God. If so, all else would fall into place. 'It is God who has chosen us even though we are all poor sinners,' she said to Père Beton. 'He has chosen each one personally for his great Work of love.'

The vocations of Foyer members

Marthe often had a part to play in the hatching of vocations to be Foyer Fathers and members. Sometimes she would be very clear, sometimes she would confine herself to asking the right questions and sometimes the things she said would prove to be prophetic. Her words were always tempered to the state of mind of the person to whom she was talking. On occasions it was just a sentence that would find its mark: 'See you soon, Monique ...' She respected the other person's timing. Père Finet spoke to her about a young woman in the room, who was wondering whether she should enter the Foyer. 'Much later. It must be left up to her,' Marthe replied, and sure enough she joined a few years later. Not infrequently she would ask that the intention to become a Foyer member be allowed to mature. 'Wait,' she told X, 'your vocation isn't ripe yet. You need to become more deeply rooted and not decide at once ... Pray with the Bible ... Spend a lot of time in adoration and offer yourself with your troubles and self-absorption and little by little silence will come. Christ will set us free.' To someone else she said, 'Wait but don't stray too far from a Foyer of Charity.'

Père Michel de Dinechin was thinking of founding a Foyer in Mexico. He went to see Marthe, saying: 'Marthe, I've agreed to be a Foyer Father in Mexico but I want to be absolutely sure that it's what God wants because it is a major risk and I already have my life mapped out before me.' Marthe answered: 'When a young man becomes a priest it is a risk; when a priest starts his ministry it is a risk; but when someone engages in something God specifically wants it is a major risk.' Reassured, he went ahead. By contrast, when, after ten years, Père Constant received permission from his bishop to go and found a Foyer in Brazil, the bishop sent him a message which, though it gave his permission also specified: 'I do not want you going off in search of adventure.' That same day he had seen Marthe who had said to Père Finet in his presence: 'Don't let him go off in search of adventure.' One person had needed reassurance; the other needed his enthusiasm tempering.

At times vocations became the subject of general debate. Some people had their personal plans and were not prepared to have them disrupted. Y wanted to become a Franciscan Missionary of Mary and could not conceive of her life any differently. But her parents did not want to lose her and had other views. Her father had even gone on hunger strike when she told them what she intended doing. Her spiritual father sent her to Châteauneuf where she told Marthe everything. Marthe was quite direct: 'Your parents will never accept your entering a contemplative community. You are not responsible for their problem. What they've done is infantile. They want to keep you for themselves and find a husband to suit. But then you are not ready to do your novitiate. If the Lord puts barriers in the way he has good reason for it. If one day he wants to remove them, he will do so. Come to the Foyer.' Y replied that she was not interested in doing so. Contrary to what she usually did, Marthe insisted and showed her that what she had been through to date had been preparation for life in the Foyers. And she added: 'The Lord does not want you in

six months time but straight away ... Hurry, hurry, give yourself
completely to Jesus. It is not the form of consecration that counts
but the magnitude of your gift to the Lord.' But Y, still
unconvinced, told Père Finet when she met him afterwards that
she wanted to be a religious. It was later as she was praying before
the Blessed Sacrament that she was flooded with peace and joy. All
became clear. She went back to see Père Finet who said, 'I know,
Marthe told me.' A way of inducing her parents gradually to
accept that their daughter had a vocation had been found.

Other vocations were very easily identified. It depended on the
state of the persons concerned. Z had a position with a middle
class family and was worried about her future, hesitating between
marriage and the religious life. She hoped that Marthe would
shed light on the problem. Seeing the young woman's simplicity
and availability, Marthe said to her: 'Why don't you come to us?
We have a real need of someone like you as soon as possible.'
Without hesitation, she gave her employers a fortnight's notice,
entered the Foyer in 1955 and after a few years at the girls'
school, worked at Marthe's farm and looked after her.

Marthe was sensitive to the 'yes' that had one day to be said to
the Lord, a 'yes' which was sometimes delayed. One young
woman who came to see her in 1961 told her that she had been
wondering for some time whether God was calling her. 'What are
you waiting for before you say yes to the Lord?' Marthe asked,
then: 'Why don't you come to us?' She knew that there were steps
and when necessary, helped people to take them. 'I realised that
Marthe nurtured my abandonment to the Lord's will before she
suggested I come to the Foyer,' someone else said. Once that
'yes' had been said, however, for her it was radical: 'You give
yourself completely to God. You give your life unconditionally.'
Once the time had come, there should be no more delays. 'It
seems to me that you intend entering the Foyer,' she said to W.
'Be careful. Don't wait too long because the devil will work on
you and you will no longer know whether it is yes or no.' To XY

who told Marthe her life was empty, she responded: 'This is the time to decide. You mustn't wait any longer.' But she also knew how to take possible obstacles into account. 'She asked me,' XY went on, 'if I was afraid to join the Foyers of Charity. She asked me if my parents would oppose my coming.' There were a multitude of other examples.

There were times when Marthe mysteriously knew in advance that people were coming. Sometimes she would tell Père Finet. A priest of the Missions étrangères de Paris, expelled from Burma, was on retreat at Châteauneuf. Seeing Père Finet, suddenly an idea flashed into his head like a shooting star and he blurted out: 'Father, if ever one day you need me, just let me know.' And Père Finet answered simply, 'We've been waiting for you for a long time.' In response to Père Reyniès surprise Père Finet explained that when the news of his expulsion from Burma reached Châteauneuf, Marthe had said: 'He's for us. We can expect him.' Sure enough he founded the Thu-Duc Foyer in Vietnam. One retreatant experienced 'an enormous shock to [her] heart and the conviction: this is for you' when she heard Père Finet talking about the Foyers. When she told him what had happened, 'Sitting facing me, Father rubbed his hands and said: "When I read out the list of retreatants to Marthe and she heard your name she said: 'You remember, Father, she came to see us. She is for us. The Blessed Virgin wants to give her to us.'" How many times has that remark, forever engraved on my heart as it is, helped me in times of difficulty?'

The founding of Foyers

Clearly Marthe thought on a very large scale when it came to the Foyers. She wanted them to radiate light and love all over the world. 'Every country with its own language should have a Foyer,' she used to say. She also paid considerable attention to the founding of each Foyer. Whilst in Japan, Père Alain Quennouëlle, a missionary there, had been invited by a former Châteauneuf retreatant to go to Châteauneuf for a retreat. On his arrival a mysterious inner peace and joy came over him. He went up to see Marthe and gave some thought with her to founding a Foyer in Japan. But he did not want to be in charge of it. What he offered to be was 'a small element to help with the foundation should the need arise'. 'Oh no! An important element,' said Marthe. 'I was stunned,' he confided. 'There was so much authority in her voice! I kept quiet, enthralled. What was said to me then was to remain engraved on my heart. There was to be no arguing. The Lord wanted this foundation, they had been praying [for this] for ten years etc. I can't remember the exact words. With my heart full of indescribable joy, when I left Marthe's room and walked back down to the Grand Foyer I felt as if I was flying. In a matter of moments all objections had been swept away. I had decided to found that Foyer in Japan come hell or high water.'

Père Jacques Beaudry was giving thought to a Foyer in Haiti but had a number of reservations, not least his lack of readiness for such a task. He did not mention this to Marthe, confining himself instead to saying that his bishop wanted a Foyer and him to be the Father. 'So get started!' said Marthe simply, adding: 'But you have a Foyer and you don't realise it.' 'It was as if she were saying: "You are ready because everything you have done to date has been a long and specific preparation for your responsibilities as a Foyer Father ..." Without knowing my objection about not having time to prepare myself at Châteauneuf, Marthe had removed it. She had removed it by doing what Jesus did to Nathanael: by reading the secret objection in my heart and responding with the revelation of a situation I had not had time to explain to her, and showing me that this situation (this specific but unrecognised preparation for my role as a Father) was itself the response to an objection that I had formulated in my heart alone.'

Father Atangana from Cameroon had asked for a meeting with Marthe. He turned up an hour late and Père Finet was not impressed. 'To appease Père Finet's anger I said to him: "You see the colour of my skin?" – "What do you mean?" – "Back home in Africa the sun tells us what time it is but here I can't see yours." He smiled. "Alright. Let's go."' The conversation with Marthe surprised the visitor greatly because she identified a problem he was harbouring and which he had not mentioned to her at all. She ended up asking him to start a Foyer of Charity in Cameroon. Well, he had already gathered together a group of very poor children in what he had happened to call a 'Foyer of Charity'. 'That's good, Father. You're already part of the Foyers of Charity, because you already have children's prayers. Now go and preach about children's prayers and never abandon those children. The Lord values their prayers greatly.'

Conversely, Marthe could sometimes have reservations about or even be opposed to foundations. One priest wanted to set up a Foyer and Père Finet was in agreement: 'He is not a Father,' she said. 'He's a problem … He should not start a Foyer. That priest is dangerous.' That was the end of the matter.

There were times when people felt she knew where future Foyers would be located, or at least that she knew something very specific about the place. Père Girouard, founder of the Foyer in Sutton, Quebec, was talking to her about establishing a Foyer when Marthe came out with: 'What about that house that was sold, not sold?' This enigmatic remark became less so when it was realised that a religious house that would make an excellent place for the Foyer had already been sold but was back on the market because the previous agreement had fallen though. The Foyer bought it. When people were considering founding what was to become the Foyer in Courset, Marthe declared: 'For the Foyer in the North I see a large property with tall trees'. Then, when she was broached about an initial idea, she asked, 'Why not closer to the sea?' The attractiveness of the buildings was important to her. 'Father,' she said, again in connection with Courset, 'your Foyer must be beautiful … We have to build for the twenty-first century.' She asked that every room there should have a bathroom with a shower.

She also seemed sometimes to know when the time was right. In 1951 Père Ricart went to see Marthe to talk about a possible foundation. 'It will take time, plenty of time,' she said but later, in 1964, she told him: 'You must start straight away. Even if it costs you a hundred million[8] go ahead anyway.' That was how the Foyer in Saint-Denis was born.

Many of the Foyers being founded encountered major problems and Marthe assumed them in her prayer. In Agen there were plans to have an enormous refuse dump close to the Lacépède Foyer but by some miracle the project was abandoned. In Bunia (Zaire, now the Democratic Republic of Congo), a shady businessman was after the land envisaged for the Foyer, land which belonged to the diocese. All seemed lost until an unexpected turnaround sent the businessman to prison and gave the land to the Foyer. There was no lack of financial problems. In Thorn, Marthe was worried about finding the money to buy a house. The project came to nothing. When, however, a short while later a viable plan presented itself, the Foyer contracted a loan to be repaid over twenty-five years. It was settled in just nine months. In response to Father Van der Borght's anxiety over Tressaint, Marthe said, 'The Lord will test our faith to the absolute limits,' and she was not disappointed. She had given some very sound advice about the choice of location for the Foyer in western France. People were wavering between Pontmain and Tressaint and discussing it heatedly in her room while she said nothing. Running out of patience, Père Pagnoux said to her: 'Marthe, you may not sleep but we do. So which is it to be, Pontmain or Tressaint?' Immediately a little voice was heard to say: 'Tressaint would be quieter than a place of pilgrimage,' and the matter was settled.

Often delicate decisions were referred to her. The Foyer in Roquefort-les-Pins wanted to start either a rest home or a school.

They were inclining towards the former, despite the requests of several local Christian families. 'But we have to have some Foyers with schools,' Marthe declared when she was consulted. And when she was asked where it should be, she replied: 'You mentioned a small house by the side of the road ... The first classroom can be built there backing onto the house.' That was what was in fact done and in this way they saved on one of the four walls. A few years later, the school had ten classrooms and three hundred children. Marthe also saw the Foyers as linked to the local Church with its particular situation and struggles. Thus when she met Father Claessens, who was teaching at the small seminary in Rwanda at the time, she affirmed: 'Yes, the Lord wants a Foyer of Charity in Rwanda. The kind of charity that transcends what divides and separates must be preached there. You see, all those differences of race, language, ethnic group and culture ... all those differences are a visible sign of the infinite richness of love.' As if she sensed the fighting to come and the need to take things further, one day she said to the same priest: 'We have to think of the Foyer in the year 2000.' The history of the Foyer in Burundi includes a reflection Marthe uttered with great sadness: 'Burundi at the moment is the world's Garden of Olives.' On another occasion she added: 'It will be a Foyer of reconciliation ... You will not say so but you will live it.'

Everyday life in the Foyers

When she met the Foyer Fathers and members Marthe would take an interest in every aspect of their daily life, asking very concrete questions, sometimes giving judicious advice, shedding light on and anticipating situations. She would intervene at the spiritual level as well as the material.

Marthe had a strongly developed sense of the beauty and grandeur of the vocation to be a Foyer member, and showed it in many ways. She knew that the Foyers were contributing to the salvation of the world: 'We are saviours of one another. We should be people who believe we are saved.' She insisted on the total and real gift of one's life: 'To be happy you often need greater simplicity and renunciation. So you no longer have time to think about yourself.' She also insisted on the fact that community members were called to live a truly contemplative life and not just one of work: 'Oh yes! You must ask for this grace of contemplation. The Lord wants to give it. We are all called to contemplation.' It would bring about profound inner change in the form of a special purity. Questioned one day about virginity, she replied: 'Complete virginity … is not just physical virginity … It is virginity of the soul, mind and heart … virginity of our whole being and especially our thoughts which we must discipline and elevate, and our words and deeds … And then our love, the purity of our love.'

She was concerned that relations between Foyer members should be good, knowing full well that difficulties and hurt were inevitable in community life. It was when the person in charge of the Foyer in Mexico admitted to having difficulties with the Foyer Father whom she nonetheless loved, that Marthe said simply, with great truth and wisdom, 'Love brings suffering'. One had to go beyond the suffering. 'Unity and charity,' she said to Rachel W. 'Try gradually to overlook the minor frictions, don't stop at them. Be unity and love.' She emphasised the fact that unity was primarily supernatural: 'Unity is not created round the person in charge! Unity is created around the Blessed Virgin with the person in charge. And that's not the same thing!' and again: 'You must not observe others or you will judge them. It is at the level of the heart that we must know and make ourselves known.' Sometimes she would intervene more directly. 'I thought at one point that I was right and the rest of the community was wrong,' a member of the Châteauneuf girls' school recounted. 'Then Marthe sent word through Hélène Fagot to tell me that I was completely wrong, and helped me with her words (and her prayer and her offering) to restore harmony in three hours. I was straying from my vocation.'

She valued the family spirit highly: 'A Foyer is … a home,' she would say. People must act together and not independently of one another: 'Our vocation is essentially one of community. Sharing makes a Foyer's atmosphere. The community prayer is primarily an act of sharing.' She knew that relationships were more demanding when there were not many people, that more importance was then attached to little things which must be transcended in love: 'People must live in communion, hold onto the essential, live the beautiful now of God, doing the Father's will, being all for Jesus.' With regard to the relationship between members and the Foyer Father, she answered Marie-Thérèse A: 'It must be beautiful, great, supernatural and human too, because we are not angels. It is made up of respect and obedience.' Often she would support faltering vocations. To Monique B she said: 'People think, you know, that when they leave the community things will get better but that is not the case. Be a soul of prayer, thanksgiving, a soul like the Virgin Mary. Take into your life and carry the needs of others. Embrace things on behalf of others,' she said to Irène Z. She also knew that each Foyer had its own distinctive character, dependent on the country in which it was implanted. 'You must be completely Dutch,' she told a member of the Thorn Foyer in the Netherlands.

She was very attentive to the way in which people spent their retreats: 'Are people keeping silent during the retreats?' she would ask the Foyer Fathers. 'People come on retreat to calm and purify themselves. A retreat is the open door through which they subsequently enter more and more deeply.'

A good illustration of Marthe's close attention was the setting up of the Saint Joseph's home for the elderly. She took a special interest in the first people to be taken in. Presented with a list drawn up by the Grand Foyer, 'Marthe ruled nearly all of them out but insisted on taking a certain gentleman from Aix-en-Provence whom she seemed to like very much.' He was a childless widower. She provided the chalice and paten for the chapel, a lovely table and made sure there were enough pillows. For Christmas dinner 1980 she asked: 'What are you going to give them to eat?' – 'Turkey' – 'How? With olives or chestnuts?' – 'Chestnuts' – 'Don't forget to baste it frequently during cooking so that it isn't too dry.' She was particularly concerned to give these elderly people's lives meaning. She wanted them to be kept occupied, to be asked to perform small services such as peeling vegetables or laying the table. Above all, she believed that the home could be 'a cathedral of prayer' for the Foyers, the Church and the world, and she asked that the Rosary be recited there every day.

People's health was another of Marthe's preoccupations. She knew that Foyer members gave generously of themselves and sometimes overworked. She said to Père T, 'Father, be careful about your girls' backs.' Like a true Frenchwoman she attached great importance to food. 'And what about cheese? Father, you must give your retreatants cheese,' she told Père T. 'Retreatants have been battered by life. They must be given a fulsome welcome.' She even went into the details of fixtures and fittings. To a team leaving for Burundi she said: 'What are you going to put on your tables? You should use Formica. It seems it's very practical ... And don't forget a coffee grinder. Go and buy one from Monsieur L. Bring me the bill.' She was also concerned about the well-being and comfort of retreatants. Of Mme Jean D who had come to see her, Marthe enquired: 'How are you?' – 'Very well.' – 'Why are you not frank enough to tell me that you're very tired because you didn't sleep last night, because you've been put in a room with a bed not suitable for a person in poor health like you? Tell them from me to change your room for one where there's a really good bed for you.'

VI. The question of the canonical status of the Foyers
Thus the Work of the Foyers developed in much the same way as a human body gradually grows. The question of its legal status within the Church had, however, still to be settled and at the time

it was no simple matter. In the Church, as in civil society, if you want a work to last you have to find a status to guarantee that the founding intuitions will endure. The beginning is all fire and flames and the legal aspect seems cumbersome, constraining and unnecessary. As time passes, however, difficulties arise and memories fade. Things are often then seen more subjectively, at least by some, and are reread too much in the light of the successes and failures of individual lives. They have to be rendered objective for the benefit of generations to come. The problem is to find a suitable legal framework. The initial intuition must not be distorted, forced into a framework that is not meant for it. Many founders and foundresses have found themselves facing this problem. Sometimes, not without difficulty, they have helped to bring about a change in the law. Marthe and Père Finet were themselves confronted by this challenge.

In the case of the Foyers, in the beginning the situation was particularly delicate. The Catholic Church had always maintained separation between the priestly life, the religious life and the lay life out of respect for these different states, the desire to safeguard their particular characteristics, and in order to allow each individual to give the best of him or herself in a clear context. Secular experience had shown that there was nothing worse than a confusion of roles. Now, the charism of the Foyers was to have priests, laymen and laywomen living, working and evangelising together. But that was not all. Foyer members wanted to make lifelong commitments, something which the Church reserved for priests, religious and married people. Such commitment also brought with it specific, reciprocal rights and duties. How was this to be admitted in the context of life as a lay person?

At the same time it was clearly apparent that the Work of the Foyers was stamped with the seal of God. An enormous amount of good was being done. There was holiness about it. The Foyers were presenting a new and beautiful face of God and the Church, and bringing hope for the future. The local bishops where they were implanted had faith in them and other bishops were asking for Foyers. The Foyers had the right to the Church's protection. Some form of legal status must be found for them but which? In the aftermath of the Second World War, then during the great period of the Foyers' expansion, this question was to remain without a satisfactory answer.

The search for a solution
The truth is that Marthe Robin was in no hurry. She thought that the important thing was first to exist: 'Live, and then we shall see,' she would say. More categorical and a little naïve, Père Finet, no doubt interpreting Marthe's more nuanced statements too radically, maintained the Foyers would never have statutes. Marthe was sure of the charism of the Work and resolved to defend it. To one priest who in 1950 remarked to her, 'The Foyers of Charity are an improvisation,' she responded, 'An improvisation! They are a work which is already the result of twenty years of bloodshed! If it had been just my blood it would never have got off the ground but it is the blood of Christ.' Be that as it may, it was decided, with the agreement of Père Beton from La Léchère who played an important role in the process, to attempt some preliminary exploration.

In 1952 meetings went on for three weeks with Canon Naz from Chambéry. Raoul Naz (1889–1977) was one of the great French canonists. He published several learned works, among them a *Traité de droit canonique*[9] in seven volumes that took him thirty years (from 1935 to 1965) to write. There was no greater authority to be found. At the end of these meetings Canon Naz could recommend no other status for the Foyers than that of secular institute: 'I can see nothing else.' But secular institutes are connected to religious orders, seeking to extend their work into the world. Their members are quasi-religious, subject to the jurisdiction of the Roman congregation for religious and secular institutes, and although recent, their status did not in any way correspond to the life of the Foyers. Marthe reacted sharply. After Canon Naz's expert opinion had been submitted to her, she was silent for a long while, then declared frankly: 'A Foyer of Charity is not something added on to something else. It is something very new which has never previously existed in the Church. It is up to the Church to take us as we are.' It took a certain amount of courage to make such a declaration in 1952. A little later in the same year, Marthe went further and declared: 'The Foyers of Charity must never have constitutions. Constitutions would restrict us and make us like religious orders. Members of the Foyers of Charity are not monks or nuns. They are communities of lay men and women consecrated to God, without vows, with a priest at their head: the Father.' 'The Foyers of Charity must never have constitutions' did not mean 'must never have statutes'. Marthe was using the word in the sense of 'religious constitutions'. Those she did not want at any price, but she was not against a minimum of organisation provided it respected the charism of the Work. A fresh attempt with Cardinal Philippe, a Dominican and a friend of the Work, was no more successful, an anticipated meeting not being able to take place. In all this Marthe remained entirely obedient to the decision the Church would one day reach: 'I would rather be wrong with the Church, than right without the Church.'

'In-house' progress

To make up for the lack of statutes, internally it was necessary to be very precise. The Foyers needed an ever clearer idea of what they were and what they wanted. They needed to avoid, for example, the monarchic-style government, to which Père Finet's personality and authority would have lent themselves. To prevent this, Marthe asked Père Beton, in whom she had great faith, to tell Père Finet frankly what might not be acceptable: 'With Father, fraternal correction is your duty.' She did not want Père Beton to be submissive to Père Finet. Sometimes he would show her the drafts of letters he wrote to Père Finet. When he concluded 'With my filial affection', Marthe would make him write 'With my fraternal affection', thus obliging him to place himself on an equal footing with Père Finet.

On 17, 18 and 19 December 1960 a gathering of the first Foyer Fathers was held at Châteauneuf.[10] The place of lay people in the governing body was not yet clear and they were not represented. Talk was of the recent failure to meet with Cardinal Philippe, as a result of which it had become even more important to identify the Work's standing. Suddenly Père d'Heu from the Foyer in Bonheiden, Belgium, insisted with the seniority his years afforded him, that the Foyers be allowed to see what Marthe had written. The founding texts had never previously been passed on. Père Finet hesitated, fearing he might be violating a spiritual secret, but then realised that it was indispensable for the understanding and future of the Foyers. Next day he read the founding text: 'I wish to create something new here ...'

Another important step forward was the first ceremony of commitment. To make quite clear that the Work was not a religious order, there had never been a ceremony of official commitment, even though Marie-Ange Dumas and Hélène Fagot had consecrated themselves in Marthe's room on 8 December 1936 and Père Beton had, together with Père Finet, dedicated his priesthood to the Work of the Foyers during the Passion of 8 October 1943. It was the custom for each person to welcome the Virgin Mary into his or her life at the dawn of each day. From 1956 onwards the first commitments had taken place in private. Should more not now be done to mark the seriousness of this commitment in the Foyers? The twenty-fifth anniversary of the Work was approaching and it was decided that from then on members' commitment would be sanctioned with a public ceremony but without canonical form. Fathers Pagnoux and Marcel made theirs on 10 February 1961. From then on, members were given a medal of the Virgin of the Foyers and a copy of Saint Louis-Marie Grignion de Montfort's book, *Secret of Mary*, to mark this family ceremony.

This was very important for members' stability. It involved initial discernment and a personal desire to give oneself for life. Marthe used to say that it was a very serious undertaking which meant whole-hearted commitment. One Foyer member 'snatched' his commitment from Père Finet and left six months later to get married. Marthe suffered hugely as a result, saying, 'You do not make a mockery of God'. Someone else left years after committing herself. When Marthe was shown the medal she had left behind, she asked that it be placed on the chest of drawers near her bed, adding: 'I shall buy it back.'

The twenty-fifth anniversary of the Foyers (1961)
One happy event was to enable the Foyers to take a more official place in the Church, albeit still without canonical status. A ceremony to mark twenty-five years of their existence was held at Châteauneuf on 11 February 1961 in the presence of Cardinal Gerlier, Archbishop of Lyon, and six other bishops. The Foyers were moving out of the private domain. Speeches were made, giving thanks to God for their good work, emphasising what was new about it and identifying Marthe's prayer as its source. One Foyer priest gave this testimony: 'We have experienced and are still experiencing in all our retreats that astonishing phenomenon of the early Church known as "Paraclese", in which we see the Spirit of Jesus take over the minds of men and transform them into fire and light. We are clearly witnessing a manifestation of the One whom the Canon of the Mass rightly calls the "living and true God"… and, confounded by this demonstration of power which works through our weakness, we think with wonder of the richness of the hidden source whose blood, mysteriously shed, whitens souls and clothes them in the raiment of the lamb.' He was referring, of course, to Marthe's experiences of the Passion.

What Cardinal Gerlier, Archbishop of Lyon, had to say was very significant. For a long time he had kept his distance from the place of the Work. His presence was therefore a sign of considerable official progress. He had gone to see Marthe while she was going through the Passion and had joined with her in prayer. In particular he declared: 'Today I have experienced ... a great day in my episcopate. I am thinking of the woman whom everyone talked about, about whom I shall say very little, you may well imagine why. You know what I feel, dear Père Finet, and you know how I have always held in veneration, without seeing her, the one who may be said to be at the origins of all the good being done here. So I bless the Good Lord for having once again chosen so humble and poor an instrument, a little peasant girl from this area, much as in Lourdes the Blessed Virgin chose a little peasant girl from Bartrès by the name of Bernadette.'

The formalisation of the charism

In 1973 a document was issued by the Foyers, specifying what their charism was. It is an important text in the history of the Work, in which the Foyers were defined as:

> A community of lay men and women who, following the example of the early Christians, have their material, intellectual and spiritual goods in common, in order to live out their commitment in the same spirit and to be, with Mary as their Mother, a truly Christian family, under the guidance of a priest, the Father, striving unceasingly for charity in their spiritual and working life, to be a witness to light, charity and love in the contemporary world.

The important aspects of their life were emphasised: the love of Mary, through whom consecration to Jesus was daily renewed, the importance of the daily Eucharist extended through personal and community prayer, unity and fraternal love in diversity, and the Foyers' mission to teach and welcome people.

No progress was made, however, on the question of statutes. True, a Foyer of Charity could not be set up without the agreement of the local bishop. There was, therefore, a *de facto* recognition on the part of the bishops concerned, but there was no general recognition guaranteeing the unity of government of the whole, the durability of the charism, the rights of committed members, the reciprocal duties and rights of religious and lay members or the manner of discerning vocations. One way forward might have been to ask for diocesan recognition in Valence as a pious union under the Code of Canon Law of 1917. That would at least have been something. Such recognition had one disadvantage, however: the impossibility of having priests (and *a fortiori* religious) and lay people working together. Conscious of the limitations of Church law, the Second Vatican Council had asked for its revision but considerable work was involved and it would not be finished until 1983. Meanwhile the Foyers could not be left indefinitely in a state of simply existing, especially as their very expansion called more and more for a stable and universal structure. The question remained in the air, therefore, until the end of the 1970s.[11]

In the Holy Year of 1975, the Foyers of Charity went on a pilgrimage to Rome and were greeted at an audience by Pope Paul VI: 'We appreciate greatly the excellent spiritual work being carried out in each of your houses thanks to the demanding retreats that you offer the various members of the people of God.' Paul VI was familiar with Marthe's life. His Secretary of State, Cardinal Villot, had never been to see Marthe when he was Archbishop of Lyon, but he had come to talk with her at length on 4 May 1967 during a visit to France as Secretary of State. 'In twenty-seven years of discussions with Mgr Montini, Paul VI,' Jean Guitton states, 'inevitably I talked to him about Châteauneuf and the Foyers of Charity. In essence what he always said was this:

"My Secretary of State, Cardinal Villot, has drawn my attention to this work. They are Foyers of love which spread like flames, as love calls forth love, and the Foyers found other Foyers." The Cardinal also told me that the Foyer had, if I may venture to say so, a mysterious hearth, flame of flame, light of light, in which the mystery of redemptive love was consumed.' There could be no better way of expressing the way in which the Foyers were at the heart of the Church.

NOTES

1. Foyers with names in italics were subsequently closed.
2. Despite wanting to remain faithful to the spirit of Marthe Robin, has distanced itself from the work of the Foyers of Charity.
3. The following Foyers were opened thereafter:

1982	Ile-d'Orléans (Canada); Bunia (Democratic Republic of the Congo)
1983	Koudougou (Burkina Faso); Bambari (Central African Republic); Medellin (Colombia)
1984	Klein Sion (Netherlands)
1985	Nana (Peru); Bujumbura (Burundi)
1987	Ziguinchor (Senegal)
1988	Chicoutimi (Canada); Tainan-Taiwan (ROC); Laoag (Philippines); Vellore (India)
1989	Antsirabé (Madagascar)
1990	Mbalmayo (Cameroon); Combs-la-Ville (France): Phu-Dong (Vietnam)
1991	Cotonou (Benin)
1994	Rogow (Poland)
1995	Kpando (Ghana); Gowripatnam (India); Pointe-Noire (Congo-Brazzaville)
1996	Rome, transferred to Ronciglione in April 1999 (Italy)
1997	Kaliszany (Poland)
1999	Murro (Uganda); Adonis Jbeil (Lebanon)
2000	Taipei-Taiwan (ROC); Bonjongo (Cameroon)
2001	Naves (Savoie) to replace La Léchère
2002	Ngozi (Burundi)
2003	Les Cayes (Haiti)
2004	Kigali-Rebero (Rwanda) Foyers currently under preparation: Germany, Austria, Colombia, Congo-Brazzaville, Ireland and Italy.

4. Comment is made only on the Foyers founded while Marthe Robin was still alive and not on those founded since her death.

5. To the former café-restaurant in La Léchère.

6. Marcel Clèment, *Pour entrer chez Marthe* (In order to see Marthe) op. cit., p. 55.

7. Jean Guitton, *Portrait de Marthe Robin* (A portrait of Marthe Robin) op. cit., pp. 33–34. The date, 1936, given by Guitton, who had this story from Couchoud, does not appear to be correct. The incident happened later.

8. Old francs.

9. Treatise on Canon Law.

10. Père Finet, Père Beton from La Léchère, Père Callerand from La Roche d'Or, Père Eberhard from Poissy, Père Oury from Spa in Belgium, Père d'Heu from Bonheiden in Belgium, Père Bonnafous from Roquefort-les-Pins, and Père Ravanel from La Flatière.

11. In civil law the question was settled in 1972 by the creation of a Foundation drawn up with the help of members of the Conseil d'Etat consultative body which provided a solid and practical legal base.

CHAPTER 12
Marthe and her Visitors

One of France's prominent neuropsychiatrists with a considerable caseload had 21,000 patients on file when he retired at the end of the 1980s. He was a long way short of Marthe who, records suggest, had 103,000 people come to talk to her in her room during her lifetime. True, some came several times but then some also came without their names being registered. At any rate, the number of Marthe's visitors was huge. Many of them gave testimony after her death: some within the legal framework of the cause for beatification; most outside any imposed structure. The majority were very ordinary people. Others were well known and included prominent politicians, a prince and a composer.[1] The combined relevant documentation is considerable and only a brief indication is provided here.

I. Access to Marthe

How did people get to see Marthe? Mostly it was in the context of a retreat. After talking about Marthe, Père Finet would as a matter of course suggest that retreatants put their names down to request a meeting. Otherwise people would come during less busy periods. Either way a selection had to be made because Marthe actually only received retreatants on two days a week: Wednesday and Thursday. Even squeezing in as many visitors as possible, she could not see more that sixty to eighty a day. At some retreats there were as many as three hundred, so some who would have liked to meet Marthe were unable to do so. There was also a period after Easter when she was so affected in the core of her being that she was unavailable for several weeks.

Usually it was Père Finet and his secretarial staff who drew up the list of visitors. If he was away the Foyer's reception office would try to ascertain whether the visit was justifiable and then refer it to Marthe. Père Finet used to say to Foyer members responsible for the farm: 'This is Marthe's home. If anyone comes without having arranged an appointment through the Foyer, you must always ask Marthe and do as she tells you.'

The criteria were simple. Anything that looked like idle curiosity, the pursuit of the sensational or magic, or anyone obviously unbalanced was turned away. Journalists were not welcome. At least two reporters who wanted to see her, one of them from *Le Monde*, came on retreat and lied about their profession in order to gain access. The ensuing interviews were very disappointing for them. Priests, consecrated persons and young people were given priority. In principle there were no restrictions as to any particular type of person. Subject to available slots and the number of retreatants, the name of anyone who wished to see Marthe was automatically put down.

On Tuesdays the family and people from the valley known to the Foyer would go and see her without the need for permission from Père Finet. If Marthe's schedule was too tight Père Finet would suggest postponing other meetings or reserving a day. In the beginning he was very attentive to Marthe's family and some Tuesdays were even kept free for them. 'It was my job to let them know,' one Foyer member stated, 'and I would often go and fetch them. It was good to see Marthe with other members of her family, especially her sisters. They would often have their meal at La Plaine.'

Some applications were made in writing. Père Finet would inform Marthe who had applied and sometimes Marthe would refuse a particular individual. It was not unknown for Père Finet to stand his ground. Then Marthe would say, 'Oh Father!' but she would succumb. There was one instance where Marthe refused outright but Père Finet had the person go up three days later regardless, and Marthe did receive him. On the other hand there were times when Marthe wanted to see someone she had not yet met but about whom she had heard. She would more often than not then ask a visitor who was a friend of that person to set up the meeting.

Marthe did not only see visitors with problems. She liked to exchange ideas with people who were good company. One friend was convalescing at the Foyer after an operation. 'Marthe has no one with her at the moment,' Père Finet had her told, 'go and give her some relaxation.' 'So I went and joined Marthe and we spent a long while together, over an hour.'

During retreats a list would be hung up at an appointed place in the Grand Foyer so that people could go up in small groups at a given time. Often the retreatants would get together and go up in the same car. They would park near the farm. 'A small farm that looked just like any other farm in France,' was how one retreatant described it, 'with a slightly peeling façade and wisteria that wound its way from one end of the house to the other above the ground floor windows. In the courtyard three small children were playing, a cock crowed, chickens picked about, a cat lay stretched out in the sun, a herd of white goats gambolled past and reached the nearby pasture in a joyous scramble. Contrary to what one might have imagined the farm was fully operative.'

People would go into the kitchen. 'We gathered round a stove in Marthe's antechamber,'[2] recounted a doctor. 'An elderly lady was doing the cooking. Several people were already waiting there, among them an African priest.'

A Benedictine Abbot gave a vivid but accurate description of the kitchen:

Impression of peace in the small farm. We wait in the kitchen with the wood fire crackling in the stove and a servant busying herself here and there,[3] keeping an eye on the cooking, putting wood on the fire, going from one room to another, not stopping for a moment. Outside cockerels are crowing. On the ceiling are slender joists. Flies buzz about here and there, but there are no sticky papers hanging from the ceiling such as you see in some farms. The tick-tock of the old grandfather clock behind me. The rustic table made out of very smooth planks pointed up with filler that is coming away. On the walls old painted plates, solid chairs on which eight or nine of us sit. The social background[4] seems well-to-do with possibly an elderly retired farming couple, five men; one of the women, elderly, has the lines of deep intellectual concentration; a businessman, at first in a great hurry gradually settles down. No one speaks other than now and then softly to a neighbour ... There is nothing taut or tense about it. One could stay there for a long time with one's entire being in repose. The fire quietly gives out heat and the open door brings in the cool of Autumn. A tentative sun begins to light up the courtyard.

Sometimes, if there were too many waiting or if they were accompanying someone who had gone in to see Marthe, people preferred to wait outside. A Passionist Brother described how: 'Outside a ninety minute wait gave me 1) contact with nature – all the farm animals; and 2) the grandiose and sweet solitude of the place. A view of the hills.'

The waiting time would vary. Sometimes it was protracted. Signs of impatience were rare. One lady from Lyon was accompanying 'a couple who were friends of mine, no longer all that young, he a divorcé. We waited for over three hours in the small kitchen before they got into Marthe's room. Habitually a man of very little patience, he was unusually calm and patient. When they came out of Marthe's room they were both happy and radiant.' Another man, renowned amongst those who knew him for his impatience, had waited for two and a half hours. He came out in tears, underwent a conversion and later died a beautiful death.

Thus the kitchen served as a kind of filter, a place of appeasement. Much anger and many a fear, worry or false concern would dissolve in the atmosphere of silence and peace maintained by the Foyer members responsible for the farm. Conversely, it could be that anxieties, fears and tensions mounted during the waiting and were subsequently expressed when the person came into contact with Marthe.

II. Initial contact

At last the door would open and the previous visitor would come out. Often the radiance of a face spoke for itself, especially if it had previously been seen entering looking very different. The next person would rise from his chair and find himself first in a dimly lit corridor, then enter the room.

The Abbot just cited gave a good description of a visitor's first impression of Marthe's room: 'Père Finet called me when my turn came. First there was a minute antechamber through which electric lighting made it possible to find our way. Then Père Finet turned off the light and switched on a small, very subdued torch to light up our feet. I entered the room where a darker half-light prevailed than I had expected. It took me quite a while to get used to it. On my left as I moved forward a very diffuse light fell on some pictures that I did not look at. At the far end was the white bed which seemed very small to me. The room itself was very small. Père Finet offered me a chair at the foot of the bed and he sat facing the bed head, but we were close to each other.'

It was indeed surprisingly dark. Marthe's eyes were as if burned by blood and she could not bear light so only a small glimmer of daylight would be allowed to filter from behind a dark blue curtain behind her head. A medical student pointed out that people cannot live in darkness for any length of time because they are deprived of the D vitamins necessary for mineralisation. Yet this was how Marthe lived.

The room was not easy to heat. The window behind the curtain was kept open even in winter but the shutters beyond it were permanently closed. There was heating only in the corridor. At night warm bricks were put in the bed beside her. In summer cool water and blocks of ice were placed in her room. Some people smelt blood; others picked up pleasant and inexplicable smells but that was rare. If people did smell anything it was usually the fruit or flowers put in her room.

After a while people's eyes would gradually adjust to the darkness. 'After a few minutes,' said Little Sister Magdeleine of Jesus, 'one could manage dimly to make her out.' A very small face became identifiable. Eventually one could spot the photos of her parents and her brother Henri on one chest of drawers and on another, called 'the communion chest of drawers' because it was on this one that the custodial was placed when Marthe was brought Holy Communion, a large crucifix. The picture of Mary Mediatrix of all Graces hung on the wall above the divan.

The chairs on which visitors sat were positioned very close to the bed. They had only to reach out a hand to be able to touch Marthe. In the darkness this physical proximity created a form of emotional closeness. People felt at home.

If someone was slow to sit down, they would hear Marthe say, 'Do sit down.' Visitors would previously have been asked to introduce themselves, but if Père Finet was there he might do it. Some people were so moved and taken aback that they had difficulty speaking, in which case Marthe would do the talking and ask: 'Who are you?' in a small, pleasant and reassuring voice. Usually the mere sound of Marthe's voice was enough to make people relax. 'As soon as she answered me,' recounted one priest, 'I felt at ease.'

Marthe had a real gift for making people feel welcome. 'As to her welcome,' someone said, 'it was really extraordinary. She had a friendly, cordial way of welcoming you as if she had known you for ever.' 'What struck me most,' someone else remarked, 'was the way she made me welcome and put me at my ease as soon as I arrived in her room.' 'I would like to emphasise,' said a third, 'the feeling of welcome and her way of being present to the other person.' Without exception they remarked on her kindness.

Once one had got over the surprise at the darkness of the room, the second surprise – and a very pleasant one – was in fact hearing Marthe's voice. Marthe did not make gestures. Because it was difficult to see in the room she could not use facial expressions, and because she herself could not see – or hardly – she could not read the reactions on the faces of people speaking to her. All she had was her voice. Marthe Robin lived and communicated through her voice and this she had perfected.

It was indeed surprising to find that Marthe had a youthful voice (a 'girl's voice') that was clear and remarkably expressive. She spoke simple French. Every word came as it should, slowly, conveying its meaning perfectly. She always found the right one. She addressed each person with a pitch and tone that suited. With Père Finet one could sense affection and trust, with others respect, and with yet others a little more distance. Her voice transmitted not only her ideas but also her emotions and this without any effort or special effects. It was very unaffected and totally comprehensible.

Not surprisingly, her voice interested people whose job entailed speaking. One academic said he had never come across anyone who used such clear and precise French in its simplicity and voice pitch. Jean Guitton tried several times to describe her voice in his notes. In 1958 he wrote: 'This time a clear voice, alert, lively, cheerful, devoid of repetition or irritation, sometimes with a Provençal mountain peasant's accent, sometimes sweet, childlike … But the voice itself changes a good deal. In this respect her voice is much more musical and subject to variation in intensity, faint like a small trickle of water, but never low, never what is called "in a low voice" or whispering, that is to say with a deliberate act of will imposed on the voice. Although swallowing is impossible, the larynx would appear to be supple. She does not shout but there is something in her which reinforces sound. Sometimes this sound is loud in volume and she talks in a strong voice with a latent enthusiasm and an ardour that wants to communicate itself. But this is in order to reproach, to give impetus. Her ordinary voice is at times slow to express itself. She slows down, softens, searches for words, "almost irritated": "Let's see, how can I put it? Help me, Father … Come on, tell me …" Generally the flow is fluent, and sometimes without realising it she happily coins new expressions: "*Il opère ce qu'il fait.*"[5] And ordinary words are taken in their common meaning.'

Visitors would have been told that after the introduction was over they could talk about themselves, so the conversation would then begin.

III. Conversations at Marthe's bedside

Generally the exchange would develop in a very trusting and friendly way. 'What struck me,' said one frequent visitor, 'was the simplicity, the ease with which one could talk to her, just as one would talk to a friend, without any difficulty. If we did not agree we would argue. She would laugh and tell jokes. Marthe's crystal-clear laugh will always be among the sounds I remember.' Another person who saw her often said: 'Everything was simple and almost natural with Marthe, when you were in her presence! Despite the affectionate respect you spontaneously had for her, how at ease and safe you felt in the presence of this loving, attentive heart which gave God to people and led them to him quite simply. It was only afterwards that you became aware, that you realised.' The conversation usually fell into three sections:

The introduction
First Marthe would want to know with whom she was dealing. She was not usually satisfied simply with the social position of the

person to whom she was talking but wanted to know about their concrete circumstances and the focus of their interest. 'Marthe would listen and ask questions. She was very, very practical. A bit like the big Teresa, a countrywoman with her feet firmly on the ground ... She was really intelligent. She always asked pertinent and essential questions in a few words ... She would end up with a wide range of knowledge by dint of asking short but pertinent questions.'

People were usually touched by this interest on Marthe's part: 'What struck me most ... was her very simple way of talking, of asking all kinds of questions about my family: how many brothers and sisters I had, what my background was and even whether we had any chickens.' 'I noticed Marthe ... taking an interest in apparently banal, insignificant things which revealed a great perspicacity on her part.' Of a student in Lyon she inquired whether her room was well heated and what colour the wallpaper was. Of a midwife she asked practical details relating to her profession. She wanted to know, for example, the precise reasons why women asked for abortions.

She seemed to have great curiosity even in those areas in which she might be thought to be ill qualified. Of someone from the Ecole Polytechnique engineering college, she enquired, 'What is fission?' She asked a professor at the University of Geneva to tell her about his work on nuclear magnetic resonance. Of a petroleum engineer she asked the diameter of the pipeline under construction in the Galaure valley. She did not agree with him and in fact turned out to be right. With an intellectual she talked about the sterility of 'cultural correctness' prevalent in his country. A chaplain in Morocco said: 'When I talked to her about Muslims, I was struck by her interest in them. She had had some visit her'. People found her to be well-informed. A religious from Sénanque who came to see her on behalf of his superior said: 'I was surprised to find in the course of conversation how up to date she was with situations and people, although she did sometimes mix things up.' One sphere in which she excelled was Châteauneuf and the Galaure valley. She knew exactly what was going on there. 'She knew everything that happened in the village ... She had kept up the relationships of her youth, at least with those who had stayed in the area. A part of Marthe's conversation was devoted to friends. She was interested in anything to do with people. Visitors would report to her in detail only to find that she already knew. 'You could pick up plenty of news from her.' The mayor of Châteauneuf himself was impressed by her competence in this respect.

If the visitor had been to see Marthe before, she would generally remember the previous conversation, even if it had taken place years earlier. Sometimes it would take a little time for her to get her bearings. Sometimes there were gaps but more often than not she would show herself to have an exceptional capacity to remember: 'She had an extraordinary memory. She would ask after every member of my family, for example, remembering what I had told her, when in the meantime she had had so many visitors.' She had 'a fantastic memory, remembering everyone she had seen and all their children and everything I might have told her over the years ... She remembered what had been said to her in the last but one visit.' She would ask a teacher about lessons he had told her about years previously. She could even remember circumstances that the people directly concerned had forgotten.

More surprising were her references to things she could not have known by normal means. The mother of a family from Moulins who had met Marthe several years previously was surprised to hear her ask for news, by name, of children who had been born in the interim. 'Someone who had done advanced medical studies, who had a very good mind and gave lectures, said to me, "I was dumbfounded." Marthe had told her all about what the woman was doing.'

The case in point

The conversation would then move on to the case in point. Sometimes people would have difficulty speaking. 'Are you worried about something?' she would ask to open the discussion. She would have the ins and outs fully clarified if necessary, always in plain words and with an eye to what was essential. All gossip was banned. Often people were facing complicated situations and wondering how they could present them to her. Well, things became very clear. It was as if there was a grace of light in the room itself, perceptible in the mind of the person talking. She had a special way of listening. People did not feel themselves judged in any way. She took things as they were, with a favourable bias, positively, without suspicion or filter. Sometimes people would stray from the point a little. Then in her small voice she would say, 'I don't understand', but without irony or annoyance. Often people found her to be exceptionally lucid: 'I had the distinct impression when I was talking to her that she was reading my heart, whilst still remaining discreet and sensitive. For this reason I have immense respect and great affection for her.'

She would next adopt one of three attitudes:

'Either she would say nothing and people would think she was asleep or absent or dozing. That meant she could not see, that it was not clear. As they left, she would say, 'Come back, we'll pray'. Sometimes visitors were disconcerted and even disappointed. But often then, either during the hours that followed or soon afterwards, they would understand something or something would happen to resolve their problem. They would feel then that they had been in Marthe's prayers.

'At other times it was clear. Then she would say, "Don't you think you should ..." or "You should do so and so", or "Oh no, don't ..." She would encourage and guide people.' Some examples of such advice will be provided later. As a general rule her approach was prudent but not at all timorous. It was positive and inclined towards hope, progress and life. Where people were concerned all was respect and compassion. 'There was in her a power of love for this soul and this person, which enabled her to find the right way to help him. There was not a shadow of negative judgement of the person, not a shadow of criticism, only a kindly way of looking that offered a response to the question posed.' 'Usually she had a solution ... There was always something that had not been thought of, something simple.' The knot, if there was one, was often unravelled in the gentlest and easiest way. Sometimes she thought the solution would appear of its own accord. To a young man considering the priesthood she said, 'Truth asserts itself. It becomes clearer and clearer, more and more apparent'. Sure enough he became a priest.

'Sometimes,' said Père Colon, 'I saw her angry, but only rarely. At people who were in a state of sin and did not wish to emerge from it, she could hit hard. But that was exceptional. She was annoyed with their evil, not with them.' In fact she wanted to unblock people. One could see the effects very quickly sometimes. She asked an engineer if he evangelised in his job. When he started to laugh she became slightly angry, insisting on the need to do so. During the following week, much to his surprise, three of his colleagues came and asked him to tell them about God. More often though, Marthe showed no irritation, even when she was extremely tired. There were those in her immediate circle who had never once seen her lose her temper.

In general people might well be moved but the conversation was not strained. With people she knew, Marthe was often animated. One of her friends described her as having 'a heart overflowing with compassion at the same time as being very cheerful, making you laugh, ready to joke'. Another said: 'Marthe loved having a laugh with me. One day Father reproached us for it. "What we're doing here is all for the Good Lord," I replied, and Marthe was very much of the same mind.'

At the same time she was very serious and not flippant or in any way lacking in attention. She sought to bring peace to people's hearts so that the Holy Spirit could work freely in them. If necessary she would try and defuse a drama. To parents worried because their future daughter-in-law had had no religious education, she said: 'Don't over-dramatise the situation, the outcome of which belongs to God. Commit your troubles to Mary who is with you all through life and above all don't change the way you behave with your family at all.' On the day of the wedding, they were pleasantly surprised to see their daughter-in-law make her First Holy Communion. She had been secretly preparing for it. For Marthe it was a question of seeing the real problem. She condemned anything that was illusion or pretence.

The end of the conversation

During retreats the allocated time was short. A discreet knock at the door would indicate that someone else was waiting and the conversation would come to an end. Generally it would last about eight to ten minutes but when the need arose, Marthe would prolong it. She would do so even if the conversation was not crucially important but was diverting her. One of her friends was entertaining her when there was a knock: 'Père Beton is here.' – 'Fine, let him wait.' After a while there came another knock: 'Marthe, Père Beton is waiting.' – 'Yes, well let him say a little more of his breviary.'

The meeting would end with prayer: 'Let us pray.' Then more often than not a 'Hail Mary' would be said. Sometimes, however, Marthe would ask her visitor to choose the prayer. There were times when hearing Marthe pray was a determining factor in a conversion. When the conversation had been really intimate it would conclude with an embrace. Ange-Marie Mattéi, foundress of the primary branch of the SGEN (General syndicate for national education) in Savoie, and then a member of the secular fraternities of Charles de Foucauld, had just had a deeply moving conversation with her. At the end of it Marthe, who had never met her before said to her: 'If only I dared ...' 'I was breathless in anticipation of what she was going to say: "Why not dare, for Jesus?" She went on: "I would embrace you so that you could take my kiss to M R's mother." I had that kiss, Oh Lord.'

Then the visitor would leave. They would usually have got used to the darkness and it would be easier to find the way out than in: through the little corridor and back into the light of the kitchen. 'When you came out of Marthe's room you would be bathed in peace, it was an ineffable feeling. She took everything, bore everything, and you could sense the suffering that atones tirelessly and with joy. But how was Jesus not overwhelmed by our faults? You felt light, illuminated without deserving to be so. All you could do was pray and give thanks.' Marthe regularly received young people – girls in difficult circumstances – from the Good Shepherd Sisters in Valence. 'When they came out,' recounted one teacher, 'I can assure you they were not the same girls. Grace was at work. Their faces were no longer the same. You could see the joy in their eyes.' One Foyer member who often helped at the farm, confided: 'I have always been pleasantly surprised by their silence ... They would come away from Marthe in a rather reflective and focussed state. I never witnessed any unpleasant scenes of any kind. Only once did I see someone annoyed: it was Père P as he left Marthe's room on 7 February 1980.' We shall come back to that.

Once outside the kitchen door people would find themselves in the courtyard in front of the farm. Often they shone with joy, peace and gratitude that a problem had been solved. The world had changed colour and they could move on. Often people close to them would notice a change. One teacher confided that at school 'everyone had noticed my radiant face'.

Special cases

Marthe usually received people individually or in very small groups. Her room was not made for holding larger gatherings. There were, however, some exceptions: one after another, every

year, classes from the Châteauneuf schools would climb up to see
her. A first-year secondary school teacher described their
meetings:

> The children would sit on the ground and the conversation
> was delightful. They would give their names and where they
> lived and say whether their parents were former Châteauneuf
> or Saint-Bonnet pupils. Then she would say: 'I knew your
> mother well', or something like that. The children would sing
> and Marthe sang songs from her childhood. It was the voice
> she had always had, a little broken, but sweet.
>
> I remember [one] first-year visit because there was one little
> girl who was unbearable. The teachers were giving up on her.
> After the meeting with the whole class I kept her back and said
> to Marthe: 'Here's a little girl, Marthe, that I would like to be
> good but she can't seem to manage it. It's too difficult for her
> and she's always having to be punished.' Marthe said to her: 'I
> shall pray hard for you that you will be able to make a really
> good effort.' Then she said: 'Now, give me a kiss.' The little
> girl went home and told her parents: 'I've kissed a saint.'

IV. The gift of wise counsel

People who went up to see Marthe usually had two types of
request: they needed advice or were asking for prayer. It was not
uncommon for people to need consolation either. Many times a
day Marthe was thus asked to counsel people, a task for which she
undoubtedly had an unusual gift.

Submission to the Holy Spirit

Marthe did not usually give definite, let alone categorical advice.
She would ask questions, make suggestions, clear away any blind
alleys and allow people to come to their own conclusion. She had
great faith in the action of the Holy Spirit in souls and wanted
them to discover it. 'You don't need advice but prayer,' she

informed one person. If necessary she would refer people directly to the action of the Holy Spirit as when one day in 1975 someone came to see her to talk about problems at a newspaper:

> Although Marthe Robin had agreed to answer my other questions she did not want to answer those relating to my publication; so when I asked her if I should continue or suspend publication, she said: 'I don't know. I can't tell you anything. I shall pray with you for your project.' It was unusual for her to be evasive, so I insisted. Our conversation went on. All of a sudden, Marthe Robin quite happily said to me in a tone of some relief: 'Do you realise you're committing a grave sin?' This remark made me burst out laughing. I thought she was talking about the girls who were being kept waiting outside her door. Marthe Robin insisted: 'You see,' she said, 'your sin is serious because it constitutes a lack of respect and an affront to the Holy Spirit. If you were to leave more room for the Spirit in you, you would hear what you should do. It is not for me to act as a substitute for the Holy Spirit. Rather you should get used to seeking, together with the Holy Spirit, solutions that conform to the will of God. If you are not hearing, it is quite simply because you are seeking advice elsewhere that is the Spirit's to give, because you lack sensitivity to divine inspiration.'

Marthe's concern to allow the Holy Spirit to act, particularly through people in positions of responsibility, also found expression in her relationship with the Châteauneuf schools. She kept herself abreast of what was going on in them, knew the children and encouraged the teachers, for whom she prayed and offered, but she did not take their place. There was no parallel government on Marthe's part.

'When I went to see her about questions relating to the school,' said one of the teachers, 'I would talk about such and such a girl or such and such a difficulty. It could be very brief and Marthe would generally reply, 'We shall pray about it' and add, 'but, Father, it is up to you to resolve the matter.' So I became very aware of a tendency in me to want Marthe to solve problems. I thought it would be simpler and that she would tell me what she thought on God's behalf.'

Another one said:

> When I went to see her it was to ask advice, either from a practical point of view or about my relationships with the children and Foyer members. I would arrive at Marthe's with some suggested solutions. Sometimes Marthe would remain silent and that meant – or at least this was how I interpreted it – that another means, another way had to be found. But Marthe never gave me another solution. She would help me discover an alternative which might be more costly but which would ultimately prove to be better. Sometimes she would make me think by asking a question. For example she once asked me: 'Are the children getting enough recreation on Wednesday afternoons?' That was the sort of question Marthe would ask. As a result I realised I needed to see to the girls' recreation, to sport, to activities or classes to which they were more naturally inclined. She had a lot of good sense whereas I had a tendency to 'force' education.

Advice about direction in life

There were times, however, when Marthe would go further. She willingly advised many people with problems and a large number of her interventions related to orientation. People came to see her about their choice of profession, a vocation or a change of activity and she would generally manage to put her finger on the salient point, on the factor that would trigger development:

A young man, Marcel Clément, came to see Marthe on 14 March 1946. He had already travelled to the United States and as far as Asia. He had published three books and held some important posts.[6]

As soon as he entered Marthe's room, she asked him straight out: 'Where have you come from?' Taken aback, he did not know how to answer: 'From … from … from the Foyer!' – 'Ah yes! The Blessed Virgin has brought you on retreat!' Marthe asked him how he was getting on with it, and he spoke highly of Père Finet's instruction. Once again Marthe disconcerted him by talking about him: 'Yes … You'll see … This is the start of something!'

But there was another surprise in store for him. A knock came at the door and he was about to go when the following exchange took place:

'I'm going to have to leave you.'

'On your way up did you see my goats?'

'On my way up to you? … No!'

'Ah! … Because I'm worried about them. I've called for the vet. They must have eaten something … He says it's their livers! It's the same with poor Father. He's not well at the moment. I think he has the same problem as my goats … It's his liver!'

These incongruous remarks left Marcel Clément completely at a loss. Much later he asked Marthe why she had talked to him like that about her goats' livers. She replied: 'If you had only seen yourself! I couldn't get you to thaw out. You were like a proper plaster cast saint! You had to be brought down to earth!'

The conversation had not finished, however. Taking no notice of a second discreet summons at the door, indicating someone else was waiting, Marthe asked:

'But when your assignment in Washington is over, what are you going to do?'

'I'd like to come back to France and work in journalism. There are tensions in the Church! I'd like to work for Catholic unity!'

'There is no way you can stay in America any longer?'

'Oh yes! I've been offered a teaching post in Canada.'

'I would give that some thought instead!'

This last sentence of Marthe's was to prove decisive. She had given no specific instruction but had raised a question, pointed in a direction. Marcel Clément, who had not taken the invitation to teach in Canada seriously, reconsidered and did in fact pursue his career in that direction for many years.

A young man of twenty had just passed his ENA[7] exam. He had been influenced by the Scout movement and was considering the priesthood. A young woman appeared to be attached to him. He was hesitating. A priest friend recommended a retreat at Châteauneuf. He went to see Marthe. 'I asked her advice about the choice presenting itself and passionately interested in my studies as I was, how likely it was that I would ever again encounter such a clear crossroad along my way. The exchange was very straightforward. She encouraged me not to delay as the Lord was calling me, and I had already taken a higher degree. One month later I entered the Carmelite seminary at the Catholic Institute. I shall never forget the decisive turn I took during that retreat, after receiving the advice I had asked for from Marthe Robin and in the certainty of being supported by her prayer.' Today that retreatant is a bishop.

In this way Marthe furthered a large number of vocations to the priesthood. Over forty people testified to the fact that God had used Marthe to bring them to it and there were no doubt others. A Breton teacher talked to Marthe about his work and she pressed him a little, apparently not convinced he was doing everything he could with his life. In the end he said to her, 'But Mademoiselle, surely I am not supposed to become a priest?' 'You should be taking that question up with God, my dear. It's not for me to answer it. It's up to you!' He was ordained in 1987 for the diocese of Bordeaux. Many individuals with vocations counted on Marthe's prayers during times of discernment and at the seminary: men such as Mgr Delaporte, Archbishop of Cambrai, who during his time studying at the French Seminary in Rome, felt 'carried in her prayer'.

Many priests came to her for advice about the direction they should take. A Marist, Père Joseph Berne, was hesitant about an appointment to Verdelai in Gironde, a long way from his place of origin. Marthe recommended he devote a year specifically to prayer and work. The question of contact with a religious community then arose. 'You mustn't keep Jesus waiting,' Marthe told him. He became a Dominican friar. She also helped some to persevere: 'There was a point when it was not going well,' said one Good Shepherd Sister. 'I'd had enough. I wanted to pack my bags and leave. The Sisters sent me to Marthe. What she said had a profound impact on me and helped me in my life with young people ... What she said was: "No, you must not leave the Good Shepherd. You must stay and be the link between the Sisters and the young people." I have tried to be that link.'

On several occasions Marthe encouraged marriage. One young woman who came to see her had been proposed to but she had reasons for hesitating. 'Is there no one else?' Marthe asked. Sure enough the girl knew a French soldier on an exchange posting in the Canadian army. 'You should write to him,' Marthe said. 'And don't give any more thought to the first man.' The story ended with her marrying the soldier.

The following story which took place in 1954 is an illustration of similar advice about orientation: 'We had told her about our intention to go to New Zealand because of my fear of communism which had removed any desire to bring up a Christian family in Belgium. Her response, which we have never forgotten, was: "Yes, it would be good to go to New Zealand to start a Christian home", but after a moment's reflection she added: "But don't you think that if the Lord had wanted you there, he would have put you there? Don't you think he wants you to start a Christian family in Belgium?"' That couple was subsequently to have a great impact in Belgium.

Work problems provided rich material for consulting Marthe. So it was that she suggested to a university lecturer in the law faculty, who was having difficulty with his doctoral supervisor, that he change his subject and do an arts doctorate. He did so with happy consequences. To another man who talked about his business, she had no hesitation in saying, 'Someone in the business wishes you ill. You must look for work elsewhere.' And her assessment turned out to be right. She advised one family over the purchase of a hotel. The business had started badly for complicated family reasons and they had been heading for total destruction, but everything was sorted out.

Spiritual advice

The advice for which Marthe was asked was frequently of a spiritual nature, and in this she would sometimes take the initiative. A countrywoman came to meet her: 'When I talked about the work I did in the garden she asked me if I sang as I worked and when I said "no", she went on as if that troubled her: "At a time when your heart should be full of joy, nothing but joy."' A Foyer member said to her: '"When I pray, when I pay a visit to the Blessed Sacrament I am eternally distracted. I can assure you. I am Jesus' little butterfly." Marthe did not answer. I said to her: "Did you hear Marthe, I am Jesus' little butterfly." And Marthe replied: "Yes, it feeds off his substance ..." That was the sublime answer I was given.' 'One day when I told Marthe that I had started a book by Marie d'Agréda,' another recounted, 'Marthe advised against it because there was too much of the supernatural in it: "There are angels at every turn. You'd do better to read theological books."' The rule of life of Abbé Talvas' Institut du Nid was completed largely during the founder's stay in Châteauneuf and Marthe contributed to it. She had such love for the victims of prostitution.

In her spiritual counsel was a desire for people's conversion if that was what was required. 'With one or other of the retreatants, Marthe found the small, very straightforward trigger that would bring about their conversion. Take the senior executive in the oil industry who lived exclusively for his work. She asked him one or two simple, specific questions about his home life, on the basis of which during his retreat he called a number of things into question.' Sometimes Marthe did not give advice but merely voiced a reaction. The introduction to this book recorded the instance of the young man for whom the two words, 'And yet ... ' opened up the way of faith.[8]

Other miscellaneous advice

Marthe was asked about everything from children's future careers to farming or family problems. One could fill an entire book with the wise counsel she gave different people.

But she also gave advice without being asked for it. She would encourage people to evangelise, for example. To a music teacher who said it was difficult to talk about God in a State school, she responded, 'It's particularly important to talk to them.' Then, as he was leaving she remarked, 'How wonderful those apostles are, evangelising in difficult places.' In an entirely different vein: 'In 1970 Marthe advised me to look for work in the provinces to be near my parents. "Where do your parents live then? ... You could go to Tours. Your sister is getting married. They will be very alone."' On several occasions she advised teachers and priests to go behind the Iron Curtain to maintain contacts, not to be afraid, and to support not only Catholics but Orthodox too. This may have had important consequences.

Sometimes her advice was not immediately applicable so then she would pray: 'Against our wishes, our eighteen-year-old son Dominique had made arrangements to travel to Holland on his own. It was more than ever the fashion in those post 1968 years ... We were aware of all the dangers ... lying in wait for a timid and still very naïve boy. Père Colon who was leading the retreat had said to us: "You should talk to Marthe about it." She listened and remained silent for a moment. We thought it was so that she could reflect but we have since learned that it was the silence of intense inner prayer. Then she said, "This journey shouldn't be made." To which we objected that Dominique was most likely already on his way, given that he had been ready to set off when we left for Châteauneuf. She did not add anything, and the visit concluded with our saying the Our Father, the Hail Mary and the Gloria together. Well, what was our surprise when on our return to N we found our son at home: "You didn't go off to Holland then?" – "Oh! No." And that was it.'

She did much to counsel those in mourning or suffering in different ways, keeping her good sense even in times of trial: 'My son Pierre went deaf at the age of four. Marthe was very much with us in this problem. She helped us a great deal psychologically, telling us that if our son was to be cured, it would be by medical science, that we should not count on a miracle but that there would be compensations. So we did everything we could to get him cured and now Pierre has a very good job.'

From the 1970s onwards Marthe found herself increasingly confronted by the question of abortion. She felt deeply about it. When it was explained to her that in Lyon a major hospital had equipped an entire floor to carry out abortions, she said, 'It's a real abattoir … People are indignant about all the war deaths yet allow these little innocents to be massacred. Can that be right? No! People can't think that's right … And those little ones suffer.' She also devoted much thought to the parents of the aborted children and believed that the children were praying for them in heaven, 'Father, those children are their parents' saviours'. Even in the midst of the greatest injustice, she continued to hope.

V. Marthe's intercession

Other meetings involved intercession. Usually Marthe would pray with her visitors and tell them clearly that she would hold them in her prayers but sometimes she was asked urgently and explicitly to intercede with Heaven for difficult cases. This was often true of married couples who could not have children. One couple came on retreat to Châteauneuf a year after their marriage, lamenting the fact that they had no children. 'Then you must ask the Lord,' she said. Their daughter was born after some ten years of marriage. Another couple was in a similar situation. The in-laws met Marthe and confided their concern. 'Ah!' said Marthe, 'children, fine children!' That simple sentence helped the couple to hold on for ten years, after which they did have three fine children.

There were also plenty of requests for prayer for people's health, and some results verged on the miraculous. A doctor's wife had been seriously burnt at Chatillon-sous-Bagneux in Hauts-de-Seine. She was urgently transported by plane, then helicopter to the Edouard-Herriot hospital in Lyon. She was thought to be lost. Her husband rushed to Marthe who prayed much for her, asking not only for her recovery but also that she would not be left with scars on her face or hands so that the children would not be upset. Not only was she saved but the skin recovered substantially, much to the amazement of her surgeon.

The Second World War was similarly an occasion for numerous requests for prayer. A soldier was captured in 1940 and his wife, who had just had their child, had no news of him for months. 'Marthe invited me to pray and assured me that my husband would come back and I would have a large family. I wanted to make a promise to go to Lourdes and Marthe told me that my husband would go to Lourdes with me.' Seven times they went there together.

VI. Marthe's correspondence

Marthe also kept in touch with and 'met' the outside world by correspondence. She never got used to people's distress. Sometimes she could be heard sobbing when a letter was read to her. 'I was astonished,' remarked one secretary, 'at her intelligence and clarity: a single sentence would say everything in a few words.' Her last secretary categorised the letters she received as follows:

'1. Letters describing people's suffering and asking for Marthe's prayers. Her response was that of a heart that shared in that suffering and at the same time conveyed thoughts of faith and hope.

'2. Letters from religious Sisters having difficulty relating to their superiors. In her answer Marthe would never say that the writer was right, but would invite her to see meaning in what she was going through and come to a better relationship by other means. I also noticed the importance of obedience to superiors which Marthe expressed delicately but firmly.

'3. Letters of gratitude and thanksgiving but not so many because most of the letters were asking for graces. Marthe was thrilled when letters were absolutely gratuitous.

'4. Letters from Foyer Fathers and members. I would not answer them. Marthe would be made aware of their contents and she would sometimes make casual conversation about them to me. Marthe would have me take them down to Père Finet with the parcels or to the secretariat for the information of the community.'

Many of these letters were deeply moving. One such was written by the great poet Paul Claudel of the Académie francaise, Nobel laureate for literature. It is dated 9 October 1950 and asks for Marthe's prayers through the intermediary of Père Finet:

How can the remarkable privilege of your parishioner be explained other than in terms of the duty she has to share the benefits of the immense grace she has received with the distressed and the suppliant?

An old man of eighty-two and a whole troop of innocent children are imploring her.

I ask for nothing temporal. I ask only for the salvation of those two wayward souls[9] by whatever means it pleases God to employ. I place myself completely in his hands. I give him complete freedom. And I fervently await a word of consolation and hope from the mouth of that saintly girl. I have faith in God, who has never abandoned me.

Many of the letters Marthe dictated have been kept but are not easy to use because they are replies to letters that have not been kept. Usually letters addressed to Marthe were burned once they had been answered. The following three documents will give some idea, however, of the kind of answers Marthe gave.

The first, dated 14 November 1964, is addressed to a family whom Marthe clearly particularly liked:

> Mlle Marthe has dictated the following to me for you: It is an ever renewed joy to receive your letters and news of you all, and to know that you hold me in your affection and your prayers ... And I do so reciprocate. Perhaps it is indulgent to tell each other so again, but I shall say it anyway because it is always good, both for those expressing and for those receiving, to testify to their feelings and give an assurance of prayers borne on the Father's waves of love, with Jesus, through our 'Maman chérie'.
>
> How conscious we are of all the strength of the communion of saints in this great, final week of the Council,[10] which will conclude on the day of the Presentation of our Mother of love.[11] We hope and pray that the Holy Father will speak forcefully, not only about her presence but about her maternity in the Church and about her universal mediation in and through the unique and sovereign mediator Jesus.
>
> We shall be happy to welcome you here in 1965, if as we hope, the Lord grants you the joy and the possibility of travelling to France.
>
> In the Foyer we are continuing to apply ourselves to doing the Father's will and being true children of the Church. Père Finet is preaching a retreat with ever increasing faith and with quite supernatural energy.

We are having a very beautiful autumn so bathed in sunlight, clear and luminous that it spurs us to thanksgiving. But we could do with a little rain.

I reiterate my great affection for you all in Jesus Love and our beloved Mother, and give everyone an affectionate kiss from me.

The second is a completely different kind of letter. It was addressed to a person aggrieved by the remembrance of her faults despite having confessed them:

Mlle Marthe Robin has taken all the contents of your letter very much to heart and prays for you with all her soul that God may grant you peace and complete faith in his mercy, in total and loving abandonment, whatever your past may have been. With a childlike heart you must cast all your wretchedness on the infinite mercy that is calling to you. Since you say that you have confessed to everything that is upsetting you, this is not the time to succumb to discouragement but, freed by your admission, be a soul on its way to eternal Love, increasing your acts of faith and cultivating immense hope through the exercise of charity. You must not just aspire to intimacy with Jesus but set about wanting it with all your soul.

The third letter is more delicate in nature. This one was addressed to someone who was suffering greatly. Marthe wanted to help her find meaning in what she was experiencing:

Mlle Marthe has dictated the following for you: Yes, I pray that Jesus may immerse you in his divine will and that you may offer your suffering in love, to the very end. He is making you a proposition: are you willing to offer me this suffering, do you wish to share my cross for the Redemption of humanity in spiritual distress, for my priests, for my Church, for all those I wish to save through you, with you, in union with me and with the Very Blessed Virgin, our Maman chérie? But be sure that I will ask beloved Jesus and our Mother of Love to comfort, strengthen and sustain you tenderly and maternally in your faith and trust.

VII. Relations with families

It is not possible to conclude a chapter about Marthe's visitors without mentioning the on-going relationships she had with certain families, sometimes over several generations. A significant part of Marthe's contacts, verbal or through writing, were 'piecemeal' but many others were of a more long-term nature. There was a reciprocal fidelity that must have given Marthe much pleasure.

This was the case with one family in Blois with eleven children. Marthe prayed for the conversion of one member of the family. The process spread and the other brothers and sisters converted in their turn, which brought Marthe numerous contacts. M P had taken part in the first retreat to which men were admitted. His son B married and his wife was then to say, 'I discovered how important Marthe was in my in-laws' family'. Love of Marthe transmitted itself to the third generation. The family produced vocations to the permanent diaconate and to the priesthood.

Another family, that of M. and Mme V, met Marthe in 1943 during a retreat in which the father took part, a retreat initiated by their friend Robert Garric. He came away a changed man. 'He came back having discovered treasure. A place where surprising things were happening for wartime … Amidst the chaos of war, the division of France, its condition as a conquered and occupied country, dad was returning from a place where hope was being reborn … He was amazed by his find and moved when he told us, in shared confidence, about his meeting with a woman who had touched his heart because she was so close to the Lord … After that my father took my mother on retreat. They came home joined in sweet complicity.'

They had twelve children and seven out of nine of their daughters were boarders at Châteauneuf. Several of the children had lovely voices and used to sing to Marthe: 'We sang to her in two parts, three parts, maybe four, with the tenor being sung as soprano. And out of the darkness came a bright, young voice, "You see, that's how life is. Each one sings her own part but in harmony with others."'

Marthe intervened in the lives of several of the children. To one she said, 'With a name like Chantal you are meant to spend your whole life singing to the glory of the Lord.' She had the sensitivity to let the girl know that the young man she was thinking of was already taken, thus sparing her unnecessary suffering. She also said of another boy, 'You can't marry someone out of pity.' To another of the daughters she said, 'You should think about getting married.' And she helped the girl extricate herself from an initial relationship. During her next visit Marthe told her, 'that a boy was getting ready for me. He was working in Africa', which proved in fact to be the case. Marthe kept on asking her whether she sang even though her sisters were more gifted singers than she was. So the girl took up singing, which helped her to get rid of a potentially dangerous hypophyseal adenoma. Another was having difficulties in class and when she did not succeed, considered entering the religious life. 'Have you thought of dropping back a year to go through everything you have chosen again thoroughly? Suggest that to your father. After all what's one year relative to eternity?' she said to her. This determined her future. She realised during the same conversation that she was called to get married. Marthe prayed for children who were slow in coming and for the health of family members. Her protection extended as far as cousins. To one of them who was in the Resistance she sent a message not to return to Vercors, and sure enough the Maquis were wiped out shortly afterwards.

Contact with the Foyer and with Marthe had a lasting impact on the family and it meant a great deal to the children to have

Christian families in their turn. The family of M. and Mme V (who died in 1996) had 187 descendants in 2005, if the 'additions' were included. Several of them entered new communities.[12]

'During the some twenty years when one or other of our daughters was being educated at the Châteauneuf school,' said Monsieur V, 'we would be called to the Foyer several times a year. We always had some reason to visit Marthe Robin, to try and join with her in prayer or ask her opinion. Sometimes she would help us come to a decision. Sometimes too, we would think our exchange had been unimportant at the time but in the period after our visit, the words we had heard would gain in significance and enlighten our minds or hearts, sometimes both. We always left Marthe with peace in our hearts.'

One family from the Galaure valley among many others benefited on more than one occasion from Marthe's friendship:

M. and Mme M had a café in the village of C. They were not practicing Catholics and on Sundays their establishment was open to men who came for a drink rather than go to Mass. One day Monsieur M said to his wife, 'I'm going up to Marthe's.' He came back two hours later and said simply, 'I've been converted.' His wife did not question him but next Sunday he disappeared while she was serving customers. She went looking for him and found him in their room in the process of putting on his Sunday clothes. 'Where are you off to?' she asked. 'To Mass.' The café was at the lower end of the village, the church at the top, and at the time there were several cafés on the road that climbed from one to the other. Everyone saw him go past and in a village where anticlericalism was rife, people were so amazed to see Monsieur M going to Mass, which very few men attended, that no one dared say anything. He subsequently played an important part in the evangelisation of the village, the spirit of which gradually changed.

M. and Mme M had a son who got married. The young couple had a child which died at birth and the wife could no longer conceive. One day she went up to see Marthe and told her tearfully, 'Marthe, it's awful. We can't have any more children.' – 'Yes, you can,' Marthe said to her, 'you can. Off you go and do the necessary and I will pray.' A short while later the woman found she was pregnant. 'This is definitely Marthe's doing,' she told her husband. 'Let's go and thank her.' They had hardly entered the room and had not yet said anything, when they heard Marthe's voice: 'Ah, it's you! You're coming to tell me the great news ... Yes, I obtained it from the Virgin on Good Friday. He will undoubtedly be born on a Friday because all my children are born on a Friday.' He was indeed born on a Friday and two years later he had a little brother, also born on a Friday. They asked Marthe to be the elder boy's godmother but she declined, 'Oh no. I have too many godchildren now.'

Monsieur M senior thought one day that his café would not provide an adequate living for his family and considered turning it into a hotel-restaurant. It was in a good position but the business would take all his capital and it was risky. He spoke to Marthe about it. 'Yes,' Marthe said to him, 'do it. You will be able to provide for your family.' But he explained to her that if the hotel was to be cost-effective it must have a certain number of rooms. He had been thinking of constructing a new main building but also wanted to add a storey to the old one. Well, that was going to be very expensive because the roof would have to be taken down, the new storey built and the roof put back on. 'But why do you have to take the roof down?' asked Marthe. 'Lift it on hydraulic jacks, build your storey, then put the roof back on top.' – 'Hydraulic jacks? What are they?' – 'Ask the architect. He'll tell you.' Amazed, Monsieur M submitted the plan to the architect without telling him where the idea had come from. The architect was surprised but studied the plan and came back shortly afterwards, saying: 'Your idea is excellent. It would save a lot of money but it is impracticable for the following reasons ...' Monsieur M listened carefully to the expert's objections, went back up to see Marthe and repeated them to her. Marthe listened in silence, then declared, 'He didn't understand. That's not where he should put the jacks.' They did what she said, all went well, much money was saved, and the architect never knew where the brilliant idea that had initially daunted him had come from.

⁊⁊

If it is true that a human being's existence is measured largely by relationships, Marthe Robin was one of the great 'existers' of the twentieth century. She had a rare richness and intensity of life. From where did she draw the energy to receive and help all the souls that turned to her? From God alone. Yet she also remained extremely human, which enabled her to nurture some exceptional friendships that warrant special scrutiny.

NOTES

1. For example: the philosophers Gabriel Marcel and Gustave Thibon; Robert Garric, founder of the 'Equipes enseignantes'; minister Antoine Pinay; actress Martine Carol; journalist Jean de Fabrègues; Lanza del Vasto; Veronica O'Brien, who introduced the Legion of Mary to France and inspired Cardinal Suenens; Jean Daujat, founder of the Centre for Religious Studies in Paris; Marie Michelet, wife of the minister; B. Gavoty the composer; Prince Felix Yussupov who assassinated Rasputin; Marshal Leclerc; historian Maria Winovska; Yvonne de Galard, the heroic nurse of Dien Bien Phu, etc. (to mention only those now deceased).
2. A wonderful name for a kitchen!
3. He is in fact referring to a member of the Foyer.
4. Of the visitors.
5. Literally: 'He accomplishes what he does', intended perhaps to convey that 'He does what he says'.
6. From a conversation reported by Marcel Clément in the book he wrote on Marthe: Marcel Clément, *Pour entrer chez Marthe* (In order to see Marthe) op. cit. He wrote some thirty works.
7. Ecole nationale d'administration: a prestigious university-level college preparing students for senior posts in the civil service and public management.
8. See p. 6.
9. It is not known to which two souls the poet is referring.

10. Marthe is probably referring not to the conclusion of the Council itself (in December 1965) but to that of one of the sessions.
11. 21 November – the feast of the Presentation of the Blessed Virgin Mary.
12. Claire Amitié, l'Arche, the Chemin Neuf, the Soeurs de Saint-Jean, Emmanuel, etc.

CHAPTER 13
Exceptional Friendships

Although we have plenty of testimonies about meetings with Marthe Robin, because of their personal and spiritual nature there is often a reserved quality to them. There were some people, however, who had close relationships with her, contacts – some very brief, others longer – that were more than just meetings. Marthe, who was very aware of how valuable they were, had some real friends, among them: Gisèle Boutteville (Signé), Mother Lautru, Père Beton from La Léchère, Père Garrigou-Lagrange, Doctor Ricard, Little Sister Magdeleine of Jesus, Marie-Ange Anstett and Thérèse Cornille to name but a few and only those now deceased.

Marthe remained very attached to her friends. One day a young academic who had received a calling to the priesthood in her room, having finished talking to her, was about to leave. He felt that what he was about to do was risky and needed her prayers. Standing at the foot of her bed, he said to her (in a sudden outburst): 'Marthe don't let go of me!' She did not answer but Père Finet who was there told him with great conviction, 'Marthe never abandons her friends'. These words were to remain with that priest for the rest of his life. For her part, Marthe needed the support of friends and felt it cruelly when, one by one, her dearest ones died. 'I have lost my last friend,' she declared on the demise of Doctor Ricard. She did still have some but none with whom she had quite the same degree of intimacy and trust. Some people said little. Others were more forthcoming, as the following examples will illustrate.

I. Gisèle Signé

Gisèle Signé was the married name for young Gisèle Boutteville, who had first come to see Marthe in the summer of 1924. Their relationship – one of friendship, pure and simple – was to last until Marthe's death. 'I don't understand why she became attached to me. Perhaps because I was so small ... I could not give her anything ... It was as if there was a spark.' When she married, her husband too became a great friend of Marthe. 'Whenever I was leaving,' said Gisèle Signé, 'our goodbye embrace would go on and on. I would always be the first to kiss her.' One day she asked M. Signé: 'Aren't you going to kiss me. Will she [Gisèle] be jealous?' 'I was waiting my turn,' said M. Signé. 'I had to lean across the chest of drawers. You had to find the space.'

Gisèle Signé thought that in 1942 she had benefited from Marthe's prayers. She had experienced terrible pains in her abdomen and it had been decided to remove one of her ovaries. She referred herself to Marthe who told her just to keep up her treatment and to do whatever the Good Lord wished. But she prayed for her. Shortly afterwards, to the astonishment of the surgeon, the ovary recovered. So Gisèle 'very frequently' referred people who were seriously ill 'and had very often been written off by their doctors' to Marthe. Several times Marthe intervened in a similar way in the same family, first for a little girl, Renée Chevauchet, then for her brother, André, and also for Mme Chevauchet herself, who was considered to be in an extremely grave condition. Later, Mme Chevauchet went to thank Marthe for praying for her: 'She was moved when she saw Marthe. She promised to go on pilgrimage to Lourdes and did so when she had the necessary money.' Marthe used to ask after any developments in the health of the patients for whom she prayed.

'I am often asked to intercede,' she said, 'but people forget to keep me informed afterwards.' 'The graces were too numerous for me to recall,' said Gisèle.

II. Paul-Louis Couchoud

Jean Guitton devoted a chapter entitled 'A Visitor in the Night' in his book on Marthe Robin[1] to Paul-Louis Couchoud (1879–1959), an important figure of whom Guitton penned a very interesting portrait:

> There was at that time in France the freest of free thinkers, a radical unbeliever, a gentle and peaceful detractor, who was quite convinced of his hypothesis, a disciple of Spinoza, about whom he had written. Paul-Louis Couchoud, philosopher, exegete and doctor, had made a rigorous study of the immanent logic in the problems raised by the intellect in relation to Jesus. He was known for having been an adviser to Anatole France, the founder of an 'anti-Christian' series of books at Rieder's, and the organiser of a Jubilee celebration in honour of Monsieur Loisy at the Collège de France.

An *agrégé*[2] in arts and a doctor of medicine, at the beginning of the century, with a grant from the Kahn Foundation, Couchoud had travelled extensively in Asia. He had brought back with him the haiku poetic form, which was unknown at that time in France, and together with his friends, the painter André Faure and sculptor Albert Poncin, became the first Frenchman to write this kind of poetry. He was simultaneously a teacher at the Ecole pratique for advanced studies and a doctor at the Salpêtrière. He was thus a man who enjoyed considerable prestige, particularly in rationalist circles. 'In the company of Anatole France,' he said, ' I have met some of the greatest contemporary minds.' He was France's equivalent of Germany's most radical Biblical critics.[3]

'What was novel about him,' claimed Guitton, 'was that he never admitted the historical existence of the Nazarene. How many times did he say to me with that sweet, sphinx-like smile of his: "I subscribe to everything in the Credo ... except *sub Pontio Pilato.*" At the same time he would say to me gravely, looking deeply thoughtful, almost sorrowful: "Jesus is the greatest 'exister' on this earth. How many people have died for him in the course of two thousand years! How many souls live only because of him!" But he did not confine himself purely to criticism. He knew well that "to adhere to the Gospels in their historic sense, you need faith, and that is not within my power". He also had a highly-developed sense of human suffering. Having sought a solution to the problem in Buddhism he had come to think that Christian mysticism was superior in its attentiveness to human suffering. "If the pain is beyond cure, Christ with you will endure," was an adage he quoted to me. Alas this historical Christ never existed!'

He was still interested in mystical phenomena and especially in stigmatics. At the Salpêtrière hospital he had treated cases of mystical madness and thought he knew something about the subject. Whilst living in Vienne, not far from Châteauneuf, he conceived the desire to visit Marthe. Knowing his reputation, Père Finet refused him, so he tried again through his friend and colleague Jean Guitton. But Guitton was renowned at that time for being a 'progressive' Catholic and Père Finet turned both of them away. Finally, Jean Guitton, who knew Cardinal Gerlier, Archbishop of Lyon, went through him and Père Finet was obliged to open the door. 'Slowly a very warm friendship then developed between Paul-Louis, probably one of the greatest atheists of Biblical interpreters and Marthe, the most remarkable mystic.'

Couchoud, the intellectual who had mixed with some of the greatest thinkers of his day, was very impressed by Marthe's mind. He also set about analysing her relationship with Père Finet and gave an account of it to Jean Guitton, who noted it down that same evening. In Couchoud's words:

'This little peasant is a superior woman. This struck me on our first meeting, and even more so on my second visit. Illness has concentrated Marthe ... Marthe does not sleep. Consequently she is constantly thinking. She is a brain – possibly one of the keenest brains on our planet.

'She is all brain, but a reflective brain. When I say that she "reflects" or "meditates", I am using the word in its truest meaning. Most of us say that we reflect or think or again pray, but our thought is a vague dream; our prayer is not meditation: it is a whirring. Marthe goes deeper. And this little French farm-woman has reflected at length about how, despite her immobility, she can make an impact on the planet.'

Couchoud understood that Marthe's objective was to bring about the reign of love. To that end different people and social classes must be brought together, hence the idea of the silent retreats. He was impressed to find that Marthe had plans and a vision for the planet. Even if in this respect he was a little short-sighted, he had at least recognised the greatness of her character.

'So,' he went on, 'she realised she could not be on her own, but needed a companion to provide not so much material help as the education she lacked. With the help of this angel, she has been able gradually to acquire a language remarkable for its clarity, firmness, density and exactitude.' This was how he described Père Finet: 'To help her in this Work she had to find a guide with almost contradictory qualities. He must be cultivated, pious and very knowledgeable about spirituality. He must, above all, be a big businessman, a Balzacian character. She even thought that this requirement to be a practical man was of primordial importance ... They met and ... as Saint-Simon put it, "what was sublime in each of them merged."' This was no mean assessment by one coming from outside.

'I am going to amaze you,' continued Couchoud: 'Do you know who I think of when I am with her? I hardly dare say it but I think of Pascal. She has the same kind of mind only with greater simplicity. What she says is clear in its contours, sober, accurate, well-chosen.

'Combined with that, she has the memory of an elephant when it comes to small details. And always what in France we call *esprit*,[4] which is never bitter, but spiced with humour and playfulness.'

He told Marthe how he saw her and she reacted in a way that was both clear and trusting: 'Marthe you are all head!' She answered him sweetly: 'Don't you think I'm heart too?'

Fascinated by Marthe, Couchoud had no hesitation about being quite open with her. He talked first about a book he was writing on war and peace, which he was evidently having difficulty in finishing. Marthe advised him to lay his sheets of paper out side by side 'until they are filled with immense hope'. Couchoud noted that these last words 'were uttered in a voice that was stronger and seemed already to contain the realisation of that hope'. Then he went on:

'After talking about my writing problems, I broached a more personal matter. "Marthe," I said to her, "I have no faith." And she replied, "Alright then, I will carry you." "But God does not want us to knock next door when a large door is standing open," she added. A silence ensued and then she said to me, "What's more you would not be seeking him, if he had not already found you."'

It is worth noting that Couchoud, who was there out of curiosity as an observer, having come to the end of his thinking and being in his heart of hearts unsatisfied and troubled, had already progressed to another register that touched on his innermost being. The conversation ranged from the book he was writing and the research being done by his daughter, a chemist. From there it progressed to wild clematis and other plants Marthe knew well.

Later Couchoud came back to see Marthe and resumed their earlier conversation. She remembered their previous meeting well and his daughter's research into wild clematis. 'Then I braced myself to say to her, "Do you realise, Marthe, that you helped me correct one of Pascal's thoughts? When I told you about my difficulties in believing, you quoted a famous thought by Pascal and said: 'You would not be seeking him if he had not already found you.' But Marthe, what you do not realise is that you misquoted Pascal. What Pascal wrote was, 'You would not be looking for me if you had not already found me.' You corrected Pascal! It's possible that it was a slip of the pen on Pascal's part. I've noticed, when editing his *Pensées*, that he often substituted one word for another when he was writing quickly."

'Whereupon Marthe said to me, "Pascal could not have written: 'You would not be looking for me if you had not already found me' because Pascal would not have said something that was self-evident. Pascal wanted to say that God seeks us first. Look at how Saint Paul was converted. God acts first. He starts ahead of us."'

This was the level of their conversation.

As they finished talking, the arrival of a peasant woman was announced. 'Oh, this one will be easy, Monsieur Couchoud,' was Marthe's reaction. She made no secret of the fact that her round with him had been demanding. "Let's embrace," Marthe said to me. I embraced her and as I kissed her on the forehead, I saw a drop of blood.

He left thinking he had seen 'one of the most unusual people on the planet'. A short while later he wrote to Jean Guitton: 'I hold Marthe to be an intellect full of insight at the centre of a privileged experience and an ineffable sacrifice.' And one day on Vienne station platform as the train was about to depart, still talking about Marthe, he recited these four lines:

What you do not know, I do not know.
What you know, I would like to know.
The fragrance of what you pray for reaches me.
Do not forget me, oh living one!

In the nature of a confidence, they were the last words Jean Guitton heard him utter. 'A quarter of an hour before his death,' Guitton added, 'he received a chance visit from a priest. He died in faith, as I was able to say at his funeral.' Marthe was later to tell Guitton, 'I loved Professor Couchoud. I embraced him.' 'It was reciprocal,' Guitton replied.

III. Jean Guitton

Jean Guitton (1901–1999) was to step into the breach left by Couchoud. He too became a friend of Marthe and visited her regularly from 1958 until her death. Twelve times he saw her and they had long conversations, out of which he compiled a book.[5] He even became a valued friend of Père Finet who showed himself to be capable, in this as in other instances, of rising above his prejudices and befriending him. Jean Guitton's wife often accompanied him and she too entered into this circle of friendship.

One of Jean Guitton's claims to fame was that of being a great friend of Paul VI, about whom, with the Pope's permission, he produced a revealing book.[6] Jean Guitton had always been Catholic and always a seeker. He had mixed with Christians who were passionately concerned about truth and ill at ease in a certain troubled, even repressive environment of the post-modernist period, among them M. Pouget, a Vincentian, about whom he wrote two works.[7] Guitton was also an assiduous associate of Bergson[8] and took an interest in exegesis on the one hand and on the other mysticism. The genre in which he excelled, however, was somewhat surprisingly, given that he was a professor of philosophy at the Sorbonne, that of literary portraiture. In addition to portraits of M. Pouget and Paul VI, he also wrote ones of Père Lagrange[9] and Cardinal Saliège.[10] Marthe Robin, it would seem, was in good company. His literary merit earned him election to the Académie française where he represented Catholic thinking. Quite humorous in his way, he left a book in which he described his own funeral and people's reactions to it.[11]

Passionately interested in mysticism, albeit from a different perspective from his friend Couchoud, Jean Guitton proved to be no less drawn to the personality of Marthe Robin. Père Finet interested him too. This was how he described Père Finet's activity in Lyon when he was deputy director of Church schooling: 'Like Napoleon's minister, Daru, he found his equilibrium, joy and wellbeing in overwork. The more such characters are overloaded, the more available they become, knowing full well that, as the Chinese proverb puts it, in a barrel full of nuts there is still room for several measures of oil.'[12]

As a highly sensitive man, when Jean Guitton went to Marthe's house, he did not fail to be struck by the Galaure plateau scenery near the farm and by the farm itself. He waited like everyone else in the kitchen and depicted Marthe simply as, 'A woman having people into her home'.[13]

Guitton's conversations with her were concerned with what made up his world: the thinking in full ferment in the France of that time. He found Marthe to be well informed about it. They talked about Jean-Paul Sartre. Marthe might have been expected to assess him harshly, for if there was one man who counteracted all hope in life and humanity, and was greatly mistaken in his choices in support of communism, it was Sartre, but she did not. After 1968, however, she did make some gently ironic remarks about him: 'I knew that, during the May events, he had been treated like an old shack. Imagine, an old shack.' But she did not regard him as someone to be taken on. Her sights were set higher. She was interested in Simone de Beauvoir, his partner, about whom she asked for details that Guitton was at pains to give her. She did not believe she had done all her thinking yet: 'I am praying for her because she has not finished her work.'[14] She seemed to have less faith in the outcome of Merleau-Ponty's[15] work. She took an interest in the wives and daughters of well-known men: 'As one who knew what suffering was, she inquired after Anne de Gaulle, guessing that she was the General's sorrowful angel.[16] "They are together again," she said.'

Jean Guitton was particularly struck by the way Marthe viewed people. She had her opinions and, amongst friends, did not keep them to herself. At times they could be quite categorical. Of one statesman she said, 'I disapprove of him strongly', of one minister in office, 'Don't worry, he'll fade away', and of another, 'We've had enough of him'. But she did not belong to any party. Even whilst fully present to people and situations, she was elsewhere. Guitton put his finger on it when he wrote: 'In these judgements her perspective was that of eternity and not of the ephemeral. She situated responsibility within the mystery of evil, pain and redemption. But she did not talk about those unfathomable things as we might talk about them because we do not feel directly involved in the salvation of others and we can wash our hands of them. The salvation of others was part of her very existence. The conflict between good and evil was not for her, as it is for us, a spectacle. It was a battle in which she was fully exposed on the front line.'[17]

Marthe talked to this illustrious philosopher in a very straightforward way. When he asked her if she had any happy memories, she answered: 'Of course I have happy memories. I've always liked laughing. Even more so now. I love to laugh. You know how to tell stories. Tell me some stories to make me laugh.'[18] She told him about his amateur painting and advised Guitton, who was trying his hand at religious art, to make Christ young and not too bloody.

Marthe was very attentive to Guitton's 'ministry' at the Sorbonne and supported him in the steps towards his election to the Académie française. She attached great importance to having a Christian in such circles. She kept up with his publications: 'I have just had your speech about Pierre-Henri Simon[19] read to me. Oh! How good it is. There is everything in it. You go into everything. And there's some humour. It was a real treat for me.'

Guitton tried to get her to talk about her mystical life. She let out a few confidences but did not go into any great length. She agreed, as we have seen, to talk to him a little about her stigmatisation, visions and 'travels' when God transported her here and there. But she did not reveal too much. He also tried to induce her to talk about the future, about the Pentecost of love for which she was giving her life. He asked her how she saw it: 'Oh, not in any extraordinary form. I see it as peaceful, slow. I think it will come about gradually. I even think it has already started. As for the future, you know people credit me with lots of ideas about the future. I know nothing except one thing: the future is Jesus.'[20]

Jean Guitton, on the other hand, did talk about himself. He needed consoling after the death of his wife in 1974, whose final illness had been very painful, and felt understood by Marthe, who told him, 'I know what it is. When one is in this sort of state, one has to throw oneself on God with all one's might. It is more than just action. It is self-abandonment. And of course it is not always easy. You tell me that your wife cried out. But Christ did too. It is a case of throwing oneself into it. When Marie-Louise told you, "I can't pray any more", ah how I understand her! It is well said: one cannot pray then. But that is real prayer.'[21]

Thus Châteauneuf became a sort of rear base for Jean Guitton. He could lead his university life as a Christian, Academician and philosopher more easily because he had Marthe's affection and prayers, and the friendship of Père Finet and members of the Foyer at Châteauneuf, which he appreciated. He did not find in Marthe some sort of guinea pig, someone on whom he could test out his theories about mysticism. Like Couchoud, he found a friend and support.

IV. Marie-Ange Anstett

Marthe Robin had many female friends but we do not have all the documentation about them that we would like. Her relationships with Thérèse Cornille and Little Sister Magdeleine of Jesus will be referred to later. Alas, her relationship with Mother Lautru is not

documented, but I would at least like to recall her friendship with
a prison social worker, Marie-Ange Anstett.

Marie-Ange Anstett had started work – or rather her ministry
– in the prison social services in Baumettes in Marseille in 1949
and had already heard of Marthe at that time. She had been
encouraged to go and see her but hesitated because of 'what I had
been told about her total fast, her stigmata and her experience of
the Passion'. She only made up her mind when a vicar general
from Besançon, a friend of her family, Mgr Maurice Pourchet, the
future Bishop of Saint-Flour, told her he had just come back from
a retreat in Châteauneuf and that Marthe 'was quite someone'.
He 'was excited about Marthe Robin'. So, in 1951, she put her
name down for one of Père Finet's retreats, and she and Marthe
were instantly drawn to one another. Marthe adopted Marie-
Ange and her prisoners. To Marie-Ange she immediately became
'more a sister than a friend – and she still is – her gaiety and her
very youthful voice used to dispel all my worries'.[22] Marthe had
Père Finet write to her immediately after the retreat to say that
she would like to see her for longer. From then on, despite her
work commitments, from time to time Marie-Ange Anstett
would go and spend half a day at Châteauneuf: 'It was always a
great joy for me and I think my visits brought her pleasure.'

'Marthe's help and affection, her smile and her prayers were an
extraordinary grace in my life,' said Marie-Ange Anstett, looking
back over their relationship. Marthe's freshness and youthfulness
made an impression on her: 'She would talk with her girlish voice.
She did everything she could to cheer me up.' She remembered
'how happy I used to be on the train' on her way to see Marthe.
Some of their meetings were entertaining: 'We spent a morning in
the company of Marthe and Père Finet and it was quite funny.
Marthe reproached Père Finet for eating too many biscuits.'
Marthe did not talk all that much about things that were spiritual
in themselves, 'but I felt her to be spiritual'. She said little about
herself but did not hide what gave her joy: 'Marthe used to talk a

lot about the new Foyers that were being founded. That made her happy.' She was an example to her friend of how 'to accept suffering cheerfully'. Marie-Ange Anstett always found her 'welcoming and cheerful' despite what she had to endure.

The friendship between these two women was swiftly turned towards the prisoners for whom Marie-Ange had, in a way, given her life. 'What struck me,' she said of Marthe, 'was her love for the most disinherited and the most culpable.' Marthe had a certain fellow-feeling for prisoners. 'I can understand them well,' she said, 'because I'm in prison like them.' She also had a good understanding of Marie-Ange's ministry: 'When I talked to her I could have been talking to a colleague at the La Santé prison, she was so in touch with my work and my personal problems.'

So began a close collaboration between the two women to help prisoners. Most of them were poor. 'They need everything: clothing, food, cigarettes, books. I used to receive magnificent parcels for them and would invariably find in them the suit, pyjamas, pullover we'd been waiting for.' Marthe did not just want to help the prisoners anonymously. She was prepared to put her name to her interest in them. 'Marthe had given me permission,' her friend said, 'to give some of them her address, and they wrote and thanked her themselves.' Her concern extended to their families and she would receive their mothers and grandmothers, and even prisoners who had been released. So it was that General Vanuxem, a political prisoner after the Algiers putsch, rediscovered his faith after meeting her.

'Those condemned to death were most in torment. Marthe helped them especially through her prayer.' 'A certain Stanislas Juhant, a Yugoslav who was very isolated, told me, "I used to write to her as if she were my mother." Marthe accompanied him right up to the end. He certainly appreciated her letters ... and her cigarettes.' Marthe also concerned herself with Buffet and Bontemps, the last two men sentenced to death and actually executed in France. Contrary to what is often written, Marthe did not, however, have any contact with Jacques Fesch.[23] She did not know about him while he was alive. It was only after his death that Marie-Ange Anstett told her about him and gave her a souvenir picture.

Support for prisoners was important in Marthe's life but it was bound up with a great friendship.

V. Jacques Lebreton

Her relationship with Jacques Lebreton, whose real name was actually Jacques Beaugé, was quite different.

During the Second World War he had lost his eyes and hands in a grenade explosion. As an act of revolt he joined the Communist Party but then underwent a spiritual evolution. In his bestseller, *Sans Yeux et Sans Mains*,[24] he wrote about his religious conversion and mentioned Marthe as the person to whom he largely owed it. After the book was published he met her and they talked about it. He had tried to be discreet but Marthe felt he had not been discreet enough. 'You understand,' she said to him, 'that I cannot promote your book, but it did interest me and I would have liked to.'

As the conversation went on Marthe suddenly started to speak again and asked Père Finet: 'And what are we going to do with the tall one there?' – 'Who are you talking about?' asked Jacques Beaugé – 'You.'

She asked him about his life: 'Are you married? Do you have children?' She made no reference to his membership of the Communist Party. He was surprised: 'So what am I to do about the Party?' 'Her response seemed to me a marvel of humility, a marvel of submission to the Church. Turning to Père Finet, she asked him: "What do you think, Father?" In her simple words, a very brief conversation, I sensed all the humility of her position, the extreme respect she had for the Church.'

Another conversation with Jacques Beaugé was about another book: 'I had given it a title which my editor did not like. He found it too shocking and I would have been very happy for Marthe to suggest another. So I mentioned it to her and waited for her response. But it came in the form of a question, "If your editor isn't happy with your title, what alternative would you suggest?" – "I would have: *Unless a Wheat Grain ...*" Marthe responded in a voice in which I could discern a smile: "Oh! You know, people will take that for an agricultural treatise!" "I might well have gone for *Light in my Darkness*," I answered, "but it's already been used for a biography of Miss Helen Keller." – "Shame," she replied. "That would have been good." Then she added: "So what title have you gone for?" Embarrassed, I replied: "Oh! Well, I called it: *Life's Enough to Knacker You.*" Marthe burst out laughing: "Well, that's certainly true. Life's enough to kill you off." Oh! That laugh of Marthe's.'

'You know, I'm very fond of you!' she informed him affectionately on another occasion.

⁂

When we consider Marthe's friendships we are entering the delicate domain of love. We may feel we are on the fringes of something very beautiful but it remains nonetheless quite private. We know very little; we can sense more. The historian can only pause for a while before the mystery.

NOTES

1. Jean Guitton, *Portrait de Marthe Robin* (A Portrait of Marthe Robin), op. cit. pp. 23–39. The quotations not drawn explicitly from this book are taken from the Châteauneuf Archives.
2. One who has a prestigious professional qualification for teachers in France.
3. He had summed up his thinking on Jesus in his work *Le Dieu Jésus* (The God Jesus), Paris: Gallimard, 1951. His memoirs were published after his death by Robert De Montesquiou under the title *Les Pas Effacés* (Insignificant Steps).
4. Wit.
5. Jean Guitton, *Portrait de Marthe Robin* (A portrait of Marthe Robin), op. cit.

6. Jean Guitton, *Dialogues avec Paul VI* (Dialogues with Paul VI), Paris: F.-X. de Guibert, 2001.

7. Jean Guitton, *Dialogues avec Monsieur Pouget* (Dialogues with M. Pouget), Paris: Grasset, republished 1999; *Portrait de Monsieur Pouget* (A Portrait of M. Pouget), Paris: Gallimard, 1942.

8. Henri-Louis Bergson: A major French philosopher (1859–1941) whose mother was English. At the beginning of the twentieth century at the Collège de France in Paris, he developed a philosophy which contradicted the then prevalent Kantism and Positivism and was open to the supernatural.

9. Jean Guitton, *Portrait du Père Lagrange* (A Portrait of Père Lagrange), Paris: R. Laffont, 1992.

10. Jean Guitton, *Cardinal Saliège*, Paris: Grasset, 1957.

11. *Mon testament philosophique* (My Philosophical Testament), Paris: Presses de la Renaissance, 1997. Its complete bibliography runs to ninety titles.

12. Jean Guitton, *Portrait de Marthe Robin* (A portrait of Marthe Robin), op. cit., p. 51.

13. Ibid. p. 69.

14. Ibid. p. 83.

15. Maurice Merleau-Ponty (1908–1961): French phenomenological philosopher.

16. General and Mme De Gaulle had a little daughter with Down's syndrome, Anne, whom they cared for very lovingly. When she died they set up a foundation for disabled children.

17. Ibid., pp. 83–84.

18. Ibid., p. 92.

19. Pierre-Henri Simon (1903–1972): French intellectual, literary historian, essayist, novelist, poet and literary critic.

20. Ibid., p. 107.

21. Ibid., p. 226.

22. *Post mortem* in some way because this testimony was written after Marthe's death.

23. Jacques Fesch (1930–1967): A young man who killed a policeman, was sentenced to death and executed. In prison he underwent a conversion.

24. Paris: Casterman, 1967 (Without eyes or hands).

CHAPTER 14

For the Renewal of the Church

The years 1948–1978 saw considerable developments in the Catholic Church, which was obliged to adopt new positions in relation to the contemporary world. Europe, and France in particular, were at the heart of this process, which was in some respects positive but in others more painful. As a daughter of the Church, Marthe was keen that faith should be accessible to all. All through her childhood until the Second World War she had known anticlerical pressure in Châteauneuf itself. She was therefore eager for announcement of the faith to be renewed but knew that it necessarily entailed a rejuvenation of the Church. For this she was ready to strive with all her heart. She spoke lovingly of the Church. 'Beyond the actual words,' one visitor indicated, 'my meeting made me aware of the joy Marthe felt when she talked about the Church and awakened love of the Church in her visitor.'

I. Marthe Robin and the Church's major problems from 1948 until the Second Vatican Council

The period we have now come to is made up of very different elements which should be examined separately.

Challenges to the Church in the aftermath of the war

In the post-war period, Catholicism in general and French Catholicism in particular formed an imposing entity. There were plenty of priests and male and female religious, and practice had increased. For practically every one of France's 38,000 villages there was a priest, unless it was absolutely minute. The contemplative life was flourishing with 120 Carmelite houses and 100 Benedictine monasteries, and all of them had people seeking entry. France was still sending missionaries all over the world. However, society had been very shaken up by the conflict. New questions were arising and fresh ideologies such as Marxism and Existentialism were surfacing and exerting a corrupting influence. France was also making a considerable effort to improve itself socially and politically. The birth rate rose again very rapidly. Thanks to everyone's hard work there was substantial economic growth. Economically, the period we are looking at was a 'Glorious Thirty Years', a time when the growth rate was generally between four and six per cent a year. France suddenly became a rich country and its standard of living improved considerably. That too could be corrupting from a faith point of view. People could take advantage of it to resort to egoism, pleasure and indulgence. Faith and the Christian way of life were thus under threat from all sides.

Marthe was one of the first to recognise that if Catholicism stood by and did nothing, it would be unable to meet challenges too great for the existing ecclesiastical system. It must therefore be made to evolve and move towards a different form of Church. But how?

Marthe's thinking was based on a very positive vision of Christian life. What was a Christian? Someone who had been called to be holy. A Christian should have no lesser ambition than sanctity. Unless we wished to damn ourselves, we were all called to see God. And in order to see God we must be absolutely pure, which is to say holy. Marthe's thinking revealed itself particularly when she talked about purgatory, which she called 'the purificator', the place in which one became holy if one had not been holy on this earth. If, then, that was our destiny, why not start at once? Why miss out on life by leading a mediocre and ideal-less existence down here?

By affirming this, however, Marthe was in tension with a whole section of current doctrine. Often it was claimed that a Christian must first earn his or her salvation, and that this consisted of avoiding hell, which was in itself an achievement! Holiness was reserved for the experts who were usually religious. For the average Christian a life of moral integrity, faithful prayer and observance of liturgical law was enough. This vision was reflected in a number of Catechisms of the time. It was also shared by virtually all the Protestant world. A much-debated question before the Second World War was whether all Christians were called to a truly mystical life, a life of contemplation of God. There were those authors who said no. Sanctity was only for some.

Marthe, as has been seen, thought exactly the opposite. In line with Saint Francis de Sales, the spirituality of the Sacred Heart and especially with Thérèse of the Child Jesus, she wanted to make holiness accessible to all. She was also in consonance with a whole movement, to which, together with Père Garrigou-Lagrange, Père Finet had belonged even before he met her. Marthe stated loudly and clearly that Baptism was a sacrament, the aim of which was nothing less than holiness.

The implications of this stance were considerable. Firstly, when life is directed at sanctity, Jesus is present and active in the heart of the person seeking him. And if he is active, he cannot remain hidden: 'You do not light a candle in order to hide it under a bushel.'[1] This meant that all Christians must make Jesus manifest in their daily life, work and social activities, which is to say that all must evangelise. Hitherto, evangelisation had been the work of experts: priests, religious and members of Catholic action groups. People were still reliant on a Christian order in which roles were very carefully divided up. Precisely, however, because people were emerging from this Christian world, the Church must function differently. All the baptised, called as they were to holiness, must evangelise just as the clergy must. It should be pointed out that this meant a Copernican change in prevailing thought. Many were not yet ready for it. Respectable, conservative religious would even see Marthe's position as a shocking doctrinal deviation.

If it was true – and it is true – Christian thinking would have to be completely revised and there would be inevitable repercussions at the level of Church organisation itself. The first requirement was to re-evaluate the role of the sacrament of Baptism and of what are known as the sacraments of initiation. Without formulating a theory, this was something Marthe preached throughout her life. Next, the relationship between priests and lay people would have to be rethought. The priesthood would have to revert to what it was at its most profound: the celebration of the sacraments, the manifestation of divine paternity and of the goodness of God. It should not in any way be conceived as mastery over the laity within the framework of a pyramidal view of society. Marthe was thus abandoning an exclusively hierarchical conception of the Church in favour of a much wider vision of the Church, as the Mystical Body of Christ, for example, which was how Pope Pius XII defined it.

We should note that there was nothing progressive about this. There was in fact a section of the European Church inclined to think that the Church should bow to the world, adopt society's values as they arose and abandon positions that were too demanding. This was the approach of priests and religious leaders influenced by Hegelianism and Marxism but of others too, who accepted the ideology of progress driven by liberal capitalism. Marthe had no desire for the salt of the earth to lose its savour, but felt for that very reason that it would be good to look into its chemical properties and the state of the saltcellar.

The challenge was enormous: the Church must be transformed. But it was not going to be transformed from outside by violent means. It must be conquered gently, from within, by love. Then people would let it happen, move forward and integrate progress. It was this transformation by love that Marthe always advocated.

The Foyers as instruments of innovation

The Foyers of Charity were a part of this. The Foyers preached a God of love and not (to use Père Finet's expression) a vulture God. They called upon people to strive for sanctity. The presence of lay people and priests working together was a demonstration of how the priesthood and the laity could evangelise closely together. It is not possible to evaluate the influence of the Foyers on a Christian elite but it has probably been enormous. Now, at the beginning of the twenty-first century, it is rare to find a committed Christian in France who does not know the Foyers.

They were set up moreover as instruments of innovation. The liturgy played an active part; the faithful sang. Well before the Second Vatican Council, Père Finet was one of the very first French priests to celebrate Mass facing the people. In the Foyer chapel he had the tabernacle placed to the left of the altar, and on the right a form of altar with the Bible on it. By this means he wanted to show the importance of the Word of God, which needed emphasising in the Catholicism of the day. In so doing he aligned himself with a movement that Mgr Pic had supported in the diocese of Valence. All this was done without criticising the Church in any way but as a demonstration of a desire for renewal. Little by little the Foyers prepared people's minds for the reforms of Vatican II.

Another line of approach was to give support to Church leaders by encouraging and, when necessary, enlightening them. Reference will be made later to Marthe's role in relation to bishops and priests. Suffice it here to emphasise that she prayed especially for the popes. Marthe Robin had a great love for Pius XII. In 1939, at the time of the conclave, she remarked quite suddenly, 'That's it. He's elected'. She felt particularly at one with him. 'He is so transparent,' she told Jean Guitton. 'He is already everything.' 'If he had died, I would have died with him,' she said of his serious illness in 1954. No doubt she offered her suffering and possibly even her life for him at that point. At the onset of his illness she said, 'He will not die this time. He hasn't finished his mission.' The Pope had had a terrible cough. When he began to get better, Marthe had a cough for two weeks.

Pius XII knew about her not only through Père Garrigou-Lagrange but also through Mgr Pic. The Pope had asked the latter to put down in writing what he had told him about her.

Another part of the process was the founding of new religious groups. The Catholic Church has always renewed itself through communities. A man like Saint Francis of Assisi, for example, had an original experience of God. Companions joined him and had the same experience. A religious order is then founded, which changes something about the face of the Church and often society itself. This process did not stop in the twentieth century – far from it. In totally different ways, men and women had powerful experiences in various places, and new and often very original communities sprang up. It is interesting that several of these founders and foundresses went to see Marthe Robin, who was like a compass, a model and an intercessor for them. Marthe thus found herself in touch with some of those representing what was most elevated in ideals and holiness in post-war French Catholicism, and was to draw some of her greatest friendships from among them.

Marthe's encouragement of the founders of new religious families
The friendship with Little Sister Magdeleine of Jesus which had begun on 25 February 1943 continued throughout their lives. Little Sister Magdeleine (1898–1989), foundress of the Little Sisters of Jesus, was one of the great witnesses to the Christian message of the twentieth century. Her life was an adventure story in itself. After stepping down from the leadership of her Sisters, at enormous risk she undertook a series of journeys behind the Iron

Curtain, even venturing as far as Communist China to support Christians there. Marthe had asked her to look upon her as a daughter, and called her 'Mother'. That did not prevent Little Sister Magdeleine from seeking her advice. The foundress was driving herself too hard and overreaching her strength, and so asked Marthe one day whether she should be a little more moderate or whether she should continue her 'folly'. Marthe began by laughing 'with that laugh that was so childlike and so human that it made her seem just like anyone else and prevented you from being too upset by all that you guessed was going on in her … Then she added cheerily, "Of course you must carry on. When you're mad you have to do mad things. If you stopped doing mad things you would no longer be mad. Even when you can do no more, you always have the energy of God. He is with you. He is in you."'

Thus encouraged, Little Sister Magdeleine went on with her ministry. Marthe took a close interest in the spread of the fraternities and offered her suffering for them. Seeing Little Sister Magdeleine was 'one of the nicest gifts' anyone could give her. 'It's true that we both love each other very much,' the Little Sister acknowledged. She continued to ask Marthe's opinion about sensitive matters: 'She has an answer for everything, a joyful answer showing astonishing good sense.' She remarked on how Marthe did not seem to age with the passage of time and how her incredible memory remained intact: 'She remembers everything I've told her over the last forty years.'

Marthe's affectionate relations with Thérèse Cornille (1917–1989) were of the same order. From a working-class family in the North, Thérèse had left school at eleven and found in the JOCF (Jeunesse ouvrière chrétienne féminine)[2] something to which she could devote herself. She went on to found the Claire Amitié homes for young women in need. Her work spread across France, Africa and as far as the Far East. Thérèse Cornille met Marthe for the first time in 1948 and it was, she said, a source of 'happiness' for her. 'Thérèse, Jesus wants these homes,' Marthe had told her. 'He wants to do much good in them. Come back and see me often.' Thérèse did not fail to do so and stated that each time she did 'a peace and joy came into me'. Marthe received her kindly and with affection, talked to her with emotion about young women in distress, but also about the seasons and about nature: 'You felt she was fully integrated at the heart of the world through the interest she took in each person and what was going on in their lives.' Thérèse Cornille was moved to find that 'Marthe was impassioned by divine love. When we were with her we felt the presence of Jesus and Mary in her very powerfully'. As each of the various homes opened, their leaders and Thérèse came to commit them to Marthe: 'The leaders too were given a warm welcome. She always asked each one's forename so that she could commit it to memory.' Marthe took a particular interest in the Claire Amitié foundation in Cambodia, and was broken-hearted at the genocide perpetrated by the Khmer Rouge when Claire Amitié members who had retreated to Europe told her about it. This friendship lasted throughout Marthe's life. 'We are greatly indebted to her,' said Thérèse Cornille, 'for her wise and valuable counsel over the forty years of our Claire Amitié homes' existence.'

With the Dominican, Père Epagneul, Marthe talked about the Frères missionaires des compagnes. She had encouraged him to found them and was later very positive in what she had to say about them. During this period of her life, among the people visiting her and for whom she prayed, was another friend, Sister Marie (Odile Dupont-Caillard, 1922–1999), foundress of the Sisters and Brothers of Bethlehem, who in 1950 had heard a call to found a new contemplative family in the Church. After much difficulty, Sister Marie managed to begin her community. By 2005 it had some thirty women's monasteries and four men's houses. Marthe also received Père Voillaume (1905–2003), who founded the Little Brothers of Jesus in the spirit of Charles de Foucauld;

Père Perrin, a blind Dominican (1905–2002) who founded the Caritas Christi Secular Institute; and Père Henri Caffarel (1903–1996), founder of the Equipes Notre-Dame, which spread throughout the world, and of the Troussures house of prayer.

They were all part of a creative impetus that was to continue in various ways after the Second Vatican Council.

II. The Second Vatican Council and its consequences

On the election of John XXIII Marthe was delighted. At the time of the conclave Père Finet had put forward Mgr Montini, Archbishop of Milan's name. 'No! Afterwards,' she responded. Then when Père Finet suggested another name Marthe replied, 'You think so, Father? I'm for Cardinal Roncalli,' which meant that she was later able to say, 'Mine got through'.

When the Second Vatican Council opened Marthe prayed much for it. She thought it important for the Church, had the decrees read out to her and was wholeheartedly behind the direction of its thinking. The Council marked a turning point in the Church's attitude to the contemporary world, initiating a dialogue with modern society. In order to be in a better position to evangelise, it began transforming not what lay at its heart, but some of its forms. It insisted on the sanctity of every Christian. *Lumen gentium*, the dogmatic constitution on the Church, solemnly proclaimed the principle that every baptised person was called to holiness. It presented the Church as the body of Christ before it broached its hierarchical constitution. It positioned lay people very positively within that constitution and affirmed their role in evangelisation. The shared priesthood of the faithful and the clergy, whilst safely preserving the ministerial priesthood, was one of Marthe's great intuitions. 'For Marthe the shared priesthood was one of the most important revelations of the Second Vatican Council, affording each individual, be they layperson or priest, a specific but complementary mission: "Not one without the other but always one with the other, and not one the same as the other!'" The liturgy was also presented in a manner of which Marthe could approve. The Council thus moved beyond the right-left divide which dominated part of social and even ecclesial life in Europe. It defined the position of the Church in a new world to which Christ must be announced. One priest said of Marthe: 'She talked about the Second Vatican Council to me in a way that made it possible to imagine all the hope she had vested in this event in the Church, before it had even been announced and convoked.' Beyond the difficulties, she thought and said, 'We are moving towards a Springtime in the Church'.

Unfortunately, the Council was also accompanied by extensive media hype. 'Progressive' groups were practically the only ones represented even in the Catholic media and they gave the Council a revolutionary image which was not true to the documents actually voted for. There was a tendency to give the impression that the Church was rejecting its past and colluding with what was most questionable about the modern world. Some bishops and priests felt destabilised and no longer knew where they stood. Amidst the universal chatter Marthe adopted a position of discretion. Only rarely did she comment. By all that she was, she constantly reaffirmed her faith in and her fidelity to the Church and did not enter into the wave of criticism unleashed both from left and right.

Towards the end of Vatican II, Marthe and Père Finet prayed for a special intention which she confided to a priest friend: 'The Lord would like his Mother to be appointed Mother of the Church so we are going to pray together that she will be.' Why was this? Marthe was well aware that the aftermath of the Council would not be easy. She suspected the situation could only develop positively with the special intervention of the Virgin Mary, with her particular protection. The Church must be entrusted to her. Pope Paul VI put forward a proposal to that effect. It was rejected. Possibly Marthe let the Pope know that this was something God wanted. Be that as it may, at the closing session of the Council, Paul VI made the proclamation – against the advice of his counsellors.

Marthe was very aware of the fight the Church would have to face after the Council. She did not share the optimistic predictions of those who believed that if the Church gave way over doctrine, the world would respond appropriately. She believed it would be necessary energetically to reaffirm the faith. In 1964, when Jean Guitton said to her that the Church was coming down a peg, she answered him: 'You're not right to talk about coming down a peg. I say several pegs. They're not making the Church conform to Jesus, but to their Jesus who is a human Jesus, the sort they can envisage. But Jesus isn't easy-going … Oh! Perhaps after the Council it is important for the Pope to pick up on everything that is fundamental truth. It will reassure the faithful! There seems to be a universal debasement of faith. It is faith in the world, not faith in God, in the transcendent. And as to suffering, one can't just act.[3] It is there. And sin too!' 'It's too human. It's man. They will not gain anything by it.'

During the post-conciliar period she supported the Pope with her prayer. 'I think he'll go on for a long time,' she told Guitton, 'because I'm not seeing anyone else.' After the encyclical *Humanae Vitae* she said to him: 'He has been firm on the question of marriage and he had to be because no one knew what to think anymore and people were turning to him. I know many priests will not approve of it.' She was very struck by the breadth of Paul VI's vision and said to Thérèse Cornille: 'This pope lives from a planetary perspective. We must pray much for him.'

In the difficult years from about 1965 to the end of the 1970s, Châteauneuf became a place of refuge for many. The faithful, priests and sometimes even bishops, who no longer knew what to think, found peace and reassurance there. Marthe was not well regarded in 'advanced' circles, however. She carried in her prayer the great concerns of the Church, especially the priesthood, which was under considerable attack at the time: 'One day we mentioned the priests – many of them around 1972 to 1975 – who were leaving their ministry. Marthe cried out and started to weep in long sobs. I thought again of the prophets and their lamentations, of Jesus' weeping over Jerusalem. I was used to hearing plenty of people around me remarking about the crisis in the priesthood, but I had never seen anyone weep over this tragedy in the Church. She added, "What they lack is a real family life."'[4]

Support for the new communities

Astonishingly, in the midst of all the post-conciliar difficulties a phenomenon of religious renewal emerged in Europe. New movements were seen to appear, new communities presenting the Catholic faith in a way that was often fresh, original and adapted to different times. These communities really lived out the spirit of the Council. They were a sign that the Christian life was viable in a new age, that Catholicism was not dead, that it could constantly renew itself, and that its life plan was still relevant today.

Some of these movements or communities were not born in France. The Focolari movement began in Italy but Marthe Robin was asked to pray for it. Two of the foundresses, Chiara Lubich's first companions, Gabriella de Luca and Aletta Salizzoni, came to see her in 1962 or 1963: 'It was a very powerful experience and at the end of it Marthe Robin concluded, "I feel like Saint John the Baptist preparing the way of the Lord, and I see your Work as being like Mary. It is Mary." We felt we were dealing with a saint, a great saint, because we experienced splendid fruits in our souls.'[5]

The Charismatic Renewal movement was born in the United States where it began to be taken up by Catholics in 1967. It became known in France from 1970 onwards. Being Protestant in origin and adopting unusual forms of prayer, it was the object of reserve and suspicion. When, however, a young French Dominican, Albert de Monléon, who was the first person to write about it in France, sought out Marthe Robin, she gave him a positive welcome and encouraged him. A few years later there were several hundred Renewal prayer groups in France. 'The future of the Church lies in prayer groups,' Marthe maintained and urged Christians more and more frequently to avoid being on their own by joining them.

The arrival of the Charismatic Renewal movement in France combined with the establishment of new communities, some of which (nearly forty or so) were within its fold but others (about eighty) belonged to other spiritual traditions. French Catholicism, which had been thought to be dying, found itself suddenly partially renewed, and a look at the history of the new communities will show that Marthe and the Foyers' contribution to this renewal was considerable.

In the first place, the Foyers of Charity set an example. They reflected a vision of Christianity that was positive, in conformity with the Council and bound by the tradition of the Church, loving the world without being a slave to it. A large number of founders and members of the new communities came to the Foyers on retreat. Sometimes they were converted. By and large they adopted the theology taught there. On one specific point, the relationship with the Virgin Mary, the impact of the Foyers on many is clear, particularly in the way of consecration to Jesus through Mary. It would not be exaggerating to say that Marian devotion was renewed in France largely through the new communities, and that they owed that devotion first to the Foyers. The Foyers also showed that it was possible to have priests, religious and secular, living and working together with consecrated men and women, an intuition which was to be taken up by some of the new communities.

In the second place, Marthe Robin met several founders and foundresses of new communities. The extent of her influence varied but among those with which she found herself in contact in this way were the Emmanuel community, the community of the

Beatitudes, the Saint-Jean community and Jean Vanier's l'Arche.[6] After her death, other communities, such as le Verbe de Vie, were to place themselves under her protection. Not surprisingly, she was very well known in these circles.[7] It would probably take an entire book to cover the full range of Marthe's impact on them. Suffice it here to include a few notes.

The Emmanuel community is now the most important charismatic community in the world. Recognised by pontifical law, it is in seventy countries. It was founded in Paris in 1972 by Pierre Goursat (1914–1991) and Martine Laffitte (now Catta) under the influence of the Charismatic Renewal movement. Pierre Goursat had difficulty accepting the leadership of the community. An extremely humble man, he felt uncomfortable about assuming a position of such responsibility, and he and his entourage went through a difficult period. He went to see Marthe Robin: 'You have been put there. Stay there,' she told him, 'and when they don't want you anymore, they'll let you know.' Her words reassured Pierre completely. He took charge of the expansion of the community and became a remarkable leader. Marthe also intervened in another set of circumstances. Since 1975 the Emmanuel community had been rediscovering the grace of the Heart of Jesus at Paray-le-Monial, where Christ appeared to Saint Marguerite Marie and revealed to her the secrets of his love. During one of their meetings, Pierre Goursat told Marthe that Paray was going to become the centre for Emmanuel. 'Rather call it the heart,' declared Marthe. Her words were subsequently shown to be very meaningful.[8] Marthe also influenced several of the first members of the community. It was at Châteauneuf-de-Galaure that Françou Malcor, one of the first five members, came to realise how much she needed community life. Claude and Danielle Proux, the Emmanuel community's first married couple, were in touch with Marthe and wondering whether to join one of the Foyers. Marthe was not against it. Once they realised they belonged in the Emmanuel community, however, Marthe became much less direct in her guidance, telling them that they must now address any questions they had to their leaders. But she kept in touch with them through her intercession. 'I shall pray that the Emmanuel community will evangelise with joy,' she told them.

The community of the Beatitudes, which is also now recognised as one of pontifical right and has spread throughout the world, is one of the most original creations of recent years. It owes its beginnings to a Protestant Charismatic Renewal group led by Pastor Gérard Croissant who, a short while previous had discovered the real presence of Christ in the host and the Virgin Mary. He was considering entering the Catholic Church but hesitated, not wanting to cause a scandal. He went to see Marthe, who assured him, 'There will be no scandal, I promise you. There will be no scandal. The time has come.' Then she explained that she had previously received some pastors in her room who wanted to become Catholics, among them Louis Dallière.[9] 'She had prevented them from doing so then, even though they had recited the Rosary with her. She had stopped them because the time was not yet right. But now it should be done. It was in fact a duty. She interrupted my protestation – or comment – abruptly: "Just listen! Louis Dallière's sister was a Protestant. She married the philosopher Gabriel Marcel who was a Jew and both of them became Catholics." Then she fell silent. For me this alliance expressed the three identities in my life, Jewish, Protestant and Catholic, and a whole vision of ecumenism.'[10]

Marthe's prediction was to come true. Gérard Croissant (now Brother Ephraïm) and his companions became Catholics without causing a scandal. Out of that sprang a community which remained very attached to Marthe's memory. By 2006 it had over fifty houses in five continents.

The Saint-Jean community began in 1975. The Dominican, Père Marie-Dominique Philippe, professor at the University of Freiburg (in Switzerland), used to preach retreats in the Foyers of Charity where he was greatly appreciated, and would go to see

Marthe and talk to her in great confidence. Several of his students wanted to be priests but, with the current crisis in the Church, did not know where to go. They asked Père Philippe to help them find direction. He hesitated and referred the question to Marthe. 'If I did it,' he would later confide, 'it was solely because Marthe assured me that I must, that it was God's work – I would never otherwise have embarked on such a venture at over sixty. I can still remember her irrevocable words at a crucial time in my apostolic work: "It is of the Holy Spirit. You must do it."'[11] Père Marie-Dominique Philippe also drew inspiration for his teaching from the manner in which Marthe lived out 'the three wisdoms': philosophical, theological and mystical.[12] Today the Saint-Jean community comprises not only a male branch with fifty-five priories but also two female branches with seventeen contemplative and fifteen active priories with several hundred members.

Marthe Robin cared greatly for people with disabilities. Her own life brought her close to them. Jean Vanier, founder of the l'Arche[13] community that welcomes them, met Marthe Robin for the first time in 1976. Marthe already knew and liked some of the l'Arche assistants and she was also very fond of the Dominican, Père Thomas Philippe,[14] because of his love for the very poorest. 'From that first meeting and those that followed,' said Jean Vanier, 'it was clear that Marthe had a great affection for l'Arche. She had great concern for the smallest, the most disabled. She had an understanding of l'Arche's vocation in the Church and in the world, and of the vocation of people with disabilities. She was well aware of the potency of suffering and of humility ... I felt that Marthe held our various communities in her prayer, especially the ones in the Third World. She followed their growth closely and I am sure that it was her prayer that bore us along and still does so today.'[15] L'Arche now has a hundred or so communities and several hundred assistants.

Manifestly Marthe Robin became very involved in everything that was on the move in the Church. She founded only the Foyers of Charity – and still did not like the expression 'foundress' – but during her lifetime she supported over twenty new communities in one way or another, sometimes decisively, and became the protectress of many others. She did not, however, lose sight of the diocesan life of the Church. She also did her best to help the bishops and priests who came to see her.

III. Marthe Robin, bishops, priests and religious

Marthe received visits from a considerable number of clergy and religious. She always welcomed them with respect but without affectation and told them frankly what she thought. Marthe's words had an effect on many of them and through them touched a multitude of people.

In 1980, a teacher was waiting in Marthe's kitchen. On his right was a priest reading his breviary. The man was visibly agitated, worried. His face was sad and furrowed. Had discretion not prevented it, the teacher would have tried to say something to console him. When his turn came, the sad priest entered Marthe's room. He stayed there for forty-five minutes. When he came out again, the teacher was astonished when he saw him framed in the doorway. It was as if he were ten years younger. He passed jauntily through the kitchen and went off happily. It was like witnessing a resurrection. The teacher happened to find out afterwards that the man in question was a bishop. By this sort of means Marthe's ministry reached more than one pastor.

We know the names of nearly sixty bishops and cardinals who came to see Marthe.[16] Other bishops used to write to her or had letters written to her, such as Mgr Marty, the future Cardinal Archbishop of Paris, who commended his episcopacy to her.

Marthe was first in touch with successive bishops of Valence. Mgr Pic (1932–1951) loved and supported her. His successor, Mgr Urtasun (1952–1955) was initially more reticent. Mgr Pic had given his backing to less worthy mystics than Marthe and she suffered as a result. After meeting her, however, Mgr Urtasun

changed his mind and gave her his support. After Mgr
Vignancour (1957–1966), who was a friend of the Foyer, visited
Marthe often and had one of his nieces at the girls' school, Mgr
de Cambourg (1966–1977) remained very reserved. Mgr
Marchand (1978–2003) by contrast understood Marthe and the
Foyers and proved his closeness to them during the crisis of
1978–1983, which will be discussed later. It was he who initiated
and supported Marthe's cause for beatification. Certainly Marthe
prayed much for her successive bishops and her diocese. She was
a citizen of the world but at the same time belonged very
specifically to Drôme and to the diocese of Valence, carrying
within her something of the place where she was born.

The range of bishops (both geographical in that they
represented nearly thirty countries and in terms of spiritual
sensitivity) who came to see Marthe is worth noting. Marthe was a
friend of Mgr Ancel, Superior General of the Prado Institute and
Auxiliary Bishop of Lyon, who entered into a dialogue with
Marxism. He still remained a friend of Père Finet too. Marthe also
supported Mgr Delaporte, Archbishop of Cambrai, who
represented a 'wheeling flank' of the Church in France when other
bishops like Mgr Chabbert or Mgr Elchinger had a very different
approach to its problems. Marthe never meddled in the
government of dioceses but she did support individuals. So it was
that Marthe's friendship with Mgr Elchinger, Bishop of Strasbourg,
whom she had known since 1942, never faltered. Marthe gave him
advice about the formation of priests and prayed for him. This was
his testimony: 'I needed spiritual help from Marthe and I received
it in abundance both in my personal life and in my responsibility as
an educator of priests and prospective priests.'

Marthe had a profound understanding of the priesthood
thanks in good measure to her Eucharistic life and sense of
Church. She offered her life particularly for the sanctity of
priests, knowing how absolutely necessary it was. 'I think what
gave rise to my questioning,' said one of her visitors at the time

of Vatican II, 'was something Marthe said: "Lay people need priests, more and more priests, and priests that are more holy."' 'The priest is always a multiplier,' she maintained. 'As soon as he stops being a multiplier of good, he becomes a multiplier of evil.' That was why she was concerned that priests should be well formed. She was sceptical about the rush to recruit after the First World War. 'Under the pretext that the war had killed quite a number of priests,' she said to Père Beton, 'don't you think they were a little too quick to replace them? No doubt the seminarians admitted to the priesthood were adequately instructed but sometimes the primary requisites for ordination to the priesthood were forgotten: balance, judgement and wisdom.' She was no more reassured by the crisis in the seminaries that followed Vatican II. But she did know plenty of good and holy priests.

Indeed, Marthe had an experience of the priesthood of a kind that few others had. It is no exaggeration to say that in the course of her lifetime she was in contact with several hundred priests.[17] Usually they came to see Marthe whilst on retreat. They ranged from holy priests asking for prayer for their ministry, to those feeling tempted to leave the Church, with every conceivable circumstance in between. Some were assistant country clergy; others were in high profile positions. Many needed spiritual support, others advice, and yet others compassion. Some of their lives were changed through contact with Marthe. As one priest said, 'She had such a respectful understanding of the priesthood and one which was at the same time so profoundly inspired from within that she obliged us to become a little more priestly.'

She was extremely discreet in her dealings with priests and they were on the whole discreet in what they had to say about her. Often conversations were about private matters that could not be related. We do know, however, that her concern for them extended to their physical welfare: 'Monsieur l'Abbé, are you eating enough? ... And are you taking enough time for sleep?' she asked one of them. If necessary she would confront them with their shortcomings. 'You're not praying enough,' she informed another. It was not unheard of for her to tell them what they were being called to do. One Dominican said to her that he felt ill and that God was probably going to call him home to him. 'No, Father,' she responded bluntly, 'the Lord wants you to preach retreats.' 'She uttered this sentence – with such energy in her voice, such strength, such assurance that I was taken aback.' Sure enough, he recovered and preached no less than fifty retreats between 1977 and 1985. One priest testified: 'My meetings with her would have something disconcerting, unexpected about them at the time, sometimes even disappointing. We would talk so much quite spontaneously about one thing or another. But in the days that followed, especially during prayer time many obscurities would vanish and in their place [would be] the light of faith in my heart and mind. It reminded me of what the Emmaus disciples must have received on Easter evening.'

After the Council in particular, Marthe Robin suffered greatly when many priests left their ministry. But she remained very specially and in some cases commendably charitable towards them. 'For the Blessed Virgin,' she said, 'there are no fallen priests. There are only wounded priests ... The Blessed Virgin loves priests so much. Jesus loves them like the apple of his eye. The Blessed Virgin loves them in the same way: like the apple of her son's eye, especially wounded priests. They have such a need to feel loved! There are those who harm themselves when they come to midlife lust at around forty-five, because they feel the lack of love. All bishops should be fathers to their priests, be primarily fathers to their priests.'

Similarly, Marthe received many religious: at least fifteen Father Abbots and an incalculable number of priors, provincials, religious leaders, etc. She had great respect for the distinctive character of the religious life, and particularly for the vow of obedience. She was very careful not to take the place of their superiors and exercise some sort of alternative authority. Her desire to keep her proper place in this respect was strong.

There was a radical quality to the religious life and Marthe did not fail, when necessary, to remind people of this fact. When religious Sisters wrote to her about *tourière* Sisters,[18] asking about relationship difficulties, she sent the answer back: 'As for the question of your *tourière* Sisters, Mlle Marthe Robin says to tell you that if you cannot live in fellowship and love one another, where are people supposed to go to find community?[19] It is not a case of keeping them separate but [of] helping them to exercise Christ's charity towards one another and their neighbours.' And she added quite forcefully: 'Since you ask Mlle Marthe Robin's advice, she takes the liberty of saying that you should have much greater detachment, be prepared for greater renunciation and have a more spiritual attitude than any of you have. You must really be souls of faith, hope and charity, completely permeated by the spirit of the apostolate and not turned inwards on all your grizzling. She will pray much to help you.' When necessary, however, she could be encouraging and comforting. To one Sister full of doubt, asking herself whether she really loved God, Marthe responded: 'The only thing that is sure in your state is that you know you want to love. And you cannot want to love God without loving him … What is lamentable is the unhappiness that withdraws into itself, not the unhappiness that loves and appeals.'

IV. Châteauneuf, a meeting place for saints

A glance at the people who came to see Marthe reveals a substantial section of French Catholicism of the day. Particularly remarkable, however, is the number of people Marthe knew and had in many instances encouraged and counselled, who died with a reputation for sanctity. In the France of the second half of the twentieth century, there was a powerful upsurge of saints which is only just beginning to be recognised,[20] and Châteauneuf was a place for them to recharge their batteries, a meeting place for some of them.[21]

It is unlikely that anyone else in twentieth-century France met so many holy persons. When you know the effect that one holy soul can have and see what an influence Marthe had on certain people, you can appreciate what an impact she must have had not just directly, but also, and possibly even more so, indirectly through what was relayed via a number of 'saints'.

When John Paul II was elected Pope in 1978, Marthe Robin saw the new head of the Church as a gift from the Virgin Mary. She had thought that the message of the Second Vatican Council could only be implemented with Mary's supervision, and here was a particularly Marian soul who would deepen it and spread it throughout the world. Speaking to Mgr Chabbert, then Archbishop of Rabat, she said, 'John Paul II is Mary's pope; she chose him specially. We have entered the era of Mary. See her presence and her handiwork in today's world and Church.' Thus, at the end of her life Marthe hailed a new dawn for the Church. She had given her all to help bring it about.

NOTES

1. Matthew 5:15.
2. A Catholic action movement to which tens of thousands of girls belonged.
3. Implied: 'as if it were not there.'
4. This did not mean that she wanted priests to marry but that they should have people about them supporting them in their daily life and also in their apostolate.
5. Cited in Raymond Peyret's, *Prends ma vie, Seigneur: La Longue Messe de Marthe Robin* (Take my life, Lord: The long Mass of Marthe Robin), Valence: Éditions Peuple libre – Paris: DDB, 2nd edn, 1991, p.229.
6. Others with which she was associated include: Notre Dame de la Sagesse, the Monastic Fraternity of Jerusalem, the Little Brothers of Marie Mère du Rédempteur, the Little Sisters of Nazareth, the

Missionaires de Notre Dame, l'Office culterel de Cluny, the Canons Regular of Champagne-sur-Rhône, the Fraternité Bethléem-Saint-Benoît, the Foyer Marie-Jean, the Nouvelle Alliance community, the Petites Soeurs mariales d'Israël et de Saint-Jean, and the educational work of Eau Vive.

7. Olivier Landron, *Les communautés nouvelles. Nouveaux visages du catholicisme français* (The New Communities: New faces of French Catholicism), Paris: Éditions Du Cerf, 2004, pp.123–126.

8. Hervé-Marie Catta and Bernard Peyrous, *Le feu et l'espérance: Pierre Goursat, fondateur de la communauté de l'Emmanuel* (Fire and hope, Pierre Goursat, Founder of the Emmanuel Community), Paris: Éditions de l'Emmanuel, 1995, pp. 58, 90–91, 232.
   Marthe's remark was meaningful because in 1986 the sanctuaries at Paray-le-Monial were entrusted to the care of the Emmanuel community which integrated the spirituality of the Heart of Jesus progressively more into its own.

9. Pastor Louis Dalliere was part of the Protestant revival in France.

10. Brother Ephraïm, *Les pluies de l'arrière-saison: Naissance d'une Communauté Nouvelle* (The end of Autumn rains: The birth of a new community), Paris: Fayard, 1985, pp.80–81.

11. Cited in Daniel Escoulen's, *Si le grain de blé ne meurt … florilège de Marthe Robin* (Unless a wheat grain dies … an anthology of Marthe Robin),Valence: Éditions Peuple libre–Paris, DDB, 1996, p.250.

12. He testified to this in Marie-Dominique Philippe's *Les trois sagesses*, Paris: Fayard, 1994, pp. 485–573.

13. Not to be confused with Lanza del Vasto's l'Arche.

14. Brother of Père Marie-Dominique Philippe, it was Père Thomas Philippe whose holiness, love for and philosophical vision relating to people with disabilities prompted Jean Vanier to lead a life of communion with them.

15. Quoted in D. Escoulen, op. cit., pp. 236–237.

16. Among them Cardinals Daniélou; Gouyon, Archbishop of Rennes; Kim, Archbishop of Séoul in Korea; Margéot of Mauritius; Martin, Prefect of the Pontifical House; Renard, Bishop of Versailles then Archbishop of Lyon; Richaud, Bishop of Laval and then Archbishop of Bordeaux; Suenens, Archbishop of Malines-Brussels; Thiandoum of Dakar; Villot, Secretary of State to Paul VI then John Paul I and John Paul II. (Some were not yet cardinals when they went to see her.)

17. Between 1941 and 1959 alone she received six hundred. Several of them were very influential, such as the Jesuit, Père Blaise Arminjon; Canon Boulard, one of the fathers of religious sociology in France; Père Lallement, a mystic; the Lebanese, Père Mansour Labaki; Père

Lebret, the Dominican founder of the Economie et Humanisme movement; Père Philippon, a Dominican and esteemed theologian; the Abbé Pierre, founder of the Emmaus communities; Mgr Thellier de Poncheville; Canon Ladame, founder of the seminary in Paray-le-Monial.

18. '*Tourière* Sisters' were Sisters in an enclosed convent who had not done the necessary studies, they did not generally take part in the Divine Office and were responsible for external relations.

19. Community life, religious life.

20. Joachim Bouflet, Bernard Peyrous, Marie-Ange Pompignoli, *Des saints au xxe siècle: pourquoi?* (Why saints in the twentieth century?), Paris: Éditions de l'Emmanuel, 2005.

21. The names of those it has been possible to identify as having died with a reputation for sanctity deserve mention. They include:
    – bishops: Mgr Ancel;
    – religious: the Jesuit Père Monier, Jacques Cachard, a Canon Regular of Saint-Augustin;
    – numerous founders: Little Sister Magdeleine of Jesus, Thérèse Cornille, Sister Marie Dupont-Caillard, Père Voillaume, Père Perrin, Père Caffarel, Pierre Goursat;
    – members of new communities: Danielle Proux of the Emmanuel Community, Estelle Satabin of the Amis de l'Agneau;
    – lay people: Véronica O'Brien, Marie Michelet.

CHAPTER 15
A Personality in Brief

This chapter picks up in a little more detail on a number of elements touched on elsewhere in the book. Marthe Robin may pass for something of a mysterious figure. The way in which she was portrayed during her lifetime and since her death has contributed to her mystique, so it might be useful here to look at some aspects of her personality on which at least a partial light can be shed.

I. Marthe's body

Sometimes, quite frequently even, Marthe Robin is referred to as if she had no body. The suggestion is that Marthe was indeed ill but that once grace had taken possession of her she forgot all about her body. At a pinch people will acknowledge its existence as the place in which she was able to relive the Passion, but it does not seem to enter into their thinking that she might have had physical needs: Marthe is seen solely as a mind and a soul.

The exercise of the senses
But Marthe Robin did have a body. And a body that made its presence felt because it was very painful, and pain, as any sick person knows, demands attention. We cannot know to what degree she suffered because of her encephalitis, but we should

bear in mind that it never left her and was constantly developing. She suffered as a result of her uncomfortable position in bed, and all the more so because a hole, which was only discovered after her death, had gradually formed in her mattress. Every week she went through the Passion, the effects of which made ever greater inroads into her body. She also suffered from being unable to move, which made it hardly surprising that she seized every opportunity to do so when her illness permitted. Very occasionally retreatants would see the suggestion of a movement of her arms under the sheets. During periods when they were 'functioning again' she would try to drag herself about her room a little, supporting herself on them. She knew the humiliation of a disabled person having to pull herself along the ground and not surprisingly only did so when she was on her own at night. Marthe also suffered from fatigue as a consequence of visits and long sessions of listening to letters and dictating her answers. On some evenings she would be exhausted and sometimes she would admit it. Witnesses also stated that there were times when her voice was weaker. They would come back later to find it had regained its strength and volume. What caused those periods of weakness?

Marthe did not eat. She said so herself. No meals were prepared for her, and although there was fruit in her room none of it ever disappeared. Père Finet stated that she did not sleep. One day when he said so in front of Marthe she responded, 'Oh Father, I sleep in God'. Père Colon believed that her long ecstasies provided a form of compensation. She lived only on the host. So she was kept alive by Jesus for the mission that was hers. But her physiological existence was limited, as will be seen from the state in which her body was found to be when she died.

Yet Marthe did have needs. A human being communicates with the outside world through the body, which is to say the five senses. Marthe needed to live. She needed contact with the external world, so like other serious invalids she developed the senses she did have to the maximum. Let us start with the sense of smell. Marthe seems to have had a fine sense of smell and attached importance to it. It should be remembered that farms in those days were not exactly sanitised areas. They gave off powerful smells: the smell of animals, the smell of hay, of people, of rain on grass or soil, the smell of fruit. Country people's noses were used to deciphering these odours and analysing the seasons on the basis of them. They were well aware, for example, that at the end of autumn smells given off by the land declined in intensity. They knew how to recognise the first scents of spring or those caused by the summer and autumn rain. This explains why Marthe was very sensitive in this respect: 'She appreciated smells greatly because she had a very highly developed sense of smell.' 'Marthe liked the smell of certain fruits (peaches, strawberries, apples, lemons ...) very much,' which was why some were put in a basket beside her bed head. She was particularly fond of the smell of strawberries. The first fruits from the farm were brought to her. She could not eat them but she could smell them. She also liked the aroma of coffee. Père Finet would give her some to sniff once in a while. She would also have flowers placed in her room 'provided they weren't too heavily scented because she would not have been able to bear that'. 'Sometimes,' said one of the people in service in the house, 'she would have us sprinkle her room with lavender essence.'

Marthe also seems to have had a particularly well-tuned ear. Because she could only make out silhouettes at best, she would identify her interlocutors through hearing. From their way of speaking she could tell their human and social position, how open they were, their reserve or their tensions. Her hearing and her voice were the tools with which she worked. She loved singing. Whenever someone with a good voice came she would ask them to sing for her. She enjoyed the school children's singing. Her hearing also brought her into communion with nature, through the sound of the wind, the rain or the work being carried out on the farm.

Marthe's sense of taste had gone completely, but it should not be thought that this was something to which she was easily reconciled. Sometimes to console herself she used to like to suggest menus. Until the very end of her life she remained very interested in food matters, which suggests that her gustatory memory had not been entirely destroyed. As far as touch was concerned, in the state she was in she could not exercise it very much. But she liked to kiss and be kissed. She loved contact with babies, which people would place next to her on the bed. Sometimes people would also bring chicks, kids or newly-born rabbits into her room. In that way she kept in touch with the farm and the land.

Failure to eat or drink
Once her illness had fully progressed, no one ever saw Marthe eat. She might perhaps have availed herself of the fruit in her room but no evidence has been found to that effect. Nor is there anything to suggest that she drank. Nothing to indicate she did so has been discovered. Of course this gave rise to questions. For some it had to be a hoax. But the vast majority of people who came to Châteauneuf believed that she did not eat or drink. There were those who would have liked a public demonstration of this fact in order to convince unbelievers that the miraculous was possible. The Parisian neuropsychiatrist, Doctor Assailly, who was very fond of Marthe, came to see her in 1949 and later wrote a report of their discussion: "'Mademoiselle,' I said to her in a tone for which I would subsequently reproach myself, "not for the world do I doubt your honesty but you must understand that as a doctor I would love to be able to put you in a clinic for a month or two, to convince my colleagues of the reality of the extraordinary phenomena you are presenting. This sort of witness could also be part of your mission, and your testimony would carry some weight with non-believers and with the majority of Catholics who put such manifestations down to deception ... Conscious or otherwise,'" he added condescendingly. Marthe

remained silent so Doctor Assailly renewed his request, specifying that ideally she would be observed by both Catholic and non-believing doctors. Still Marthe said nothing. Then she said softly, 'Doctor, I have only one rule: that of obedience. If my spiritual director, my bishop or obviously the Holy Father, were to decide that I should be hospitalised, I would say yes at once and you could take me wherever you wished. But do you really think that the problem lies where you are looking for it?' Then in response to another remark by the doctor, she said: 'No, Doctor, that's not where the problem is.'

Marthe's mission was to pray, offer, receive people and help them. It was to found the Foyers and safeguard their development. It was not to give scientific proof of the existence of the supernatural. One can imagine the consequences for Marthe if this research had been done: she would have become a public figure, a sort of official mystic and her life would have been impossible. Discretion was absolutely necessary if she was to accomplish her mission.

The fact remains that her relationship to her body is largely a mystery for us. She is not the only one in Church history to have lived without eating or drinking. In fact there are quite a few examples. But here we come up against the limits of our understanding.

Medical care

Marthe had doctor friends. There was one, Père Colon, among her immediate circle and there were nurses in the Foyer. But she was never given medical treatment. She went through periods of tiredness. She even had an abscess on her liver which she treated by sucking constantly on ice-cubes. But what could be done with a body like hers? How could such an awkward case ever be treated? In any event, although Marthe had a high regard for medicine and was a great believer in relieving human suffering as far as possible, she definitely did not want medical care. Here too we come up against the limits of understanding. It was decided to respect her wishes during her lifetime and she was never forced to give way on this point.

II. Marthe's sensibility

Given her state of health, a decline in Marthe's sensibility could and even should have been expected. It could have been either numbed or sharpened. In fact, it was neither. Rather, her sensibility was well developed and not in any way diminished. If anything, adversity seems to have refined it.

Her capacity to feel emotion was considerable and unconcealed. She was often seen to cry when listening to people in pain or when she was read difficult letters or indeed heard distressing reports of occurrences like the persecutions in Vietnam. She really wept with those who wept and did not hide the fact in any way. Her capacity for joy was great. Her voice could express every nuance of it and she was often heard to laugh. An important part of her personality was her ability to make people welcome and show affection and tenderness, generally through what she said, sometimes through touch but always with discretion and without any cupidity or possessiveness. One day someone admitted being afraid of death to her. 'Yes,' she replied, 'but a Papa caresses, a Mamma caresses!' With particular emphasis on the word 'caresses' each time. Of course this was an unusual way of talking about death but it also says something about her capacity to speak of tenderness, especially the tenderness she received from God. She experienced affection in many of her manifestations: filial love in relation to the Father of Heaven and the Virgin Mary, the love of a spouse in relation to Christ, without any doubt a mother's love in relation to many souls, and friendship in all its forms, liking, empathy with suffering, etc. ... and all this in a very appropriate way, without anything ever being forced or intrusive. People often remarked upon the fact that she was very understanding. Her sensibility was a precious means of relating to people.

How did this sensibility survive all that she endured? Or rather how was it able to develop? Even if she was naturally gifted in that direction, she never received a refined family upbringing, the kind that nurtures the subtle expression of feelings. In answer, it may perhaps be pointed out that the same thing is found in many mystics who have sustained contact with the Virgin Mary. It is as if some form of education has been undergone. Here too we halt before something which is beyond us but at which we can at least venture to guess.

We might wonder with equal astonishment at how Marthe released the tensions she experienced. She showed exhaustion but not impatience. She was even less prone to heated outbursts. No one could have been further from hysteria. Her patience and constant attention to others are well-known if incomprehensible facts.

III. Marthe's intelligence

One thing on which most visitors who had more than a passing encounter with Marthe agreed was that she was intelligent. 'A brain', some said. Others pronounced her one of the most intelligent women they had ever met.

Starting from a vantage point in which study was sadly lacking, Marthe had, not without difficulty, tried to build her own cultural world, first in the mystical domain. Little by little she had managed to assimilate, master her readings, make them her own and through them give expression to what she was experiencing. But she had no desire to create a literary work. After the war she abandoned what she had written. She may even have forgotten several notebooks in her room which she did not give to Père Finet. They were only discovered after her death. She could easily have reworked her writings but did not. They were just a phase in her life. Her knowledge by contrast kept on expanding. She had books and magazines read to her, even those as far removed from religious matters as *Réalités, Science et Avenir* and *Paris Match*.

She particularly liked anything about medical research, especially into cancer, provided it was not too technical. She tuned into contemporary life and wanted to understand the world in which she lived, but rarely had the newspaper read to her. Conversation, on the other hand, was a valuable source of information. Encouraging the wide variety of people she received to talk, she compared what they told her and formed her own personal synthesis.

Of course this knowledge probably had its limitations when it came to music and art, but in other fields it was extensive. In the art of living, be it a Christian or a human life, she was sharp and precise. It was she who taught the Foyers how to make people feel welcome. It could be said that without even moving from her bed, she had the art of receiving people and honed it to a high degree. In this she had the understanding of the heart. Her politeness was remarkable, without affectation or complication. She had recognised to what extent the mastery of manners was a way of understanding life and relationships.

In a rather different field, she had an excellent grasp of geography, knew exactly where places were and had no hesitation about expressing an opinion about them – 'Angers is a beautiful city'. She was very curious about different peoples. Her many meetings with people of all races and nations provided a reservoir of information for her. She took a keen interest in research done by intellectuals and had her own ideas about their limitations. Yet she was not one to speculate. She reserved the right not to understand. Thus she could not 'get into' Jolivet's manual of Thomist philosophy. She even reserved the right to protest when she thought authors were unclear or using meaningless language. In the speculative domain as in others, she was sometimes heard to say: 'I don't understand, I don't know, I haven't come across that.'

Marthe's intelligence was particularly suited to counselling. She had a gift for correctly understanding the most complex situations, masterfully filtering out the important from the less so, going straight to what was essential, and asking the right questions at the right moment of the right person. If there was a solution, even if no one else had spotted it, she would find it. If not, she would move onto a different plain. Accepting that the intellect could not solve everything, she would pray, and things would then unravel themselves.

Marthe was helped by the fact that she had a memory which people described as 'phenomenal'. True, this memory was not infallible. There were occasions when she did not recall situations very clearly and mixed things up. But they were rare. For most of the time her memory was accurate, quick and remarkably organised. One might have been left wondering whether she forgot anything, had she not herself admitted that it was as if parts of her personal life were blanked out. There is nothing unusual about this in mystics who live in the present moment and sometimes forget sections of their life. When it came to anything to do with her mission, however, she was very much on the ball. And all this was effortless.

What were the characteristics of Marthe's mind? It was definitely an open, curious, enquiring mind, one that wanted to keep a firm grip on reality and understand every aspect of it. It was connected to the world in which she lived, and remarkably so. She tuned into the thinking of the people who came to see her, whatever their level. She understood, as if from within, the doctrine of the Catholic faith. Here her thinking was rooted in her life. She was talking about what she was living. We have evidence of this when she spoke of the Virgin Mary or indeed of God the Father. She certainly had the ability to understand ideas at least in some areas. Yet her practical intelligence was above average. It was helped by the sound common sense of country people that she had inherited. She had received the gift of counsel from the Spirit. Her understanding of practical situations, her sense of what was possible, and the insight that found a solution to the most delicate situations were without equal.

IV. Interiority

A portrayal of this kind might be expected to include some thoughts on Marthe's determination and energy. She herself also attached great importance to generosity and courage. When she was asked why she had a particular liking for the teachers in one school, she replied, 'Because they are valiant'. To another Foyer member she remarked, 'Love is vigorous'. It took courage indeed for her to live, to accept the Passion each week and then to resume receiving people, to struggle constantly for the Foyers and for the Church, and to shoulder everything that was entrusted to her. It is fair to say, therefore, that this woman needed considerable inner strength. She admitted as much herself. Of one Foyer member who had cancer she said: 'But she must fight it! She must get better! If I hadn't fought I would have died a long time ago.'

But the real question is more far-reaching: from where did she draw her strength? What motivated her? What was it that made her want to live and help others to do so? There is only one answer to that question: her interior life. Marthe was above all else and at the heart of everything a woman with an interior life.

There is no need to repeat here what has already been shown in the course of the book. Let us just note once more that Marthe Robin lived off Christ alone. He was her only support, her only sustenance. The words of St Paul, 'Yet it is no longer I, but Christ living in me',[1] were perfectly applicable to Marthe. She relived Christ's 'states' with exceptional intensity, completing in her body 'the hardships that still have to be undergone by Christ'.[2] She was to him, in the words of Elisabeth of the Trinity, 'an abundance of humanity'. This presence of Christ was well beyond even spiritual sensation. We do not know what she sensed, but we do know that Christ had taken over the very centre of her being. Basically Marthe Robin was a being permanently 'transfused' by God.

All the same, the Christian religion being that of a God who is such a friend of humankind that he took their flesh upon himself and lived as one of them, she did not become some kind of celestial, angelic being. On the contrary, her life with Christ made her more human, closer to each individual, more understanding.

What was this interior life? Love, love of God taken to its greatest possible lengths and love of humanity also taken to its ultimate extremity. It was out of love for humanity that she accepted her suffering and remained on this earth. So Marthe Robin is a model, not only of the observance of the first commandment: 'You must love the Lord your God with all your heart, with all your soul, and with all your strength',[3] but of the second too: 'You must love your neighbour as yourself'.[4] This was what gave meaning to her life.

V. Marthe's life – day by day

I would like to conclude this chapter with an insight into Marthe Robin's daily routine, which forms the background to her existence and makes it possible to place what has been described above in context.

Marthe's week began when she 'came back' after going through the Passion and its aftermath, at first on Saturday, then on Sunday and eventually on Monday morning, then later in the day, when Père Finet would go up and, 'call her (to bring her back to us). The length of time he stayed would vary. One of the Foyer members would then take over. Marthe was far, far away. Her voice would be very faint.' Gradually Marthe would regain her strength and her capacity to speak. A piece of blood-stained cloth she had under her chin would be changed. A shawl would be put between her head and the pillow. This was something that was done every day. On Monday evenings, Foyer members at the Farm would say the Rosary with her, as they did on Tuesdays, Wednesdays and Thursdays.

On Tuesday mornings Père Finet would return, usually relatively early, but sometimes not until about 9 a.m. He would enter the room with a small tray and a jar of water. Holding the tray under her chin to catch any drips, he would moisten her lips with cold water that had either lemon, vinegar or white wine in it. She did not ingest anything. Then he would have a bowl of hot water brought to him and wash Marthe's blood-stained face. This had to be done every day because every morning her eyes were found to have bled.

Then her mail would be read to her. She would dictate an answer to one of several secretaries Marthe had over the years. If she was tired she would confine herself to giving a general direction. Answers were written on the backs of envelopes and copied out afterwards. Tuesday was also the day when the parcels were made up.

Marthe's parcels were quite a business. She sent them to the Foyer Fathers, to prisoners and sometimes simply to people who had done her some service. She herself received parcels which were put in her room to await opening. With the donations she received she would have a number of things bought such as confectionary and mandarins. She sent out everything from sausage to bibles, cigarettes and clothing. It was she who stipulated what was to go in each parcel. Sometimes she would point out that there was still some space on the right or left to put this or that in. Yet even with normal sight, from where she was she could not possibly have been able to see inside the package. Some weighed between fifteen and twenty kilogrammes, especially those sent out to the African Foyers. Sometimes she would have crates of one hundred kilogrammes made up, as she did in 1961 for the Aledjo Foyer. She would dispatch fifteen to twenty parcels a month like this. While she was directing how they were to be made up she would still go on dictating her letters.

On Tuesdays Père Finet would often spend the afternoon and have dinner at La Plaine. Often those Tuesday afternoons would bring a 'happy interlude' as one of the secretaries put it, with a visit from one of the members of her family who would sometimes stay for dinner in the evening. Marthe would decide on the menu herself and make sure the meal was good. Two or three times a year Père Finet himself would dine with Marthe's family.

If her family did not stay, the afternoon would resume the rhythm of the morning. In the evening 'sometimes there were some small leisure activities'. When night fell, everything would be turned off, the shutters would be opened and silence would be kept or something would be read to her until Père Finet arrived. She was always the first to hear his car.

On Wednesdays and Thursdays she received people. During retreats she would start at 11a.m. after the talk and would not stop until the evening. Exhausted, one of her secretaries said, 'It was frightful'. By the evening 'she could take no more'. 'Receiving people when she was in such a state of fatigue was beyond human capabilities ... All the same she received them out of obedience because Father asked it of her.'

On Wednesday evenings she would receive Holy Communion. Members of the Foyer living at the farm, other members of the Community, Père Finet, often another priest such as Père Colon and sometimes a few guests would be present. It would begin with those attending being introduced to her. Prayer would follow, using prayers that everyone knew, with the Rosary first. She would receive the sacred host. There would then be a long silence and people would leave. This was a night of respite for Marthe. She suffered less and would go into a deep silence, probably in a state of ecstasy. In winter when there was snow about, climbing or descending the long slope between the Foyer and the farm could be difficult. It was not unknown for Père Finet to be pulled up by tractor when it was the only way of getting through.

On Thursday mornings Père Finet would come and help Marthe out of her ecstasy. He would moisten her mouth with water, and then the visits would begin at once and go on until the evening. In the evening Marthe would start the Passion. From

Thursday evening until Monday evening Père Finet would be the only one to go into Marthe's room, sometimes accompanied by certain people, especially priests, on Fridays. On Fridays Père Finet would not come up in the morning. He would arrive at about 3 p.m. and stay until the end of Marthe's Passion. Sometimes he would also come back in the evening to move her head gently back onto the pillow. After the Passion 'her chin would be on her chest and one had gently to move her head back onto the pillow and hold it there for a moment. I tried to do it,' said one Foyer member, 'but I preferred it to be Father Finet. No one could do it quite like him.'

When Père Finet was not there Marthe would be all alone. Sometimes violent noises were heard coming from her room. The phenomena of diabolic assault cannot be ruled out altogether. On Saturdays and Sundays Père Finet would only come up in the evening, sometimes late, even during retreats, after a tiring day of preaching and being constantly available to people. He came to pray at Marthe's side and there draw his strength.

⁊⯯

The above makes no claim to being an exhaustive portrayal of Marthe's personality, made up as it is of simple notes included in the hope that they will help towards a better understanding of Marthe Robin, especially in conjunction with the other chapters in this book.

NOTES
1. Galatians 2:20.
2. Colossians 1:24.
3. Mark 12:30.
4. Mark 12:31.

— PART FOUR —

THE DEATH OF A JUST WOMAN

CHAPTER 16
Marthe's Final Years (1979–1981)

A study of the history of the Church will reveal that sooner or later all great communities go through a period of difficulty and even crisis. It is not for us here to look at why, but it is consistently the case. The Foyers were no exception. Marthe lived through part of this difficult time but did not survive to see its conclusion.

I. A difficult time for the Foyers

By the end of the 1970s, the Foyers of Charity had become an element of stability and hope for the future in the Church. Since 1976, over four thousand retreatants a year had been coming to Châteauneuf. Some of Père Finet's retreats involved over three hundred people. The new hall was only just big enough to accommodate them. Not everything had been sorted out for the future, however, and the present had its weak points.

Relations between Marthe and Père Finet were as mutually affectionate as ever. The priest's workload had increased, however. Foyers were being set up all over the world. He had to look after them and he had to travel in order to do so. Preoccupation with these foundations and with retreatants took up more and more of his time and energy. Through sheer necessity he began to occupy himself less with Marthe, talk to her less and take decisions, even important ones, without consulting her. 'I don't see my Father anymore,' remarked Marthe. 'He is so weary,' she said about one matter, 'that we can't talk to him about it tonight.'

Père Finet has been described as being both 'authoritarian and easily influenced'. These character traits were the reverse side of his energy and openness. Marthe was much suppler and at the same time more detached. While they were constantly liaising she provided the perfect balance for Père Finet, but when the bond was loosened the priest's weak points came more to the fore. His relationship of trust with the other Foyer Fathers weakened. There was no more fraternal correction of him and he became almost beyond criticism. The foundation of some of the Foyers was settled upon too quickly. 'Don't decide yet, Father, it's not ready yet,' urged Marthe but no notice was taken. 'Just for once listen to me!' she exclaimed on one occasion.

In the turmoil affecting the Church at that time many bishops were also uncertain of their positions. They were perceived to be worried and hesitant about what direction to take. As a result, a lack of confidence in them sometimes set in. Foyers were even founded without their being consulted, with repercussions. At the same time Père Finet, seduced by the brilliance of other advisors outside the Foyers, started listening to them.

Marthe became aware of the situation and, extraordinarily for her, complained about it to certain others. She told them in confidence that she was not being consulted, that Père Finet had other advisors, and that she was no longer abreast of what was going on. She was beginning to worry, at least in a general way.

She was not wrong to be concerned. Père Finet had a secular priest, Canon P, come to Châteauneuf at that time. Marthe was not consulted. Père Finet did not ask the opinion of the bishop of the diocese to which the priest belonged, who might perhaps have enlightened him. When later someone told Marthe that the arrival of Canon P was being attributed to her, she responded vehemently, 'Oh no! I would never!' Canon P (who became Father P like all Foyer priests) had no sooner arrived than he assumed a position of authority at Châteauneuf and started to extend his importance. He even introduced himself to some as Père Finet's successor. Père Finet was not aware of any of this.

The canonical status of the Foyers had not yet been established. They were living by a *de facto* arrangement which could not go on for ever. Post-conciliar canonical law was in the process of being changed, however. They could wait and see what formulae were suggested for the new communities and movements, especially if there were no major internal difficulties to make a rapid conclusion necessary. Marthe was in favour of not rushing: 'The Lord will show us when the time is right.' But her position of prudence was not adopted.

An ill-timed quest for canonical statutes

What Père Finet did not know was that several priests and religious, who were friends of the Foyers and regular visitors to Châteauneuf, had together decided to tackle the question of the canonical future of the Foyers.[1] They did not consider the ageing Père Finet or any of the other Foyer Fathers capable of resolving this sensitive matter, but instead took it upon themselves to do it for them. Père X, who was one of the instigators of the affair, wrote to his colleagues on 27 September 1977: 'I did the behind-the-scenes-work in Rome.' Père P was the architect of the undertaking. Marthe was left out.

On 15 June 1977, Père Finet, upon whom influence had been brought to bear, had addressed a letter to the Congregation for Religious in Rome with a view to exploring ways of establishing the status of the Foyers of Charity. On the same day he accredited Père P as his sole representative in the matter. He did, however, stipulate that he should keep him informed of everything he did. The Foyer Fathers and the Foyers' Council were not informed. Marthe Robin was only to learn of this appointment on 13

February 1980, two and a half years later. 'Well,' she remarked then, 'something else I didn't know about.' Père P and Mgr M of the Rota tribunal in Rome did seek out Marthe to ask her opinion about the future statutes. But they did not actually take account of what she had to say, at least not on the essential points.

Père P went to Rome several times. He came back one day, saying to Père Finet that a solution had been found but that it was covered by pontifical secrecy. He could not therefore talk about it. Père Finet believed him and did nothing to check that it was true.

On 21 November 1979, Cardinal Renard, Archbishop of Lyon, who had not previously had any jurisdiction over the Foyers, went to Châteauneuf accompanied by Mgr M. They were both friends of Père P and had helped to work out a plan that they in part revealed. Cardinal Renard went up to see Marthe but did not explain the precise ins and outs of the affair. The plan was as follows: Cardinal Renard was to be appointed Superior General of the Foyers; a collegial council to run the whole was to be formed out of three priests; and Père P was to become Cardinal Renard's Vicar General with authority over all the Foyers. Père Finet was given an honorary position but in reality he had been ousted. He was not even a member of the Council for the Foyers, to which he could only be invited. As for the future status of the Foyers, there was talk of an 'association of perfection' grouping together lay people and priests, but in fact Père P and the small group associated with him in this affair were more inclined towards a religious formulation. They were leaving the laity behind. In particular, separate male and female branches were envisaged. The appointment of the Father of the Châteauneuf Foyer was to be for no more than three years, which could be renewed thereafter.

The Bishop of Valence, Mgr Marchand, to whom Châteauneuf was answerable, had not been consulted. Cardinal Renard was dealing with something which did not concern him. The Foyer

Fathers and members had not been consulted about their own future either. Yet the arrangement had been presented with all the authority of the Church, as if the Church itself were concerning itself with the Foyers and giving them their status. At first his abuse of power fooled nearly everyone. Père Finet himself did not see where it was leading, and on 17 December 1979 he sent a letter to all the Foyer Fathers informing them what had been done. The letter had in fact been written by Père P and the constitutions quite simply reiterated to within a few details what had been announced on 21 November 1979. The Foyers were officially becoming a work that was no longer lay but religious in character. The names of the Council members were announced without their having been consulted.

The document had been issued in Marthe's name which implied she agreed with it. In fact, Marthe had been read texts which had not been explained to her. She had asked for important changes. She was told in response that Rome wanted them as they were and that they were definitive: 'There were points to which I said no. They answered: "Oh no, that's the Holy See. You can't change it."' Notably she had wanted to modify the whole of the third part. Père P had answered: 'That's Rome … pontifical secrecy.' She had not been able to talk to anyone about it. In reality the texts that had been read to her were already in the process of being printed!

What might well be called a *'coup d'état'* provoked reactions in Châteauneuf and in the Foyers. On 6 February 1980, Cardinal Renard came to Châteauneuf to meet the Foyer Fathers who were there for their annual retreat, to make things official. He met with reactions he had clearly not anticipated and regarded the protest as subversive. They must obey! When the Foyer Fathers felt they should meet to discuss it, in the name of Cardinal Renard, Père P forbade any such gathering.

The situation was saved by a few Foyer Fathers and Marthe. Braving Père P's interdiction, several Foyer Fathers went to

Marthe on the evening of 13 February 1980, and again on 25 March. They asked Marthe if she agreed with what had been done. She said to them: 'Since it was read to me on the first day in Father's absence, there could be no question of changing anything. Everything had already gone for printing. That's why some people were misled because it looked as if we agreed with it when that was not the case.' False interpretations and words had been attributed to her: 'But I never said that.' After that many of the Foyer Fathers came to ask Marthe for help and advice.

For his part, Père Finet realised he had been led by the nose, which was not of course pleasant for him. He re-established his relationship with Marthe who welcomed him warmly, comforted him and gave him her full support. Later he went to ask forgiveness of the Foyer Fathers and other members for the line he had taken: 'I was wrong'.

The opposition in Châteauneuf made Father P's position difficult. He had a meeting with Marthe from which he emerged angry. Thereafter she refused outright to receive him and a Foyer member was even permanently posted at the farm to prevent him from gaining access. He left Châteauneuf in March 1980 uttering threats.

Marthe encouraged the Foyer Fathers to not simply let things happen. She gave her approval to their putting down in writing what the life of the Foyers really was: 'Say what you are actually living.' Mgr Marchand assumed his responsibilities as a bishop and defended the Work. Contact was made with the Congregation for Religious on 22 April 1980 and a dialogue established. In November that year a meeting of the Foyer Fathers and members was arranged at La Flatière, and a team set about working out an outline for the statutes. Rome sent three apostolic visitors who were open, intelligent and understanding. They gained a good insight into what had been undertaken and one of them declared that he had met 'real saints' in the Foyers. All this culminated in 1986 with Rome's recognition of the

Foyers of Charity as an international association of Christ's faithful, answerable to the Pontifical Council for the Laity in accordance with the terms of the new 1983 Code of Canon Law. From then on relations between Rome and the Work of the Foyers were excellent and full of trust.

An attempted explanation

It might legitimately be wondered how such things were possible in religious circles laying claim to high ideals and seeking to practise them themselves and teach them to others. Did they not represent some sort of failure? An attempt at explanation might be helpful, even if it is still only partial.

It should first be noted that the individuals engaged in this quarrel were not just anybodies pursuing purely human ends. They were men of merit. But then nothing does more harm than division between people of virtue. Next, the matter should not be viewed unequivocally as a clash between good and evil. It was more complex than that. Let us take a closer look at the principal protagonists.

First Père Finet. He was approaching eighty. He had not yet settled the matter of his successor because he had not seen anyone capable of taking on his role, nor that of the canonical future of an institution which at that time included some 620 lay people and sixty-five priests. He was still apparently in good form. He had survived several serious health problems including a bad attack of diabetes, and he was getting through a considerable amount of work without complaint and without sparing himself. But living with mystics is not easy: it brings with it a specific, subtle temptation: that of omnipotence, the feeling of having a direct line to Heaven. And Père Finet had witnessed some real miracles. He was even part of a kind of permanent miracle. As a consequence he was no longer very aware of his limitations and had a tendency to exceed his capabilities. In such circumstances, defects and any dysfunction tend to surface. Marthe was no longer able to restrain Père Finet because he no longer let her get through to him, but the priest's good will, his love of souls, of the Church and of Marthe were intact. They had only to resurface once the mist had cleared, and that was what happened.

From outside, some friends of the Foyers were well aware of Père Finet's limitations. They thought him unable to sort out his succession and put forward a proposal for the Foyers' status. He was unable to think as people in Rome might think. So they tried to solve the problem of the future without him. They had no desire to destroy the work of the Foyers. They wanted to spare them the destabilisation and even destruction that a number of religious communities were experiencing at that time. They did not talk to Marthe because they knew very well that she, in turn, would have spoken to Père Finet. They therefore brought influence to bear on Père Finet and by-passed Marthe, motivated by the need to save the Work from a disorganised future. But in the period of crisis the Western Church was undergoing at that time they did not trust the bishops. So they too had to be left out and negotiations undertaken directly with the Holy See. They even had to pass over the Foyer Fathers who were not considered to be very reliable, and *a fortiori* Foyer members, who must be saved despite themselves. They lost sight of the fact that they had received no mandate to act in this way.

The Holy See was keen to give the Foyers the best possible status. Mgr M, and not only he, involved himself energetically but without listening enough and without sufficient discernment or discretion. Inaccurate information was given to the Holy See. When, however, the latter realised that it had been misled, it reacted positively, accepted that it had acted in error, asked for an audit and took the proper steps.

The Foyer Fathers and members were understandably very shaken by this crisis. The fact remains, however, that not many people left. The crisis obliged the various Foyers to reunite around Châteauneuf. Only one Foyer had already distanced itself and decided to be independent. There is no reason to hide the fact that Marthe was very upset by this. But the Work survived and continued.

II. Marthe's death
By the time the crisis was resolved, however, Marthe had died. She did not live to see the Foyers emerge into the light.

Marthe's gradual decline
Clearly the trial the Foyers underwent had a powerful effect on Marthe's morale. She felt she had been betrayed, not just by Père P, whom she had not trusted, or by Père X, but also by others in whom she had put her faith. She assessed the seriousness of the crisis, especially the division caused within the Foyers themselves and realised it would take time to get over it. Yet she was ever hopeful, saying, 'It will take a long time but we'll come out of it'.

She was more particularly hurt by accusations of failure to obey the Church: 'Why this accusation of disobedience to the Church when we love it so much?' Her love of the Church remained untarnished but in a way she lost her bearings. Her pain was extreme. 'At the time of the crisis the Foyers went through, I was able to meet Marthe alone with Père Finet,' said Mgr Chabbert.[2] 'I was deeply upset by her suffering and I heard her say how much the Foyers were suffering.' 'They might just as well take me away to the madhouse,' she said. 'What have I done, poor old woman that I am, tucked away in the middle of a field in the countryside?' 'A small house in a field. I've done nothing wrong … If I've done anything wrong, let someone tell me.' 'I could shout out my suffering.' Marthe and Père Finet were in need of consolation but they had lost a number of the people in whom they might have confided.

Neither Marthe nor Père Finet broke off their usual activities, however. They found the courage, one to preach retreats, receive the faithful until late into the night and visit distant Foyers; and two, to listen to the complaints and problems of retreatants who climbed up to La Plaine in ever increasing numbers, to answer the abundance of mail and have parcels made up. People who met Marthe and Père Finet in 1980 never suspected anything was wrong. Père Finet's discernment when it came to souls was still intact and he managed to handle some very difficult cases. Marthe maintained the same welcoming spirit, the same attentive kindness and the same openness of mind. Conversions and vocations still came about in her room. Even when the pain was at its greatest, Marthe showed no concern about the long-term future of the Foyers: 'We must pray that we get back on our feet … this is a kick from Satan's hoof but the Lord will use it to the good.'

6 February 1981

During the week of 26–31 January 1981 Marthe fell ill. She coughed more and more and felt cold: 'I was like an ice-block.' It seems the shutters to her room were not properly closed. Nevertheless she still kept up her various activities. During her last week of 2–6 February, she was increasingly wracked by a bronchitic cough: 'My old carcass is falling apart,' she said. Visits were stopped. The last visitor, for whom an exception was made, was Philippe Madre, of the Lion of Judah.[3] He was accompanied by Père Bondallez. Marthe answered her letters, she was read passages from an encyclical and the Rosary was said with her as usual. On Wednesday, 4 February Père Colon gave her Holy Communion. Before receiving it she said to him: 'Help me to *offer* myself.' What she usually said was: 'Help me to offer.' After Communion she did not go into the usual state of ecstasy but continued to groan and cough.

On Thursday, 5 February her suffering intensified. It seems she was burning up with fever. Her throat was completely dry, she was coughing incessantly and from time to time she would groan. At her own request she spent most of the morning alone. After lunch, members of the Foyer came in to pray the Rosary with her. Then some letters that had arrived that morning were read to her. She was extremely weary, had difficulty in hearing and was very shaken up with coughing. There were long intervals of silence. She talked about people who were ill in the communities at Châteauneuf and elsewhere. The nurse from Saint-Bonnet arrived at 3 p.m. and tried to give her some relief. She seemed to be in a very uncomfortable position. Two days previously she had said to a Foyer member, 'Oh if you could only lay me on the ground. My bed is like a bad dog's kennel.' At 5 p.m. people came to say the Rosary with her again. She was waiting impatiently for Père Finet's arrival but did not want to ask for it to be brought forward. Sensing this, the Foyer members alerted him and he came up at 5.45 p.m. and stayed with her for a while. At 8 p.m. she gave some instructions about gifts. The little table beside her bed on which any outstanding mail was put was clear. This was noticed because it was rare for Marthe to be absolutely up to date with her correspondence. She indicated that she wanted to be alone and twice said, 'A Dieu' with a special emphasis that suggested 'To God' as opposed to 'Goodbye'. At 8.30 p.m. Père Finet came back up: she was due to start the Passion. People were saying the Rosary next to her. She fell silent.

On Friday 6 February, at about 5 p.m. Père Finet came into the room as usual. He found Marthe inanimate on the floor, at right angles to the divan, her head against the foot of the bed, next to the chair. She was clothed in her nightgown and had slippers on her feet. She was cold and stiff. He called Henriette[4] and together they put her back on the bed. Père Finet had thought he would be forewarned of Marthe's death. In the monastic tradition saints are often seen to ask permission to go to God. He had expected something similar so for a moment he could not believe she was dead. He thought she was 'gone' as in her Passions. He prayed together with Henriette, and then alone. But this time Marthe did not come back. Père Colon and Père

Bondallaz were called, then Doctor Adolfatto, the Châteauneuf doctor. They could only confirm her death.

Père Colon, a doctor of medicine, described the state of the body thus: 'When she died she weighed twenty-five to thirty kilogrammes. Her legs were like bread sticks. Her mouth was corneous ... without any teeth.' Marthe's survival with a body in this condition defies explanation. No one had been able to see the stigmata for a long time but traces of the crown of thorns were discernable on her forehead, and the nasal arteries looked as if they had been 'cut with a lancet'. Curiously, the skin was that of a very young person, without bedsores. When Père Colon gave Marthe her last Holy Communion her lips had felt fresh to him, like those of a young girl. One more surprising thing: the body showed no traces of violence. The arms were relatively supple but the legs could not be stretched out.

Marthe definitely died during the night of 5–6 February, probably on Friday 6. It was one of those times when mobility – if it can be called that – was possible for her. Exhausted by illness, she was unable to get back into bed. She did not have the glorious end of some saints, surrounded and comforted by their nearest and dearest. She died alone in the night. She had given her utmost, sacrificed her utmost. Like Christ she commended her soul into the hands of the Father, painfully and in great isolation.

❧

Marthe Robin had accepted the idea of giving her all, even her death. It was as if she had been stripped even of this. And yet in the presence of the body on the bed, dressed as she had requested, in a white alb, in her room that was lit at last, there was no horror. Certainly there was sadness but also immense hope and a great serenity. Mgr Marchand, Bishop of Valence, who at once came to see her, recited the Gospel text for her: 'Unless a wheat grain dies ... The fruitfulness of Marthe's life would not end with her death.'[5]

NOTES

1. The passage that follows is based on a considerable amount of documentation which has been summarised. The people concerned have not been named for reasons of discretion.
2. Mgr Chabbert, Archbishop of Rabbat, then Bishop of Perpignan, one of the bishops who supported the Charismatic Renewal movement in France.
3. Now the Community of the Beatitudes.
4. Henriette and Thérèse lived at the farm and looked after Marthe's everyday needs.
5. Taken from Saint John's Gospel, chapter 12, verses 24-25: 'In all truth I tell you, unless a wheat grain falls into the earth and dies, it remains only a single grain; but if it dies it yields a rich harvest. Anyone who loves his life loses it; anyone who hates his life in this world will keep it for eternal life.'

CHAPTER 17
Life Goes On

For saints real life begins after death. That is when their influence really becomes apparent, when it is at its greatest. The best example of this is Saint Thérèse of the Child Jesus, who died unknown in the Lisieux Carmel in 1897 and whose The Story of a Soul *caused a 'storm of glory'. Marthe was already well known during her lifetime but publicity about her had been successfully restricted. News of her death, by contrast, spread like wildfire. It led many to pray to her and subsequently to testify to the power of her intercession.*

I. Marthe's funeral (12 February 1981)

Within hours people all over France knew about Marthe's death. Many newspapers reported it. It was announced on television and radio and in some instances whole programmes were devoted to it. Through the Foyer network the news spread immediately to the far corners of the earth. Countless messages of affection and condolence were sent to Châteauneuf and the Foyers by every conceivable means. It was realised then just how great an impact, direct and indirect, Marthe had had on the hearts of countless people.

Marthe's mortal remains had been left in the small room at the farm. Day and night people took it in turns to pray before her. In the early afternoon of Tuesday 10 February she was placed in a coffin and at 3 p.m. she left the farm and went down to the chapel at the Grand Foyer. It was forty-five years exactly to the day, and even the hour, since Marthe's first meeting with Père Finet. Hundreds of people walked in procession behind her coffin submerged beneath magnificent flowers. Père Finet came to pray in the chapel. It was moving to see him in his grief but also his dignity.

The funeral was held on Thursday 12 February. Those who took part will never forget it. Several hours earlier thousands of people had invaded the large sanctuary where prayer went on continuously. They overflowed onto the esplanade, into the narthex and the corridors, which had all been fitted up with a public address system. It was a fine winter's day. People came from all over France and Europe in cars, trains and special coaches. No less than 120 officers had been commandeered to police the highways and the roads through Châteauneuf and around the Foyer. There was not the slightest incident. Four bishops and over two hundred priests concelebrated the Mass presided over by Mgr Marchand.[1] There were six thousand communicants and they ran out of hosts. The Mass concluded with a singing of the 'Magnificat' and the 'Salve Regina'. Then, in the midst of the cortège formed by the crowd, the coffin left for the family grave in Saint-Bonnet cemetery.

The atmosphere at the ceremony defies description. There was intense emotion dominated by a sense of great faith. Above all else there was the impression that Marthe was entering glory, as if the heavens had opened for her. People who had not known her but who were present that day were surprised by what they discovered. This was the case with Raymond Peyret, a priest journalist from Valence, who, not being particularly interested in mystical states, had never wanted to see her, even though he lived very close by. His astonishment gave rise to the first investigative report about her, *La Croix et la Joie*. Tens of thousands of copies were printed and it was translated into a multitude of languages.[2] This was the first of a succession of books together with several hundred newspaper and magazine articles in all the main languages.

II. Pilgrims to La Plaine

Visits to La Plaine did not stop with Marthe's death but the visitors became pilgrims. In Saint-Bonnet the modest tomb, often covered with flowers, did not change in any way. At La Plaine, on the other hand, access to the farm had to be reorganised. The local authority built a road giving access to coaches, a parking lot was created, the courtyard was done up and the house re-roughcast. Marthe's room was cleaned but left absolutely as she had known it. It was still a faithful reflection of her spirit of prayer and poverty.

The number of visitors recorded between 1981 and 2005 was over 432,000. There were about twenty thousand a year in the 1990s increasing to forty thousand a year in the 2000s. Every month between two hundred and three hundred letters asking for intercession were and are received, with more at times, as in June 2003 when there were 350.

III. Graces and favours

Marthe Robin is 'considered a saint by most and people respect her', said one person who knew her. This *fama sanctitatis* is strong all over the world. It manifested itself in hundreds of testimonies when the cause for beatification opened in 1986, in the thousands of letters requesting favours sent to the Foyer, and in the hundreds of thank-you letters following graces received. If published they would make up several volumes. Here it is only possible to point to some of the areas in which Marthe has interceded.

Graces of the physical order
Numerous graces of sometimes spectacular physical cures have been attributed to Marthe, such as the recovery of a person living

in the diocese of Nice, who had an incurable degenerative eye
disease. After the intercession of her prayer group, she found
herself completely cured. Her case seemed medically so
extraordinary that it was the subject of detailed documentation
for the cause. Another woman was cured of septicaemia and lung
disease. According to the chief of staff at the Roubaix hospital
who treated her, her recovery was miraculous. A person from
Mans with extensively ramified cancer underwent radiotherapy
and surgery for five years and could only tolerate very light food.
She came in faith to Châteauneuf. First she managed to cope with
the long journey, she ate normally during the retreat in which she
took part, and then she started to live again. 'There has definitely
been a special intervention from above,' her doctor concluded. A
diabetic was very badly injured. His case was looking very serious
and people prayed to Marthe for him. After three months in
hospital, the surgeon informed him: 'You can thank who you like
but you may as well know that I could not have cured you on my
own.' A man suffered an extremely serious rupture of the aorta in
Cuenca, Spain. He was operated on but warned that there was
practically no chance of success. The failure rate for the operation
was almost one hundred per cent and the rare survivors invariably
suffered serious after-effects. Marthe was asked for her
protection. The man came out of the operation perfectly, without
any negative effects. A person with heart disease was completely
cured after Marthe had been prayed to. 'Don't let's look any
further,' the doctor declared. 'It's Marthe Robin who cured you.'

The graces attributed to Marthe in connection with the curing
of children were numerous. There was one little girl who had to
be hospitalised from birth. Her body was not strong enough to
cope with treatment. A fervent prayer was addressed to Marthe.
On the same day her cure began and was subsequently confirmed.
The child grew very well and the doctors told her father it was a
miracle. Another child had fallen into a swimming pool and was
in there for ten minutes. His vital functions had stopped.

Emergency aid saved his life but it seemed certain that his brain had been affected. He spent five days in a coma, during which people interceded with Marthe. Ten days after the accident, to everyone's amazement, the child resumed normal living. A child of nine had been the victim of an accident. His condition was desperate. He was in a stage IV coma with his cerebral trunk affected. After prayer to Marthe he was totally cured, without any after-effects. A child of two was condemned never to walk. Those around him prayed ardently to Marthe and to their joy and amazement saw him start to walk completely normally.

Just as she had during her lifetime, Marthe continued to be instrumental in the birth of numerous babies. Often these children were given the Christian name, Marthe. In one family one little girl was even called Clémence-Marthe (the clemency of Marthe).

Graces of a psychological or spiritual order
Graces of the physical order are always in the service of other, more profound ones which relate to the person's intimate relationship with God. It is these that are most important.

Many people have testified that even if they were not actually physically cured, they came to a different way of looking at their trials and their life in general. It was imbued with new meaning. 'Marthe rent the veil that was blinding me,' said one woman, 'making me realise that since Christ's glory passed through his crucifixion, we must accept our burden as he did. I have since made a habit of offering my difficulties and worries to God, and a sweet serenity comes over me. Of course it's a daily struggle and every time I'm about to flounder, I reread a passage from Marthe's life and ask for her help. Marthe has taught me to accept and offer up my trials. That is the greatest grace she could have obtained for me because I really think it's the way to God ... She has given me an ardent desire to pray daily ... Yes, through Marthe's intercession, my grand return to God has come about without any fuss, very quietly.' Someone else wrote: 'Without her I would have committed suicide long ago.' She was not alone in this admission.

As in Marthe's lifetime, the grace of vocations has continued to be granted in Châteauneuf and the other Foyers. In 1984, for example, during a retreat at Châteauneuf, a young boy received a call to the priesthood. On the previous day his father had prayed for him in Marthe's room, asking her to intercede with the Lord that his son might know his will for him. Priests and religious have also been strengthened in their vocations and sometimes even undergone real conversions. One religious Sister, for instance, stated that she had experienced a profound conversion in self-abandonment, total giving, interiorisation, obedience and complete dedication to Jesus through Mary, thanks to prayer, through the intercession of Marthe Robin and her perceptible help. She also testified to the similar conversion of another Sister.

Marthe Robin had been at the origins of numerous conversions while she was alive. She continued to be so after her death. Thus a Canadian woman wrote: 'I am aware that Marthe Robin was behind my conversion over seven years ago. At that time I was interested in esotericism and the New Age, and even in the Rose Cross. After reading quite by chance a little book about Marthe Robin ... my curiosity was aroused and I rang the doorbell to a Foyer of Charity ... After a long conversation with the Foyer Father, I asked him this question: "What does one have to do to have a faith like yours?" – "It's very simple. You just have to ask for it. Faith is a gift." That same evening I asked Marthe to obtain it for me. That simple prayer changed my life completely. Marthe Robin was behind the step that turned my life upside down.' Someone else had this to say in gratitude to Marthe: 'On 26 April 1987 after a week's retreat in a Foyer of Charity I rose again after being dead, by joining the Church. I believe Marthe Robin interceded on my behalf for that conversion.' A man who went on retreat in 1990 wrote afterwards: 'I had abandoned the faith and therefore any practise of it for over thirty years ... I felt alone, utterly alone, very alone ... As I looked at the figure of the Very Blessed Virgin in the chapel choir I was seized with great relief and very profound emotion ... I was able to make my confession and receive the sacrament of Reconciliation ... Without any doubt, this was Marthe Robin's doing. She implored the Mediatrix of all Graces to have her son rekindle in me the faith he had given me at my Baptism.'

Many prayers were addressed to God through Marthe's intercession for the conversion of loved ones. A mother, for example, said: 'I asked Marthe Robin for the grace of Baptism for my daughter. I committed her to Marthe in the little church in Saint-Bonnet and eleven months later for her twentieth birthday, on Easter Day, she was baptised as an adult, with great openness of heart and conscience. I believe she intercedes much for my daughter and for me.' Someone else prayed intensely for her father's conversion through Marthe's intercession. He had not been to church since he was young and was now ninety-two. At the end of a stormy life (with a difficult childhood, three marriages and two divorces), her father died in peace, having received the sacraments of Reconciliation and the Eucharist. 'I think,' she said, 'that my father benefited from special graces which I attribute to Marthe Robin's intercession.' A Portuguese mother wrote: 'Since reading a biography of Marthe Robin it is as if I have awoken from a deep sleep. She has entered my heart, interceding with the Lord to lighten my burden. Many are the graces obtained through her goodness: my husband's conversion, as well as that of my son who has found another job after six months of unemployment; the bishop's invitation to my daughter to talk about the Portuguese Catholic faith. In every instant of my life she is a little ray of sunshine and a little flower that gives me hope and helps me to carry my cross.'

Marthe Robin had helped the new communities' movement. They remained faithful to her memory, praying to her, drawing inspiration from her example, asking her to look after them and help them to make God known in the contemporary world and to surmount their collective or individual difficulties. All over the world religious houses, prayer groups and small communities bear her name.

᠅

Marthe Robin is thus a protectress for the evangelisation of the world to come. Far from declining, her reputation for sanctity has consistently grown, not because of propaganda of any kind but simply because those who pray to her feel they are dealing with a living friend. Beyond the barrier of death she is very close to the hearts of those who love and call upon her, and is more active than ever. Her beatification is sought and expected everywhere.

NOTES
1. With him were Mgr Vignancourt, Archbishop of Bourges; Mgr Chappert, Archbishop of Rabat; Mgr Thien, former bishop in Vietnam. Cardinal Thiandoum, Archbishop of Dakar, was represented by his Vicar General, Abbé Seck.
2. Raymond Peyret, *Marthe Robin, La Croix et la Joie*, Valence: Éditions Peuple Libre, 1981 – *The Cross and the Joy*, New York: Alba House, 1983.

✦ Conclusion
Marthe Robin, a Spirituality for our Time and for the Future

Why is Marthe important for people today? Why does she have such an influence? As we come to the end of this book, I would like to respond to this question by looking, if only briefly, at the needs of our time and seeing how it is that, providentially, she helps to meet them.

I. The anxieties and desires of people today

Since the eighteenth century a crisis has occurred in the Western world, and this crisis has been gradually exported, at least partially, to the New and the Third Worlds. It manifests itself principally in the idea that human beings have become autonomous. They can create their own happiness without God, which is even something desirable because God, if he exists, is an oppressive master. Science is enough to guide humanity. These principles appear in a multitude of forms, both theoretical – in which case they are easily identifiable – and practical, and have a series of consequences.

The first result is the distancing of humanity from God, giving rise to a lack of understanding of God, fear of a God who is often poorly represented, and the perception of religion as playing upon this fear. Then there is a profound lack of understanding of the way in which God wishes to reach out to humanity through Christ and the Church which continues his presence. Christ is seen as a myth and the Church as a pernicious structure. Faith then becomes more like an ideology, a creation of thought.

But a world without God is an orphaned world, without reference points, a past or traditional values, causing many to be anxious about life, the future and commitment. The consequence of this is loneliness, the loss of landmarks and the idea that no life can really be successful. People then create for themselves a sort of inner prison. The loss of God brings with it the loss of a sense of what it is to be human: people no longer have respect for others. We saw much of this in the twentieth century, the most murderous in the history of humankind.

God, however, is at work in human hearts. There is evidence today of many mysterious recourses to God (or at least to the spiritual, the invisible world), a new sense of human solidarity, of human rights, of respect for the dignity of the individual, and concern about the management of the planet. God can make use of these desires to touch humanity.

Our world is truly, in the words of Paul VI, 'fascinating and fearsome' and 'capable of the best as of the worst'. We are currently playing the most important hand the world has ever known. The future of humanity rests with us. But who will have an influence on that future? Who will help humanity to make wise and fruitful decisions?

II. The spiritual experience of Marthe

These questions were very much at the heart of the Second Vatican Council. No one can say that the Church has not taken an interest in the future of the humanity in which it exists. The Church's magisterium informs and makes suggestions. These proposals are all the more authoritative and striking when they come from a man as powerful and saintly as John Paul II. But they are not enough. The holiness of ordinary Christians is another form of response and proposal. In what way is Marthe Robin a 'word of God', does she provide a vision of God for the world to come?

The richness of her experience means that it may be presented as an answer to this question in several ways. Let us just consider some of its dominant characteristics.

For a start Marthe's experience was a *living experience*. Marthe did not form theories about humanity or God. She lived and testified to what she was living, not by words but by her actions and by what she gave to God and to others. An experience is not a matter for debate. She countered theories with her life. That is why she was able to touch great intellectuals like Couchoud, Guitton or Garrigou-Lagrange. The remedy she offered for a world sick in its ideas was the simplicity of her life. This means that it is possible for anyone to follow the way marked out by Marthe, which was moreover a continuation of that of Thérèse of the Child Jesus and the Virgin Mary herself. Anyone's life can be fruitful if it is authentic.

True life begins with the *interior life*. Marthe's experience was primarily of this order. Marthe could not move. In a world beset with agitation, she showed that fruitfulness came from within and not from being successful in terms of power or money. This too is possible for all Christians, provided they nurture the interior life and cultivate prayer as a priority. Fruitfulness comes first from the beauty of a personal relationship with God. In a hectic world there is something prophetic and very wonderful about this.

Marthe Robin's entire life was an *experience of love*. Marthe made herself accessible by love, a love which she did not generate, but which was objective because it was God himself, an engaging and life-giving love. Her experience was one:

- *Of the love of Christ as a friend, brother, spouse, received in the Eucharist.* In her God made himself imminent in Jesus Christ. This experience was a complete rebuttal of the idea of God being far removed from humanity, that he was indifferent or menacing.
- *Of the Father's love.* This is essential in Marthe. In a world in which fatherly love was often lacking, she had an extraordinary

experience of God's affection as Father. Here again she is in line with Thérèse of the Child Jesus. She was one of the artisans of the 'return to the Father', one of the finer aspects of contemporary French Catholicism.

- *Of the tender presence of Mary.* Marthe was in contact with the Virgin Mary in a way that was rare in its intensity, simplicity and constancy. The Virgin was a real mother to her: good, understanding, effective, attentive.

Marthe's life was thus steeped in love, which is to say in the constant presence of the Holy Spirit. A life of relationship with God has to progress from fear to love, from distance to proximity. Some effort is necessary on our part and then God takes us much further.

Marthe had a *beautiful, positive vision of the world and life*. She had a very humble start in a not very supportive environment, with poor health, no friends, no education and no one to advise her. Yet she made a magnificent success of her life. She founded the Foyers, received a multitude of people and changed the lives of thousands. She is an example of success through smallness and so offers hope for everyone, especially the sick, the weak and the rejected. Marthe, like Thérèse of the Child Jesus, represents the triumph of smallness: thanks to the goodness of God, if only one believes in it, any life can be successful.

There is no shortage of ways to such success. They are primarily of a supernatural order. The first is Baptism. Marthe had been baptised. She was a daughter of the Church, who took her Baptism seriously. Baptism is the gateway to true life. The grace of Baptism is continued and developed by the sacraments, especially by the Eucharist. With the help of these supernatural forces Christians are called to restore meaning and joy to life, in the depression that is masked in varying degrees but prevalent in a fair proportion of the world.

Finally, Marthe had a *sense of the future of the Church*. The Church is God's great gift. It is a family of brothers and sisters inspired by the Spirit of Jesus. Marthe wanted the renewal of the Church and announced a new Pentecost of love which would spread to all of humanity. Through Baptism each person has his or her place in the Church. The baptismal priesthood of the faithful joins with the ministerial priesthood of priests to form a complementarity of vocations which, when it is put into practice well, bears witness to a life and love to which people are not insensible. All Christians are called to this life and, whatever their vocation, have a role to play in bringing about the new Pentecost of love sought by the Second Vatican Council.

⁊

Marthe Robin lived 'holiness' in her own simple, humble and friendly way. She was the first to set foot on a long road subsequently taken by lay members and priests of the Foyers, retreatants and all those who loved her and received her message. Marthe Robin is not some extraordinary mystical case in the way that has sometimes been suggested. That is not what she was really about. She was a loving woman who lived the life of Christ and wanted everyone to know him. She does not call people to participate in her mystical states but rather to follow her in her love of Jesus, on a journey accessible to all if only we put our trust in God and allow him to do with us what he wills.